Models of Love

THE PARENT-CHILD JOURNEY

Models of Love

THE PARENT-CHILD JOURNEY

Barry Vissell MD **and Joyce Vissell** RN, MS

Illustrations by Rami and Mira Vissell

FOREWORD BY EILEEN CADDY, FINDHORN, SCOTLAND

Contributions by Leo Buscaglia, Jeannine Parvati Baker, Gerald Jampolsky, Jack Kornfield, Jenny Dent, Joan Hodgson, Qahira Qalbi, Brian Graham, Safiya Williams, William Lonsdale, Karen Karima Rivers, T. Mike Walker, Bill Knight-Weiler, Emily Sanford, Wendy Chapler, Mary Manachi, and Rami Vissell.

Ramira Publishing

Copyright material as follows:

Portions reprinted by permission from *A Course In Miracles*, © copyright 1975, Foundation for Inner Peace, Inc.; *A Gift for God, Mother Teresa of Calcutta*, © 1975, used by permission of Harper and Row, Publishers; White Eagle quotes taken from: *The Quiet Mind* © 1972, *The Path of the Soul* © 1959, *Heal Thyself* © 1962, *Healing By the Spirit*, by Ivan Cooke © 1955, and "Stella Polaris" Magazine, Sept.1985, used by permission of The White Eagle Publishing Trust; *Touching: The Human Significance of the Skin*, © 1971, Harper and Row, Publishers, used by permission; *Spiritual Midwifery*, Ina May Gaskin, © 1977, The Book Publishing Co., used by permission; *Four Arguments for the Elimination of Television*, Jerry Mander, © 1978, Quill, used by permission; *Teaching Children Joy*, Linda and Richard Eyre, © 1984 Deseret Books, used by permission; *How To Release Your Child's Natural Genius*, Lawrence Williams, © 1984 Oak Meadow Publications, used by permission; *Teach Your Own*, John Holt, © 1981, used by permission of Dell Publishing Co.,Inc.; *The Revelation of Ramala*, © 1978, used by permission of Neville Spearman; *The Prophet*, Kahlil Gibran, © 1973, used by permission of Alfred A. Knopf, Publishers; *On Children and Death*, Elizabeth Kubler-Ross MD, © 1983, reprinted with permission of Macmillan Publishing Co.; "Loving Life Enough", Mary Manachi, reprinted with permission from Guideposts Magazine, © 1985 by Guidepost Associates

Photo Credits:

Photo of Meher Baba © Lawrence Reiter; Photo of Martin Luther King, Jr., taken from *Martin Luther King, Jr.*, Flip Schulke © 1976 Flip Schulke, W.W.Norton and Co., Inc., used by permission of Black Star Pub. Photo; Photos of Yogananda and his parents, and the quote, used with permission of the copyright holder, Self-Realization Fellowship; Photo of Navajo grandfather and children taken from *Child of the Navajos* by Seymour Reit, photographer Paul Conklin, © 1971 used by permission of Dodd, Mead, and Co.

Every effort has been made to trace and contact copyright owners. If there are any inadvertent omissions in the acknowledgments, we apologize to those concerned.

Library of Congress Catalog Card Number: 86-060823
ISBN: 0-9612720-1-5

Acknowledgments

We extend our heartfelt gratitude to our typist Beth Holland for her support, encouragement, and the sleepless nights we spent together in the final stages of the manuscript; to our beloved editors, Rainbow Rosenbloom and Eric Snyder, who loved us enough to criticize as well as support our writing; to John Hansen, Virginia Lee Jacobs, and Richard Hudson for their strategic editorial comments; to our proof-readers, Karen and Steve Backinoff, Ian Norton, and to all those who worked hard at our "proof-reading parties"; to our book designer, Jim Petersen, and typesetter, Glen White, for the magical transformation of manuscript to book; to Doris Buckley, who spent hours with Rami and Mira to capture the right photo for the front cover.

We are deeply grateful for those who helped with our children during the final months of book production: both sets of grandparents who came from great distances to help, Kathy McBride, Joseph Guido, Mark and Lisa Greene, Diane Savarna McCabe, and Kathy Hollinga.

A special appreciation goes to all of the contributors who lovingly volunteered to help us with the book, to all the parents who willingly shared their stories, and to the children who shared their feelings so freely.

Without the combined efforts of many, this book could not have been possible.

We dedicate this book to ...

... *our parents, who have patiently and sincerely guided our early steps and then willingly set us free.*

... *our children, Rami and Mira, for being such beautiful teachers of love.*

... *all children everywhere, born and unborn, who are bringing the light of peace to this planet; and to their parents, who are learning to give without thought of themselves.*

... *our Heavenly Parents and the Brotherhood and Sisterhood of Great Beings, who are the true MODELS OF LOVE.*

Contents

*"Unless you become as little children,
you cannot enter the Kingdom of Heaven."*

JESUS

Models of Love
THE PARENT-CHILD JOURNEY

Foreword

by Eileen Caddy
Findhorn, Scotland

It is a great joy to be able to write the foreword to MODELS OF LOVE because I feel it is such an important book.

As parents we have a tremendous responsibility to set an example for our children. And yet to allow that responsibility to become too weighty can take all the joy out of bringing up our children. How important it is to enjoy them. They are young for such a short time.

As a mother of eight I ought to know something about raising children, but I realize there is no blueprint. There are certain principles which can help, but each child is different. That's what makes bringing them up so fascinating and exciting.

1

Three of my sons were brought up in the environment of the Findhorn Community under God's guidance. Every birthday I would ask for specific guidance on how I was to handle them throughout the year. As each child was so different they each had to be handled differently. The guidance I received gave me insights and pointers that were such a help to me.

When my sons left home to go to University, I realized I had never taught them their prayers at bedtime, nor how to meditate. I had not even read the Bible stories to them. In fact, I had not given them any spiritual tools to use in the "big wide world." I felt I had failed them. When our eldest son left home for the first time, I had a couple of letters from him which proved to me that children are like pieces of blotting paper. They absorb from their parents and the environment in which they are brought up.

In his first letter he said how much it had meant to him to live in a community of New Age souls and that it had profoundly affected him, far greater than he or I were aware of. He confessed that being away from our physical center had induced him to look within to find himself. (I had no idea he had ever thought about anything like this.) Then he went on to say that he was hoping to use a magazine article about Findhorn to stimulate discussion with his friends. He did not want to "Bible bash" as he called it, or thrust Findhorn and New Age ideas down people's throats, because he had learned from us that force-feeding was not the answer. Through discussion, however, he hoped they would see life as a much fuller and spiritual experience—that in truth they were cosmic beings. He ended the letter by saying, "thank-you."

Imagine how I felt when I read that first letter from him? He was 19 years of age. I was quite overcome by it.

I wrote back and asked if I had failed him by not giving him any spiritual tools to use in his life. Again, the answer I got from him deeply touched my heart.

First of all, he gave me some insights about myself and my future. Then he went on to share how grateful he was for the way he had been brought up under the direct guidance of God our Beloved. He said that his heart was filled with gratitude as he felt that being in continuous communion with the Creator was far more important than kneeling at the bottom of his bed saying his prayers.

These letters from my son gave me a deep insight into how much children absorb, not from what their parents say, but from what their parents do. Now I realize that I have given my sons far more than I thought, simply by living the life I believe in.

Now, when someone asks me how they can teach their children to meditate, or what they can do to help their children find their spiritual path, I simply say, "live a life, don't talk about it."

To love one another you must try to understand one another. To understand you must be able to communicate, whether that communication be through words or in silent action matters not, as long as it is done in love. You must be loving and tolerant towards your fellowmen.

When something is clear as crystal to you it does not mean that it is so to all. Therefore lovingly, with patience and understanding, try to convey what you are experiencing and share those deep feelings within you. It may not be easy to do this but make the effort. When you love you want to share with those you love.

Love is the answer to all relationships; without Love there cannot be communication. Where there is Love no words need be spoken Where there is Love there are no language barriers. Love can be conveyed in action, a silent look, the smallest deed. Love is so great that it can be felt and sensed. When you truly love, you love all.

EILEEN CADDY
GOD SPOKE TO ME

Introduction

When we would feel the inspiration to write this book, our minds would say, "Wait until the children are a little older, or when they are grown and on their own. You'll know so much more about parenting by then." Then the intuitive voice of our hearts would urge, "Write this book *immediately* while the experience of raising children is fresh. Let each day's happenings and growth be your guide."

We started writing when our oldest daughter, Rami, was seven and our youngest, Mira, was two. It took two years to complete. There were *many* interruptions.

Most of the writing took place outdoors with the children playing close by. I remember one typical incident so clearly. The girls had built a little house out of sticks and leaves. They were happily gathering pine cones and pretty stones to use as their "food". We were peacefully writing. The words were flowing onto the pages in an effortless way. We had been trying for several days to write but without much success. Finally the writing was truly happening rather than us trying to make it happen. Every writer knows that this is a wonderful feeling.

Suddenly Mira started screaming. In her search for pine cones she had stepped into a wild bee hive. Pens and papers flew into the air as we rushed to her side. We acted quickly and she only received one sting. But of course both girls were upset and needed our attention. Writing had to be abandoned for that day.

By the time we could resume writing, the inspiration seemed to have been lost. And this kind of thing would happen repeatedly! We had to continually overcome our feelings of frustration and begin again.

However, we found that each interruption had in fact been beneficial. The experiences with the children in between writing periods had served to deepen us and bring greater understanding.

We parents sometimes feel that the interruptions, hassels and inconveniences of parenting are standing in the way of our growth. We don't realize, however, that the constant change and adjustment are teaching us every moment. They propel us forward as human beings, strengthening our ability to love unconditionally and bringing forth our true greatness. As we endeavor to teach our children, they are the ones who are truly teaching us.

With gratitude, we open our hearts to receive the bountiful gifts they bring.

Children are models of love. Their innocence, purity and joy continually teach us.

Parents are models of love. They are the first teachers of love for their children. It is from them that children first learn how to translate their inner light into caring for others.

But the true Models of Love are those who live fully in love, who breathe love in and out with every breath, and who live completely in service to love—in service to life. Some of us have seen these Beings; some of us have heard Them speak; while some of us have fully entered into discipleship with Them, dedicating our lives to become what They are.

This book is about parenting. It is about parents and children as models of love. It is about the vast pioneering journey which couples undertake by having children. But it is also about our on-going relationship with the true Models of Love. It is, therefore, about parenting in the context of that relationship. The Great Ones are the true parents, and all the parents and children in this world are *their* children.

This book is for parents and non-parents alike. It is for anyone even curious about the deeper meaning of family life and the transformation it can bring. It is for couples who want to glimpse the practical as well as the inspirational side of parenting—and even more, how they can be integrated.

For parents, this book will be like a companion on a long journey—something they can open to in times of need or crisis; at other times to share their uncontainable joy. It has been so for us. In the two years of writing and collecting contributions, we have been helped, inspired, nourished, and reassured as parents. We have more deeply understood the many-faceted gem of parenthood.

May the contents of this book serve you on your journey in this life. May its pages open new horizons for your view; new paths along which to explore. May the thoughts and stories, the quotes and contributions, all convey the utter simplicity and yet profound beauty of this experience called family.

We offer this book from our hearts to you—our extended family. We offer this book to all models of love everywhere. We offer this book for the healing of our beautiful planet.

Barry and Joyce Vissell
Aptos, California
First Day of Spring, 1986

one

The First Spiritual Teacher

Many have come to teach the holiness of God, but still there is not peace in the world. Many have come to teach the holiness of man, and still there is not peace in the world. When many come to teach the holiness of children, then there will be peace in the world.

RABBI SCHLOMO CARLEBACH

Imagine you have been on a remote tropical island for two weeks, taking a vacation from everyday life. The weather has been perfect and you have spent beautiful days in the sun and sea. You have eaten only the purest foods and have exercised plentifully, giving your body a feeling of health and well-being. You have also spent time in prayer and meditation, things have become crystal clear, making you feel very close to the source of life. Your being has become filled with the light of God-consciousness and you have felt the magnitude of your Higher Self. Looking back with this clarity, you see your life as a series of wonderful opportunities for growth. You feel eager to return to work, to serve others, and to grow. And yet there is a feeling of sadness too. You realize the difficulty in maintaining this type of consciousness once you are home again, and most of all, you will miss the closeness you felt with God.

Perhaps this hints at the feeling some souls experience as they prepare to take birth—grateful for the opportunity for more growth and service, yet nostalgic to be leaving such a paradise.

Several months ago I attended a seminar entitled, "The Secret Life of the Unborn Child" by Dr. Thomas Varney. Though the seminar was going very nicely, I was experiencing extreme fatigue, having worked late the night before. Imagine the embarrassment I felt nodding off to sleep while sitting in the front row. The instructor interrupted this embarrassment by announcing that he would lead us in an experience of our own birth. He directed us all to lie down on the floor. The minute I was horizontal I fell into a deep sleep and must have started snoring for the sound of it woke me up. At that moment, a very beautiful taped music filling the air, Dr. Varney commanded, "Now feel your birth."

Somehow, through this marvelous combination of circumstances, the depth of my sleep, the music, the momentum of fifty people in a room all concentrating on their birth, and mostly the Grace of God, I experienced myself being propelled back in time to the moment just before my soul entered this physical body. I saw the new lifetime flow before me like a dream. There was my arrival into my family, my reunion with Barry, being led to teachers and friends who would assist my awakening process, and my service and children. Clearest of all were the lessons I needed to learn which could only be learned on earth. Mastering these lessons would eventually bring me closer to God, the eternal presence I longed for with all my heart. Close by me at this moment were the guides and masters who would be helping and loving me along the way.

With this wonderful opportunity before me, I still felt somewhat sad. Taking birth meant I would "fall asleep" and be unaware of God's Presence in my life for most of my early years. It was at that moment just before entering this female body, that I had the vision of this book.

Our children need not "fall asleep" to the beauty of their heavenly state for 20, 30, or more years, at which time breaking the habit of material thought is very difficult. We can help them begin the awakening process from the day they are conceived, so that the bridge of consciousness between the two worlds is continually strengthened.

The conscious vision of this book in this lifetime has been with me ever since Rami was born in 1976. When I would think about it, a thrill of divine joy would pass through me. Then, due to the habit of my doubting mind, the thought that I am not a pure enough mother would creep in and eventually subdue the joy. When we finished our first book, *THE SHARED HEART*, the urge to write this book came all the stronger. The doubt came all the stronger too: How can we write a book for other parents on so lofty a topic, when we make so many mistakes ourselves?" As was the case in the eight previous years, the doubt won out.

While camping at our favorite spot in the Sierra mountains where most of our writing has been done, I awakened during the first night with ideas and words tumbling before me in a thrilling way. Barry also got up and I told him I had to start writing, that the words were almost being forced out of me. He felt my enthusiasm and agreed we would start writing in the morning. I lay back down filled with excitement. Then my old friend doubt came knocking on the door. I let it in again, and became painfully aware of my own imperfections as a mother. I fell back asleep with doubt as my companion.

The next morning I arose and knew I was very sick. By afternoon I had a high fever and one of the worst sore throats of my entire life. The next day I was even sicker and the day passed like a dark cloud. That night I awakened from a troubled sleep and told Barry that I was in a lot of pain and darkness. The darkness was bothering me the most. He examined my throat again, and he saw signs of a possible strep throat, and explained the medical issues to me and my choices. I started taking antibiotics, and yet I knew I would not get better until I healed whatever it was that was holding me to this illness. I asked Barry, "How could I get sick after feeling so much enthusiasm?" We both knew the answer even as I stated the question. I must triumph over the doubt and begin to write.

The next day, with Barry's help, I began to write (fever, sore throat and all!). As the words flowed onto the page, the energy once again flowed through my body and it began to heal. Within hours my throat was normal—much too fast for antibiotics to work, according to my personal physician!

Parents who insist they can't teach their children about God tell us, "I don't know enough myself. What if I confuse them? I'm not good enough." The lesson I learned while camping is this: all that is required of us in teaching our children is the desire for our children to know Divine Love. We need not be perfect parents. We are only asked to try. We do not need a lot of knowledge about spiritual matters to teach our children. We need only the courage to be honest

Joyce (1948).

with our feelings. Saying to a child, "God loves us," while inside we feel bitter for some "injustice" we have had to suffer, is going to be ineffectual. Children listen to and absorb feeling, not words, and they learn accordingly.

When I was a child of ten, I became obsessed with a fear that one of my parents would die. I worried about it before going to sleep at night, dreamed about their funerals, and would awaken in the morning very upset. Finally one night, my mother came into my room just as I was drifting off to sleep with a troubled look upon my face. She came to me gently and asked, "What's wrong?" I burst out crying and said, "I'm afraid you and daddy will die and then I'll be so alone."

Now my mother could have given me a discourse on what the church says about life after death, which would have meant nothing to me. Or she could have brushed my fear away as silly, leaving me feeling not only afraid but also ashamed to be feeling that way. Instead she met me on a feeling level and said, "My mother died when I was seven. I never missed her, for she never left me. To this day I can feel her arms around me and her comforting presence with me whenever I think of her." She felt it so strongly that she transmitted her experience to me. For the first time in my young life the gates of heaven opened and a connection between the two worlds was made. I felt loving invisible arms surround me. "Your mother loves me too!" was my happy reply. And she nodded "Yes." That night my mother gave me one of the greatest gifts she has ever given me, for she allowed me to go past my fear of death and recognize it as a friend. All this was accomplished with simple words, said with feeling.

To be our child's first spiritual teacher is one of the greatest and most rewarding privileges a human being can have. There is no higher profession. In addition, there is no greater gift we can give the world than a child who is spiritually aware. We as parents must acknowledge and feel in our hearts the sacredness of our work. The outside world rarely gives recognition for this lofty yet humble job, so our rewards must come from within.

I would rather plant a single acorn that will make an oak of a century and a forest of a thousand years than sow a thousand morning glories that give you joy for a day and are gone tomorrow. For the same reason, I would rather plant one living truth in the heart of a child that will multiply through the ages than scatter a thousand brilliant conceits before a great audience that will flash like sparks for an instant and like sparks disappear forever.

EDWARD LEIGH PELL

Barry and family (Helen and Michael Vissell and sister Donna).

Jesus said, "Unless you become as a little child, you will not enter the kingdom of heaven." This one sentence sums up one of the great rewards that comes to dedicated parents who choose to spiritually train their child. We can read every spiritual book, memorize whole passages from the Bible, the Koran, or the Upanishads, yet if we can't put all that knowledge into the simple heart-language and feeling of a child, then we will never experience God. We will have a concept of God in our mind, but not experience the Divine Presence in our hearts. Through the practice of teaching a child, we are forced to become simple ourselves, to see God with the pure, innocent eyes of a child.

Joyce and family (Louise and Henry Wollenberg and brother Bruce).

When Rami was almost three, I wanted to somehow convey that God is not some distant being, but very close and within her. Therefore, each night before she fell asleep I would lovingly rub her heart area, sing a little song, and then gently say, "God is in your heart, Rami."

We never know how things will be received by our children. We can only try, wait, and make adjustments when necessary. By the end of several weeks of this approach, I could tell something was beginning to stir and awaken. One night, while I was rubbing her and repeating about God being in her heart, she looked up at me with pensive eyes and softly asked, "Doesn't God want to get out and play sometimes?" Looking into her bright blue eyes, I vividly saw my own seriousness on the spiritual path, my wanting to confine God into a package. The door of my being opened and out came God—playful as could be, dancing, loving, smiling, eyes twinkling and full of humor. So together we changed the concept a little: God is in our hearts and also all around us, playing, singing and very happy. Rami was pleased and I learned a valuable lesson.

We can not have rigid concepts about spirituality when teaching a child. It is an ever-changing, opening process. We have to be ready to let go of how we see things moment by moment. Our children will, if we let them, teach us to loosen our attachments to our intellectual knowledge. We have to have the courage to let go of our pride, the idea that we know what spirituality is. First, our children will shatter our definitions and stretch us to our limits. Then, when we're nice and settled in to our new way of seeing things, they will pull the rug out from under us once again. Many people object to such change, or are afraid of it. However disquieting it may seem, the only constant in this universe is change, until we develop our ability to rest at our center. When we have learned to live at the still, central point of our being, we can then dwell beyond change, but at the same time thoroughly enjoy all the movement in the world. Then we will not only "be as little children," but will possess the wisdom of the ages as well.

Many souls coming onto the earth now are very advanced in consciousness, especially those coming to parents who have accepted the responsibility of spiritually training them. Bringing the blessing of so much light into our homes, their inner understanding and experience of God is vast. As we teach them with our simple heart-felt words and phrases, so much is awakened in them, and so much given back to us. In teaching them we see how we are the ones being taught.

We invite you to accept this divine responsibility of teaching your child, which will in turn transform you. If your children are grown already, perhaps you could help in the spiritual training of a grandchild. The process is on-going. If you don't have children and feel you never will, "adopt" a child of a friend or neighbor. There is not a parent alive who doesn't relish the interest another adult gives to their child.

From the moment we conceived Rami nine years ago, and Mira three years ago, we have been attempting to bring out their spiritual natures and have watched with joy their awakening process. This has been one of the greatest adventures in our lives.

The thoughts, stories, practices, and meditations in this book are meant to spark your own creative nature. When I teach classes to pregnant women, I tell them that with every baby born there comes a book of personal instructions on how the parent can assist to awaken the child to God. This book is planted into the hearts of the mother and father. To read the book, the parent must enter the domain of the heart and there receive understanding. If an idea in our book feels right as you read it, perhaps it is already written down in your "heart's book."

We believe in God and He is in our hearts.

CHIP, AGE 6

As the flower is the forerunner of the fruit,
so man's childhood is the promise of his life.

HAZRAT INAYAT KHAN

two

Parenthood as Initiation

Nothing will be given to you without the asking and nothing will be given to you until you are ready to receive it, and then at that moment the Heavens themselves will be opened and everything will be placed into your hands.

SAINT GERMAIN

BARRY AND JOYCE: "We're afraid our lives will change so much after we have children."
BABA HARI DASS: "Your lives will change anyway."

Unless you are ready to change every minute, you can never recognize the truth.

VIVEKANANDA

Before we became parents, Barry and I immersed ourselves intensely in spiritual disciplines for three years. We did Sufi dancing, Buddhist meditating, yoga asanas, read every spiritual book we could get our hands on, went to church, did a four month retreat in a cabin on the slopes of Mt. Hood, studied with numerous spiritual teachers, spent a summer in the French Alps studying meditation, and pilgrimaged repeatedly to Mt. Shasta, California for inner training. Before conceiving our first child, I was meditating several hours a day and doing a whole string of other practices. Yet there was something missing in all of this. I still felt an emptiness inside. The practices and retreats were calming my mind, strengthening my body, and bringing about a relative harmony in my outer life. But they were not touching an inherent self-centeredness which was growing stronger and blocking me from what I really desired. I could not seem to escape a subtle feeling of "spiritual prowess" while doing my practices.

The moment Rami was born, that block began to crumble and has been crumbling ever since. When I first held Rami and experienced how much love we had for each other and how totally dependent she was upon us, my selfishness began to melt. In my heart I was and am learning the essence of spirituality—to love so completely that we are willing to give up our very life for one another. When someone else's happiness and well-being is truly more important than our own, then God has entered our heart. Serving God is serving one another.

I had read and been told about these things, but I could never quite experience them until I held newborn Rami, nursed her through painful breasts and nipples, stayed up most of the night rocking her continually, and prayed constantly for her well being. In those days, spirituality became a living reality and continues to be so every time I serve and give to my children with no thought of reward or gratitude. Rami's birth was an important "rebirth" for me.

Barry and I recently traveled to Boulder, Colorado to give a workshop on relationships. This was to be a special trip. We were to connect with a close friend whom we had not seen in nine years. We had met this man shortly after we were married in 1968 and had amazing growth experiences together; civil right's marches in the south, travel and all the early pursuits of consciousness-raising. During our last time together, Barry and I were newly pregnant in Santa Cruz and he was moving to Colorado. As we all held one another in a last embrace, we somehow knew that a considerable amount of time would elapse before being together again.

Five minutes before our scheduled talk in Boulder, in bounced our friend, filled with light and enthusiasm. We exchanged hugs and felt how the time and distance had only served to deepen our relationship. After our talk he approached Barry in a very serious way.

"Barry, there is such a positive change in you. What do you feel has been the greatest catalyst for the growth? Has it been the workshops, counseling, writing the book, or your medical work?"

I watched the two men lovingly. They had always held a brotherly trust and respect for each other. I knew our friend was sensing in Barry a wonderful change that he wanted to bring into his own life.

Barry hugged him warmly and simply said, "It's because I'm a daddy now."

Never having had children, he seemed puzzled at this answer. Throughout the workshop, I could tell that he was intently studying the two of us. As we were getting ready to leave for California he again commented, "I've so enjoyed seeing the changes in you both. Do they really come from being parents?" This time our answer of yes seemed to sink in to a deep place in him where it was fully understood.

Make sure that you let God's grace work in your souls by accepting whatever he gives you, and giving him whatever he takes from you. True holiness consists in doing God's will with a smile.

MOTHER TERESA

Joyce and I feel that parenthood has catapulted us headlong into an intensity of spiritual growth the likes of which we had never even imagined. More than just the process of having children, parenthood has opened us, as a couple, to a quality of groundedness, a rootedness to the earth which has given us a base from which to soar with stronger wings than ever before ... a quality of peace which has come from fulfilling a part of our human destiny. Even more, becoming earthly parents has been awakening in us the reality of the heavenly parents, the Father and Mother Presence within, the presence of incredible power softened by the gentlest arms that ever cradled a baby.

I love small animals,
  For they are part of my creation;
But I love children much more,
  For with them, I am the eternal child
And they in their happy play are my playmates.

MEHER BABA

Parenthood is a gigantic initiation! It is a quantum leap in the growth of a human being. It means BIG CHANGE! If we're afraid of change, then we're afraid of becoming parents. Yet, despite our fear, we long for the love and wisdom that comes to us through change of such magnitude.

In a sense, the change of parenthood is a kind of death. It is the death of those parts of ourselves that we cling to as our very own, that we identify with, no matter how obsolete. We're afraid of the death of our individuality, when it's really our selfishness that dies. For by being sincere parents, only selfishness gets crucified—not us. We're afraid of the death of our childlikeness, when it's really our childishness that dies—again, selfishness and immaturity being burned. We're afraid of the death of who we are, when it's really who we're *not* that dies. A major initiation of parenthood is this letting go of our false self, so that our real self can shine forth.

Parenthood brings openness to the fullness of life. Birthing babies is life without pretension. Watching/feeling the vagina stretch, the protrusion of the infant's head after hours of waiting and working, then the gentle explosion of love out of the birth canal and the couple's naked sobs of joy—this is life!

If we are quiet inside, we become aware of a gentle irradiation at the moment of a child's birth—a warm influx of radiant energy. This begins from the moment of conception and builds gradually (and sometimes not so gradually). It is as if some invisible link has been made with a higher frequency of energy, like a doorway to heaven. Our children bring with them this influx of light, this refreshing energy. Just look at them. We must remember, however, that this light is also power, and can do extraordinary things.

Imagine a surfer picking up his (or her) surfboard and eagerly heading for the breakers. He rides the waves with confidence because he has done this many times. Suddenly he sees the largest wave he has ever seen rapidly bearing down on him. His first feeling is one of utter terror, and he holds his breath, tightens every muscle in his body, and prepares to die. Then he realizes his choice in the matter. He breathes, relaxes, and soars up to the towering crest of the wave, where he then has the ride of his life.

The towering wave is this influx of enormous energy that parallels the incarnation of a soul onto the earth. This is especially true of a destined birth, a soul who goes through conscious preparation leading up to the conscious, perfectly-timed, decision to incarnate. The surfer (parent-to-be) who has invited parenthood, has also invited this gigantic wave, but then often balks in fear at the enormity of it. This is the initiation of parenthood for those on the journey of love. No matter how many giant waves the surfer has ridden and mastered, this one will always be the biggest. To give in to fear is to go under. Physical or even mental strength will do no good. When the wave is welcomed with love and embraced with an open heart, only then will the surfer be raised to the crest for the ride of a life-time. The initiation of parenthood, like the ride of the surfer, will provide an unsurpassed opportunity for mastery of the soul. It will provide the joy of selfless service which all initiates know, and will open horizons of consciousness that were never dreamed of.

The new role of parenthood calls for major internal changes on the part of the parent. This in combination with light that radiates from these little beings is an extremely powerful catalyst to bring transformation to the individual and the couple. All the while this personal transformation is occurring, the parent or parents are serving the world in the highest way by giving the gift of their child. And the change in consciousness is so subtle that, for the most part, the parents remain unaware of what is happening inside them.

A person can fight against this transformation. A father can suddenly find himself with *very* time-consuming commitments at work, keeping him there evenings as well as days. A mother can easily resent all she has to do for her child and can feel imprisoned by these responsibilities. It is possible to remain just as self-absorbed after parenthood as before. However, even the smallest amount of surrender to this transformational process called parenthood will bring great rewards of inner peace and fulfillment. Even the smallest amount of time spent "in the moment" with gratitude goes a very long way.

I am endeavoring to see God through service to humanity, for I know that God is neither in heaven, nor down below, but in everyone.

GANDHI

Look well to the hearthstone; there hope for America lies.

CALVIN COOLIDGE

It is so important for pregnant women to have some time alone before the birth of their child. This can be a time for receiving guidance for the new child as well as a time for gaining a clearer perspective on your whole life.

Shortly before giving birth to Mira, Barry took Rami on a three day camping trip, which allowed me to have a little retreat. It was not hard for me to feel Mira's beauty (though I thought she was a boy). I felt her strength, determination to serve, and the balance she would bring to our family. I was not prepared, however, for the answer to my question, "What am I needing to be a better mother for her?" The answers came lovingly, yet strongly, that I have more work to do on selfishness. I groaned inside. I thought I had done enough work on that one with Rami. But soon I realized I had only scratched the surface. I was shown that only by Mira's presence in my life could I more deeply heal the self-centered aspect of my personality. She was to be the guiding light to lead me over that step. Whenever I was tempted to give in to self-pity because of the work-load of two young children, I would remember this revelation so I could be thankful for this opportunity to heal my selfishness.

However, I never dreamed what an intense "selflessness crash course" I would receive the first year after Mira was born. Mira didn't cry—she screamed at ear-splitting volume. At times it seemed unusually difficult for her to be in her little body and she had no inhibitions about letting us know. Between trying to comfort Mira and assure a slightly jealous Rami, I seemed to be forever going at top speed. When we had just one child, Barry and I sometimes used to get into petty arguments over who was going to do all the little chores for her. Now we both just worked as hard as we could, without time to worry about fairness. I sometimes felt like I was on a never-ending race track.

Occasional thoughts of self-pity would creep in upon me, especially when I didn't feel well physically, when Barry was away and the children were more demanding, or the time my mom came from the East to help so I could get ready for Christmas, and she became so sick that I had to care for her too. Sometimes I missed special events in the evenings because I was just too exhausted. When the "poor Joyce" thoughts came, I got out my journal and read my written words before Mira was born, and remembered how this was a golden opportunity to learn the path of selflessness. When I could finally thank God for making this aspect of my growth so perfect, I knew that a warm peace would immediately settle upon me and I would receive the strength to go on.

The truth is, we are totally needed by our children for *such a short* period of time. Their utter helplessness and dependency pass so quickly. When we seize upon this God-given opportunity for our growth and yield ourselves to the changes, we are indeed blessed. Our children have then brought gifts to our own being which can never be measured or perhaps even seen, but which remain a treasure for eternity. They are leading us over a barrier within ourselves we might never be able to cross without them.

The beauty and wisdom of children are for all to enjoy and to learn from. Those who are not ready to be parents or who feel they will never be parents, can choose a child to spend special time with. Before I had children, one of my first spiritual teachers was a little boy of six years old who I was seeing in therapy. He had been expelled four times from his first grade class and came from a very difficult home situation. His parents and teachers called him impossible, yet it was so easy for me to love him in the simple setting of the play room. All of his actions, no matter how bizarre, were simply an attempt to receive the love he needed. He just didn't know any way to receive attention other than by misbehaving. Forgiveness flowed from my heart as he would tell me of his problems at school and how he was always in trouble. In opening my heart to the being in him behind all of his misbehavior, I could then open my heart to the child in myself. Through loving him I was learning about self-forgiveness.

I counseled a woman who complained that she had been dating for twenty-five years and was tired of superficial relationships, yet she was afraid to make a commitment to anyone. Although she had been through much psychotherapy and self-exploration, there was still this block within her. I asked her if she ever spent time with children. She responded sadly that she hadn't for a very long while. I then suggested that she take a special interest in a child and regularly be with that child in a mutually nurturing way. Through that contact, I told her she could overcome her fear and learn about commitment. It worked! Several years later she was happily married. Her child friend had taught her that commitment to another is not only beautiful but liberating as well. From a child, she learned a commitment to love.

Children can be our greatest teachers. Through our openness and surrender to the innocence of children and all that is gained by taking responsibility for their care, we can be led back to our original child-like condition.

Once, I was excited about meeting an older woman I had not seen for a long time. We had spent the summer with her at a meditation camp in the French Alps two years before we became parents. I had always admired and respected this woman, and wondered if she would even recognize me after so many years. In the mountains I had felt so serene, so filled with peace and inspiration, compared with my now busy and sometimes frantic pace with two small children. The woman was going to speak at a local worship service. Since Barry was away working in the hospital, it was harder to get the two girls ready on time. Finally, with one minute to spare, both girls stood ready in clean white dresses, blond hair brushed and smiles shining brightly. Then I remembered myself, threw on a white blouse and purple skirt and dashed out the door.

As we were riding along, six-year-old Rami suddenly shouted, "Mama, you didn't brush your hair!" Since I had neglected to bring my hair brush, she offered me her dolly brush, which helped a little. One-year-old Mira was busy eating a buttered rice cracker and inadvertently smeared my silky blouse with her greasy fingers.

When we arrived, I glanced in the mirror and smiled to myself. Before having children I used to spend a long time brushing my hair and dressing. I would have never dreamed of going out like this. Opening the door at the worship service, I noticed everyone was just opening their eyes from a meditation. Since we were making the only noise in the room, all eyes seemed to be on us. Holding Mira on one side of me, Rami clutching the other, and carrying my purse weighed down with bottles of juice, toys and treats to amuse Mira during the service, I moved in a most awkward way. After tripping over a young man's leg, I flopped into a chair. The girls were very good during the service, although they got me very sticky with their treats. Rami also accidently rubbed the blood from a "picked-off" mosquito bite scab onto the sleeve of my blouse. Finally, as we were saying the last prayer, I felt that all-to-familiar warm, wet sensation on my lap. Mira had wet through her diapers leaving a large wet mark on the front of my skirt.

When the service was over, Rami immediately took Mira into the kitchen for treats, leaving me with only my purse to try to cover up the big wet mark and wrinkled appearance. I was standing alone feeling slightly embarrassed, when the woman I came to meet approached me. She was now a well-respected teacher in her own community, and had come to Santa Cruz to lead a seminar. She looked at me for a long time and then said, "You've grown so beautifully, Joyce. Motherhood has brought forth your essence."

At first I was taken aback, but then I understood. I felt the positive changes that parenthood brings. Perhaps the changes can't be seen on the outside, for often the individual or couple will appear slightly disheveled and harassed because of their many parenthood duties. The beauty and changes come from deep within. It is a beauty that reflects a budding maturity, insight, and selflessness. The amount that we give our children is so small in comparison with all that we receive on a soul level from them. We may lose some of our free time, social life, privacy, and even our neat appearance by having children but, when these are sacrificed with the spirit of gratitude, we will discover the peace and fulfillment of our true inner natures.

three

The Model of Love

by Leo Buscaglia

In 1970, Leo's popularity was largely confined to his University of Southern California students. It was during this time that Barry and I had the great privilege of being his neighbors and students. We came to Los Angeles as rather immature 24-year-olds, somewhat rebellious and in need of guidance. Barry began his third year of medical studies and I entered into a master's degree program at U.S.C., ending up with Leo as my preceptor. He became like our spiritual father for 2 years, leading us from self-doubt and insecurity into the realm of love and the pure joy of living. He accomplished all of this not by his words, but by being such a powerful example that we could never again go back to our old way of being.

One cold, rainy winter day I was walking my dog in the neighborhood. The rain was bothering me and I was dreading going off to my job as a nurse. As I dragged along I spotted Leo coming out of his house on his way to work. He was singing merrily to himself as he kissed all of his plants good-by, then skipped down the walk to his car. At that point he saw me, and joyfully sang out, "Oh, isn't it a lovely day! The rain is making the air so sweet and I love to feel the drops on my face. God has blessed me with so much: a great day, wonderful work, and beautiful friend like you. I feel so thankful!" He gave me a warm, wet hug, got into his car and was off. Suddenly the day was exciting for me also as I started to feel thankful for my blessings. Now I was enjoying the rain and feeling my own beauty.

Being in the presence of such a strong model of love changed our lives. Leo showed us the power of dwelling on the positive and beautiful in life. We, as parents, have an even greater opportunity of modeling love and enthusiasm from the beginning of our children's lives.

The following is excerpted and edited from a TV appearance for PBS broadcast in 1983.

It is very difficult for me to separate life from love. I think they are one and the same thing. It bothers me to think how many people don't live life, when it is the greatest gift that we have.

Recently I had three bouts with death. They told me, "Buscaglia, this is the end for you." I told them, "No it's not. I have things to do, trees to plant, people to love."

Life and love are not taught. The schools don't teach it. Media perverts it. Madison Avenue exploits it. Hollywood debases it. Scientists all but ignore it. We seem to accentuate pain and despair more than glorifying life and love. Life is pain, but it isn't only pain. What a shame to accentuate the pain, when life is so glorious. It is essential that parents accentuate life and love, for they are models of love and we need all the models we can get. We have enough models of hate, and they are always the ones who are the most vocal. Maybe the models of love have to begin speaking up more. Canon Drinkwater, the great English theologian, said a beautiful thing: "You educate to some extent by what you say, more by what you do, and still more by who you are, but most of all by the things you love." Those are the things that you are going to pass on, and those are the things that will live beyond you. Those are the things we need to celebrate.

Children's definitions of love are beautiful. Children keep reminding me of what we were like, how trusting and how amazing we were before we got all these heavy trips thrust upon us. One seven year old said, "Loving each other is important, for if it weren't for love there wouldn't be any people." A smaller child said, "My turtle fell in love, but it made him tired."

When is the last time you sat down with people you love, and talked about love, and talked about life, and talked about death and the beautiful transitions in our lives, so that we could keep them up with who we are becoming. Nothing ever remains the same. Every one of us is changing. Verbalize it! Talk about it! Tell how you are different! Never go to bed at night the way you woke up in the morning! Make sure that in some real way you've grown and become more accepting. Because there isn't time in life for anything less.

But what do we accentuate? We have been taught to accentuate the physical self. We spend something like five billion dollars a year on cosmetics to keep ourselves young and attractive according to certain standards people have given us. Well, you could bathe for the rest of your life in "Oil of Olay" and you're still going to get old. The message that we hear over and over is that it isn't nice to be getting old. It's wonderful to be getting old! Celebrate your wrinkles! Run around with joy and say, "Look, I got a new wrinkle!" Celebrate everything about you. When the day comes that you can say, "this is what I have been given and I'm going to make the best of what I have," you'll find that other people will begin to respect who you are too.

We are more than our bodies. Each life is an eternally individual unique pattern of integrity. What matters in each is the high level of love and spirituality. Our body is a vehicle. It's nice to have a healthy vehicle, but that's all it is. It is a vehicle to carry around only what is essential about you. If we go about judging only by the vehicle, we are going to miss some of the most beautiful, sensational happenings of our lives.

I have an ex-student who was twenty-two years old and was going to be a contractor like his father. He was on a roof just before quitting time putting on the finishing touches. He slipped, fell off the roof, and broke his spine and his neck. He is now a quadraplegic. This was a boy who had celebrated his body all of his life. He worshiped the fact that he could lift weights and do incredible things with his hands. Now he is in a wheel-chair unable to move. He said to me, "I finally found out what was really essential about me. It had nothing to do with my muscles."

We need to teach our children what is truly essential about them, that there is a wondrous spirit within them that is much greater than their bodies. We need to teach our children tenderness. We are so tender towards our cars, our gardens and animals, and we are so tough on ourselves and our children. We are afraid to find out about tenderness. It's not a sign of weakness to let others come close to us. It's a sign of welcome. We do not know this because we are not shown it enough. When anyone tries, we tend to become uncomfortable. We've lost sight of the fact that we human beings are in one respect like tiny little animals without any fur or sharp teeth to protect us. What protects us is not our viciousness, but our humanity, our ability to love others and accept the love that others offer us. It is not our toughness that keeps us warm at night, but the tenderness that makes others want to keep us warm.

In a recent mental health survey, only twenty per cent of those people in America who were interviewed said they enjoyed life and were happy. One out of every seven people is going to require psychotherapeutic help before the age of sixty. One out of every three marriages will end in divorce and before the year 2000, it will be one out of every two. Sixty million Valium prescriptions are given out every year in the United States. When we are this kind of model, what do we expect our children to pick up?

Children learn from modeling. They don't learn from being told. They learn from watching, observing and picking it up. Learning is a discovery process. We are demanding that our children learn love, learn responsibility, learn joy of life—without our being a very good model. Fred Moppet, who is very involved in education, wrote a little book, *HOW CHILDREN LEARN*. In it he says, "Thus a child learns by wriggling skills through his fingers and toes into himself, by soaking up habits and attitudes of those around him. Day by day the child comes to know a little bit more about what you know, to think a little bit more about what you think, to understand your understanding."

People are always saying, "Buscaglia, you were so lucky growing up in that home you grew up in." I smile when they say that. It's true. I was lucky. I had an incredible, wonderful Papa, and an insane Mama. She was outrageous! She always brought joy and music, beauty and understanding into our home. Papa was very serious. Mama balanced him. She would do things that were

PHOTO BY FLIP SCHULKE

Martin Luther King Jr and daughter in tender moment.

outrageous. There were times when he'd come home and say, "I don't know where we'll get enough money to eat tomorrow." She would say, "Don't worry, we'll find a way to eat." He came home the next day to find an incredible dinner on the table. "What's this?", he asked, to which she replied, "so I sold a little ring. The time for happiness is now! Sit down and eat and shut up!"

I was learning all this time. I didn't know that this woman was so amazing. No one ever stopped to tell me those things, but I learned. I learned pride. We were very very poor. Some of you understand that money isn't everything. I remember one very cold day my mother said, "You have to wear a coat." I didn't have a coat, and she insisted that I wear my sister's coat. As a little bambino, that's a trauma. "I'd rather freeze to death!", I complained. "Shut-up!" (She was a really good non-directive counselor.) "Put the coat on and be grateful to God that you have a coat to keep you warm." It was one of those coats with the little fur collar and the buttons on the wrong side. She said, "Wear it with pride. There are people that don't have a coat." I was embarrassed at the time, but in retrospect I now understand. Those are the ways and those are the things that cause us to become who we are. We don't recognize that we learn in those interactions. They are wonderful.

We teach our children every day without knowing that we are doing it. I hear mamas standing in the supermarket with a little child holding onto their fingers. She is saying, "Now this is the dumb one and his sister is the smart one. It's alright though because he is cute." What is the child learning? He is learning that he is cute but he is also learning that he is dumb. The ideal is to see all children as unique and special.

Everyday we are models for our children. How can we demand that they become loving unless we model that for them? What children learn is what they are going to practice, and is what we will receive in return. In order to teach children we must forget our intellects and say instead, "I want to be the model. I want to teach life."

The first thing we need to teach our children is that each of us is a holy thing. I am so awed when I look at an audience and see the gold-mine of you. To look at a large crowd of people and realize that there are no two alike is awesome. We are all different for a reason. We all have something to do for this earth and something to say. Get in touch with this and do it! Then you'll know what life is all about.

Why do we protect children from life? It's no wonder that we are afraid to live. We aren't told what life really is. We aren't told that life is joy and wonder and magic and even rapture if we get involved enough. We aren't told that life is also pain and tears. I don't know about you, but I don't want to miss any of it. I want to embrace life and I want to find out what it's all about. I wouldn't want to go through life without knowing what it's like to cry. It's alright to cry a little bit. Tears cleanse the eyes.

So many times we treat each other as if we aren't there at all, as if we have no worth at all. I love the work of Martin Buber, especially his concept of I and Thou. He says, "Each of us is a Thou." When we are interacting with each other, we must interact as if we are holy things because indeed we are. We are all special and unique. But he says so often we interact with each other on the basis of I and it. It's so hard to be treated like an "it". I am ME! One of a kind! Buber says, "As long as we treat people as I and Thou we have a dialogue. When we treat people as I and it, we have a monologue." Children need to learn that early.

Children also need to learn that they don't find themselves by looking outside of themselves. They have to look inside. It's not an easy trip to find your uniqueness to share with others, because all of your life you are told by others who you are. Most of you are what people have told you you are. Maybe some of you have been wise enough to understand that they meant well but it may not be congruent with what you really are, because you feel uncomfortable with the role that has been thrown on you. So you smash it down and you say, "I'm going to try to find who I am." If you do, it's going to be your biggest challenge. There will often be no peace, but you'll never be bored. Self-discovery is like all discovery. It's full of wonder, but you have to get inside.

I love the Sufi story about the man who is out on the street on his hands and knees. A friend comes by and asks what he is doing on his hands and knees. He replies, "I am hunting for my house key. I have lost my house key." The friend says, "Oh, show me where you have lost it and I'll get down on my hands and knees to help you." He said, "Oh, I lost it in the house." The friend said, "What are you doing out here?" He said, "Well, it's lighter out here."

Most of us look for ourselves out here in the light. You're not going to find it. You're going to have to get down on your hands and knees where it's dark and spooky, and discover all those wonderful things about you.

No one has ever been able to find a limit to human potential. You are far more that you have actualized. You can go on and on forever.

Rami and Mira (1986).

Einstein, at the point of death, decried the fact that so little of him had been realized. That is true of all of us. Knowing that we are limitless is our greatest challenge. Find out all of that wonder of you, develop it, and stand up proudly! Don't be afraid to fail. It's alright. You don't have to be perfect. I'm just very happy to be a human person. I don't have to be perfect.

Then we need to teach our children the importance of others; that they cannot grow in this world without taking in others. The more unique others they can take in, the more they can become. We need to teach them to trust others again, for we are all frightened to death of others. We are building higher and higher walls, and longer and longer bridges. Tear them down! We have to learn to trust again and to believe in others. We have to go beyond just being. We have to get in touch with being human. There is a big difference.

There is a Buddhist story about an ant in a community rain barrel. The first person goes over, sees the ant and says, "What are you doing in my rain barrel? Yuk! Get out!" That is selfishness. The next person comes by, looks in, sees the ant and says, "It's a hot day, even for ants. You aren't hurting anything. Go ahead, sit in my rain barrel." That is tolerance. The third person comes by and doesn't think about being tolerant or angry. He sees the ant in the rain barrel and spontaneously feeds it a handful of sugar. That is love.

When you get to the point where you don't have to analyze love anymore, you have it made. Love is a spontaneous reaction. We don't love to be loved in return. We love to love.

A long time ago someone said to me, "No matter what the question is, love is always the answer." At that time I thought that was very naive. I have lived many years since then, only to have found out the truth of that statement. With all the questions that life has, love is always the answer. If you love, and I love, we can change the world.

four

The Relationship Between Parents

Your mind will naturally seek the easiest person to be with, one with whom there is no struggle, no rough edges to work out, one with whom it is easy and comfortable. But your heart, your true inner self, will seek the person who can best help you in your search for truth. The mind seeks an easy relationship. The heart seeks a spiritual partner.

THE SHARED HEART

When a couple has children, their relationship takes on a whole new purpose and meaning. The relationship between a mother and father can become the crowning glory of the male-female union. When I think back upon Joyce and my relationship before we were parents, I can hardly believe the changes that have occurred. Parenting has brought so much more love and joy into our lives.

Although our free time has been sharply diminished, we have learned to make so much better use of that time. The year before having children, Joyce and I lived the lives of monks and nuns, meditating and praying in solitude for hours each day. Our time for

37

long, drawn-out spiritual practices was shortened after Rami's arrival, and then especially after Mira's arrival, but we learned to make better use of the time we had. We learned the secret of appreciation, for example.

Appreciation is one of the most heart-opening practices a couple can do together. It can take only a few seconds to say something positive to your partner and make their whole day—as well as yours.

People sometimes ask, "but what if I don't feel anything positive about my partner?" At a recent couple's retreat, a couple shared with the group the darkest period of their marriage. During that time, neither of them felt anything positive about the other. At one point, while pondering the idea of separating, they both realized that this would be running away from something. They also had the startling feeling that they might never get back together again if they separated.

They decided to start appreciating one another. At first it felt awkward, empty, superficial, and devoid of feeling. They forced themselves to say something—anything—positive about the other, whether they felt it or not. They accepted this work as a responsibility for their young daughter as well as for themselves. They accepted it as a challenge and vowed to continue appreciating one another.

Little by little, the doors of their hearts creaked open and feeling started coming into their words. It was as if they had been priming the pump all along and finally the water started flowing. Now they are a deeply committed couple—and they haven't stopped appreciating one another!

As well as appreciation, all parents need time away from the children—time alone as a couple to renew the love they share, the love that attracted the souls of their children in the first place. A common situation is one where the mother gets so wrapped up in the lives of the children that they become her whole life. This is natural, because of the whole pregnancy and birth process and the special bonding it brings. But it can easily go too far. In fact, the mother's relationship with her children is *not* more important than her relationship with their father. Neither is the father's relationship with the children more important than his relationship with his wife. The relationship with the children may be more time-consuming but it is not more important. And very often, while the mother is wrapped up in the children, the father is wrapped up in his work or life away from the family. The reverse also holds true. We've seen overly preoccupied house-fathers and career mothers. This is almost always a mutual situation, a shared problem. One parent can't look at the other and say, "You did it first!" Each side supports the other. It doesn't create the other. However, one *or* both can realize the need for change.

Joyce and I recognize our need to be alone as a couple. We try (and often succeed) once a week to have at least an afternoon "date" and do something romantic like a walk on the beach and then out to dinner. Sometimes we write together or do some other "special" work. Sometimes we get nothing done. Then we feel how wonderful it is to sometimes get nothing done!

People tell us they feel guilty about leaving their children. As parents, we understand. We feel it too. It's very easy to think, "They're so young and they need us *so* much. How can we leave them with a complete stranger!" (It's interesting how suddenly our best friend or relative becomes a "complete stranger.") Yes they need us, but they also need time away from us—just as much as we need time away from them. It helps them in their process of separation, which is essential. It helps them to appreciate us as their parents, which children so easily take for granted. It helps them in their relationships with others.

Although it helps them, children won't necessarily make it easy for you to leave. Don't expect them to help you with your guilt about leaving. They'll be only too happy to let you know you've used poor judgment to leave them. They'll often confirm your feelings of being a "bad parent". It takes firmness of conviction and an open heart to "love them and leave them".

What about disharmony between the parents? Anger and arguments are often part of a living relationship. The growth of the relationship, however, depends more on how we resolve the arguments and our openness to change. Just yelling and screaming at one another doesn't guarantee a living relationship. It's one thing to release our anger and quite another to look at what's behind it.

We would all like to prevent our children from witnessing our lower natures in action, whether it is anger, sadness, selfishness, greed, or jealousy. However, as I mentioned before, the presence of children often magnifies whatever is going on. So arguments tend to happen especially when the children are present. They pick up on our feelings as parents and then act them out in their own symbolic way. If we were alone with our spouse we might more easily get away with repressing our feelings, ending with an unspoken tension which silently undermines our love. In the presence of our young "magnifying lenses", the tension becomes unbearable. Children often are catalysts to bring this tension to the surface in the form of anger. We can either project some of our anger onto them for "causing" us to explode, or we can thank them for being catalysts and for not allowing us to smolder and hide.

Often we feel guilty that we behaved so immaturely in front of our children. I remember one time Joyce and I were unable to control our anger. Our behavior made us feel very ashamed of ourselves. We felt Rami and Mira would have less respect for us as their parents. We felt more childish than them. They, however, had long since let go of what had happened. When we sat down with them to talk about it all, they were actually uninterested. We were the only ones holding on to the "damage" we'd done. Then they started laughing at the funny side of our behavior. That helped us to laugh too.

There are two big lessons for parents here. First, it's very healthy for our children to witness our human side. They need to learn that *we're* not perfect - but that the Divine Mommy and Daddy can come through us. And second, we parents need to remember how forgiving our children are—of our mistakes. *We can learn how to forgive through experiencing our children's forgiveness of us.* Our craziness makes them crazy in the moment, but when that moment passes, so does their craziness and so does their image of us as crazy. *We* hold onto our craziness for a long time. Our children find it much more interesting to see the love within us. This is true forgiveness. And all they ask of us, their parents, is to see one another's goodness.

When I was a teenage girl, a friend of mine confided in me the difficulties she used to have with her parents. While she was growing up, her parents seemed unable to discuss their differences. Disharmony between them would produce an icy silence. The girl's father would retreat into himself. The mother turned to her daughter for a release of her pent-up emotions, coming into her room to complain about her father. My friend shared that she strongly disliked these times with her mother, but out of respect she would listen and try to interject positive comments. When her mother finally left, she would break down and cry. It hurt her so much to hear such negative statements about her father.

One time when her mother came to complain about her father the girl burst out crying and told her mother that she didn't want to hear another word. "You are complaining about your husband, but he is *my father* and I love him." The mother never complained to her daughter again.

On some level children must all feel that they are a deep part of both their mother and their father. When a mother complains to her son about his father, the child feels she is also attacking him. In their childlike simplicity they reason, "You think my daddy is no good. Since I am a part of daddy, you must feel I am no good too."

For a father to say to a child, "I hope you don't grow up to be like your mother", this is really wounding the child. Each child strives to become the essence of what they feel their parent to be. They need to be able to nurture the ideal of their parent as long as possible, until they themselves can feel that their real parents are the Mother/Father God. To prematurely disillusion a child about his or her mother or father can disrupt their natural spiritual yearning to contact their heavenly parents. Both the mother and the father are the first spiritual teachers the child knows. To tell the child that one of their spiritual teachers is less than their ideal will create much confusion.

The one parent who talks negatively about the other is the one whom the child eventually resents the most. My friend was not as upset at her father for his icy silence as she was at her mother for her negative statements. Negative statements always rebound back to the sender. Still, a parent speaking negatively to a child about the other parent can have a great impact upon that child's life.

Parents can give their children such a gift by trying hard to express only positive comments about each other. If this feels impossible at times, then remain silent. We should just remember that children feel their mother and father are very sacred, like a holy place within their hearts. If we have slipped and stained this place by our criticism and condemnation, we can always cleanse it again with true and honest appreciation.

A newly married couple once came to us for counseling to work on their difficulty with the woman's teenage son. Although he had a sharp mind, his rebelliousness was causing him to fail in school. He had frequent angry outbursts at home, too. The boy's father had been an alcoholic and had recently died of liver failure. At the time of death there was disharmony between the mother and father. The woman traced the start of the boy's angry outbursts to a time shortly before his father's death when she was looking at his class picture and said, "You look exactly like your father did when he was young." In the counseling session the woman remembered a time when the boy was five years old. The father came home drunk, became angry at his wife and started throwing dishes, pots and pans around the house. The mother and little boy were huddled together crying when she said, "Don't ever grow up to be like your father!" Those words must have had a deep impact upon the boy, for when he did indeed grow to resemble his father it was more than he could bear.

We suggested to the couple that they have a special ceremony with the woman's son and her two other children to honor their deceased father. During the ceremony they were to concentrate on all of the man's positive qualities.

The woman called several weeks later and happily described the ceremony. They had brought out old pictures of their father and each had described their favorite memory of him. Then each expressed what they loved the most about him. Their words turned to tears and soon they were all holding each other. The mother told her children how much she had really loved their father. She had felt so badly about his drinking that she rarely showed her love and appreciation for him. The rebellious son broke into sobs as she spoke and told his mother that he had always loved and admired his father so much, but failed to show it for fear of disapproval from her. The new husband was so grateful for the experience of the ceremony; he was able to feel who the children's father really was for the first time. The other children cried also. Suddenly one of them happened to remember that it was also their father's birthday. They sang to him and wished him well in his new home. As they closed their eyes, all felt his presence in the room returning their love.

The mother further shared that the ceremony had an almost miraculous effect upon the boy. He was now freed to express his pride in his father and he felt good rather than ashamed about resembling him.

There have been times when Barry and I disagree, my feelings have been hurt, and tears flow from my eyes. Rami and Mira have a knack for appearing at the height of my crying, even if they've been sound asleep. "What happened, mama?", their innocent voices inquire. It is so tempting in these moments of weakness to speak against Barry, and to receive their full sympathy. However, through my tears I see their purity and also their deep love for *both* Barry and me. Sometimes I just say, "Mommy and Daddy are acting silly," or "Mommy and daddy both hurt each other. These tears are my fault as well." Usually one of the girls runs off to check on Barry, because they know he's feeling bad and needs cheering up as well.

While we each hold a child, our hearts are opened once again to love. Usually we just sit in silence. But as I hold Rami or Mira I can feel their deep love and respect for Barry which helps to open my inner eyes to his true beauty.

Rami and Mira's devotion to Barry is so deep and pure, as is every child's love for their parents. It is our sacred responsibility as parents to help them hold that devotion as a steady flame within their hearts. That flame will eventually cause a burning desire for God. If, in a moment of weakness, we blow upon the flame and it is diminished, it can always be rekindled with loving care.

Daddy is God. Mama, Rami and I are angels.

MIRA, ON HER FOURTH BIRTHDAY

*I feel good and beautiful when
my mom and dad are loving each other.*

CLARE, AGE 8

Affection with Children

We parents need to remember to show affection to one another as well as to our children. It can be so much easier to hug and kiss our children because there's so much less ego and personality to have to get beyond. But again, they need to see *us* being affectionate with one another. Although Mira and Rami see our craziness, they also see our hugging and kissing. They're learning all about relationship. We are their models of love as well as they are for us. They're learning that couples can get angry at each other and still be very much in love. We're learning that our affection toward one another as a couple is one of the greatest gifts we give to our children. It's amazing that whenever Joyce and I affectionately embrace, it actually attracts Rami and Mira. No matter where they are, they often come running. It's clear that they want to be a part of the show of love. Children love to snuggle with their parents in a "love pile".

We parents can easily get confused about our sensual feelings toward our children. In every one of our workshops we see men and women who have confusing, unpleasant memories of one of their parent's sexual actions toward them. Sexual fondling of children can cause great suffering, sometimes with life-long bitterness and resentment toward a parent. This is sad. Yet it's also sad when we parents, who feel such deep attraction to our child, get confused about our feelings and "turn off" to our child. This is also a tragedy for, in turning off our attraction, we're also turning off our love. Our workshops are filled with individuals who were painfully aware of their parents "turning off" to them, especially near the time of puberty, when they were needing the physical affection of their parents perhaps more than ever. This is typical with daughters and fathers, but happens often enough with sons and mothers. It also happens with daughters and mothers and sons and fathers, in part because of negative feelings about expressing affection toward a member of the same sex.

My heart goes out just as much to the confused parent as to the "hurt" child. Rami and Mira want and need physical attention from me. I feel their female energy seeking a complement in my male energy. I feel I have an enormous responsibility to stay awake to their real need. They need the energy of the Father, which comes through my heart's inner embrace of them. But they also need the gentle touches of the Father. They need my physical as well as spiritual arms to hold them in the embrace of the Father.

At the same time, Rami and Mira in their pure childlike way are expressions of the love and touch of the Mother, which is what makes them so attractive to me. I need and receive that from them. So my second enormous responsibility is to stay awake to *my* real need. It's not easy for me to stay aware of both these sides, but I know this to be my (and all parents') challenge. They both have to be balanced, our children's need for us and our need for them, the giving parent in us and the receiving child in us, our attractiveness to our children and theirs to us.

Parents sometimes get confused because they equate attractiveness with sexuality. Sometimes it's appropriate for me to hold my daughters, sometimes to speak my feelings of love to them, or sometimes simply to feel it all inside myself. What I'm really attracted to in them is their purity and innocence, and at the same time the ancient wisdom of the Mother-God which shines through their eyes. What I'm really attracted to is all of this in myself, which I have projected onto my children, yet also which is teaching me to identify with these, my higher qualities. I pray for the strength to carry this awareness through Rami and Mira's adolescence and adulthood.

When Parents Separate

Parenting is a life-long commitment—not only to the children, but also in some way between the parents. Ignoring this can bring deep suffering. The following story illustrates this.

Charlene*, a middle-aged woman, sat hunched over, crying amid the caring gazes of the other members of the workshop. Although divorced thirty years and with grown children, she still carried bitterness and resentment directed toward her ex-husband—and herself. "Even at our daughter's wedding," she sobbed, "we both parked our cars blocks from the church to make sure we didn't see each other. Then we sat as far away as possible from one another in the church, not even once daring to glance at the other."

Joyce and I asked if there were others in the group who shared Charlene's problem of conflict with an ex-spouse. Ten other hands went up. We invited all of them, Charlene included, to sit in a circle in the center of the room. It turned out that each of them not only had ongoing conflict with an ex-spouse, but also had children involved in conflict, which made it especially painful for all concerned. One man shared in a choked-up voice how he had lost his young children to his ex-wife, who deeply resented any contact he tried to make. A woman spoke of how she lives in constant terror of her ex-husband. Another man, sharing custody with his ex-wife, stated that she was totally incompetent as a mother and was ruining the children. All felt they had made a great mistake by marrying their ex-spouse in the first place. The suffering among these people was as deep as any we had seen, and much of it was due to the involvement of their children. Everyone took a turn sharing, an activity which often brings healing in itself. Each was relieved; first, to not have to hide their suffering and, second, to feel the support of others with similar feelings.

Now this group was ready for a deeper level of healing. First we directed this inner group to hold hands and silently ask for the strength to take a risk that would heal them. Next we had them look around at one another and imagine each person solving his or her problem in the highest way possible. It is always easier for a person to see someone else solving a similar problem, which then draws them closer to their own solution. Then we asked each member of the group to share, in turn, the memory of that quality that first attracted them to their ex-spouse, to focus on the most beautiful

*Name has been changed.

aspect of that person. We have learned that once the door of appreciation is opened, so is the door of healing.

Now, however, there was fear in this inner circle. If they opened their hearts to their ex-spouses, most felt that person would take the children away or somehow take advantage of them. They feared that love and appreciation would produce catastrophic results. They clung not only to their suffering but also to self-pity.

Then I remembered an experience Elizabeth Kubler Ross once had and told the story to the group. Dr. Ross was working with a young girl in the terminal stages of cancer. The girl went on day after day, her body all skin and bones except for a huge bloated belly, knowing she was dying but unable to die. Dr. Ross remembered that this girl had been a "straight-A" student in school. So at her next visit she asked the girl, "When you were at school and your teacher used to give out assignments, did she give all the children the same assignments?" The girl answered, "Oh no, the smart students got tougher assignments." Then Dr. Ross asked, "and what kind of assignments did your teacher give you?", to which the girl replied in a voice full of pride, "the toughest assignments of all." Dr. Ross looked into the girl's eyes with the loving eyes of a mother as well as a psychiatrist and asked, "If God is the greatest teacher of all and gave you *this* assignment, what does that mean?" At that, the girl looked down at her body with a look of intense pride and beamed back at Dr. Ross, "God must think I'm a very top student!" She died that night with a peaceful smile on her face.

I told the people in the circle that their "assignment" was to open their hearts to their ex-spouses and allow healing to occur. I reminded them that they were good enough students to take on this assignment.

One by one they spoke. One man said he was attracted to his ex-wife's body—and nothing else. When prodded to go deeper, he realized he was attracted to the light and love shining through her body. In that moment he opened to her inner beauty for the first time in years.

One by one, each person was able to open their hearts and appreciate their ex-spouse. One woman, however, expressed her fear that by opening her heart to her ex-husband, he would then take advantage of her softness by getting his way in their child-custody battle. That brought up another story.

Once, in counseling, Joyce and I saw a woman in a similar child custody battle. Her ex-husband was spending a fortune to legally prove her incompetence as a mother of their three small children. She was struggling to earn enough money just to provide basics for the four of them. He would write nasty, threatening letters, one of which she read to us in the session. After hearing the letter, Joyce and I felt clearly what the issue really was. It wasn't who was a better parent. His letter revealed his anger at being rejected by his wife. Taking the children away from her would be an act of revenge. We shared all this with her, telling her the answer lay in her opening her heart to him. She was able to do this and that night wrote a sincere appreciative letter to her ex-husband. She let him know how she cared about him, thanking him for all the good things he had done. And to show that miracles do happen, the next letter from her ex-husband was entirely different—no threats, no blaming, even a little show of caring.

We told the woman in the workshop circle that her ex-husband might not come around as quickly, but that on some level he would feel and respond to her appreciation and love. With this encouragement she was able to break through and pour out genuine love to him.

Finally it was Charlene's turn. She assured us that she tried many times over the years to love her ex-husband, but it never worked. By this time the whole group was actively involved in the process, and they wouldn't let her get away with a feeble excuse like that. With the support of the group, she agreed to try again.

"He's always been a good provider," she icily stated. She was still tight and holding on. Joyce moved very close to her and started rubbing her heart with exquisite tenderness. I had her look at me, then gently said, "You love him very much." That did it! The dam broke! With the flood of tears there came into her being a softness and sweetness. She admitted to the group that she does still love him and hasn't been able to admit it to herself all these years. Then she said, "You know, it feels so good to be loving him again. For the first time in thirty years I feel OK about the divorce, that the relationship wasn't a big awful mistake. Here I was afraid that by loving him I would feel I needed to be married to him again!"

What beautiful lessons! First, it is *never* too late to love, to appreciate, and to forgive. Second, the energy of love creates the highest good, whether in our own lives or our children's—love is its own reward.

Individuals and couples with children of past marriages has become a common situation. There are times in a relationship when one or both persons feel they just can't go on any longer. They've lost the vision, and they've lost hope for their togetherness. It may be that this is a test to be passed together *or* individually.

Joyce and I have been asked several times in our talks, "How do you know whether it's right to stay together or to separate?" This is seldom an easy question. We have known couples who have received clear inner guidance that they needed to divorce - - and have done so with incredible peace and harmony. What about the rest of us, often engulfed in turmoil and confusion? The secret is space. In *THE SHARED HEART*, we wrote a section called "Separation Into Oneness" and included that beautiful quote from Kahil Gibran's *THE PROPHET*:

> ... But let there be spaces in your togetherness, and let the winds of the heavens dance between you.
>
> ... Sing and dance together and be joyous, but let each one of you be alone. Even as the strings of a lute are alone though they quiver with the same music."

We've found it most helpful for couples to make this space graphic as well as symbolic... especially when children are involved. We couples tend to cling to our partners, often equating this for closeness. This is true no matter how beautiful the relationship. The problem in too much togetherness is that we're not strong enough to prevent projection. So we externalize onto our partner too much of our own thoughts and feelings and lose touch with who we are as individuals.

The presence of children intensifies this. Their purity is like a magnifying lens between us as parents—for good *and* for bad. When it's our beauty that's magnified and externalized onto our partner, it's not as problematic as when it's our ugliness or weakness. We have to take responsibility for this and do all we can to resolve this in the context of the relationship. But there are times when we're just stuck, and all our tricks aren't helping. Our spiritual practices aren't helping and our communication seems to be pulling us deeper in the mud.

I remember one couple in particular who came to see us in this condition. They had two young children (again, the magnifying lenses) and were unwilling to open to one another in the counseling session. They were really stuck and heading for divorce. Joyce and I asked them if they had taken any space from each other. Before we could explain further the man jumped in with, "That's not our problem. I spend all day long away from my family at work. I'm away from them more then I'm with them."

He, of course, was defending himself. His wife added with tears in her eyes, "Even when he's home he's not with us. I feel like our relationship is in the past."

We told them they needed a different kind of time apart from one another—a time to feel who they were as individuals, which would then help them feel who they were as a couple and family. We explained that just going to work every day was not enough real space.

This pushed panic-buttons in each of them, and thus we knew we were on the right track. I suggested that they might need to separate for a time, one of them finding his or her own place to live, and taking turns with the children.

There was a moment of brightness in each of their eyes, but it faded into dullness as their minds started churning.

"We can't afford two places to live," they both agreed. I said, "If you knew how critical it was for your relationship, you would find some creative way to have two places."

Their minds kept churning. Finally the big excuse emerged, the one we hear so often, "It would hurt the children too much if we separate." They were again in agreement.

Joyce asked, "Are your children happy when you're together?" The woman quickly replied, "No. They're happy enough when they're alone with me, and they seem happy when their father does things with them alone, but when we're together I've noticed lately they're not happy."

We shared that they were not the first family we ever counseled with this problem. Time after time, when the couples "separated into oneness," separating with the conscious intention to work on the relationship by spending enough time alone in prayer and meditation, the result was a renewal of the couple's love. Some couples of course failed and, not wanting to endure the loneliness, continually sought out distractions in the form of other relationships. Other couples moved back together after the first minor breakthrough, only to find this was premature. They hadn't allowed enough "cooking time." The heart knows when the time is right. The mind is impulsive, or else it is stubbornly proud and clings to hurt and rejection.

Then we stated that children are only happy when there's love. The highest gift parents can give their children is to love one another. We as parents so easily forget that *the primary relationship is between us as parents*, and that children come to us because of the love we share. We are easily confused because it is often so much easier to love our children, with their trusting innocence, than our spouse, who may be closed and resentful at times. *But it is our love for our partner which nourishes our children the most.* Our responsibility is to do whatever we can to bring out the most love between us as parents. If by separating we find we can more easily cut through the ego layers of our relationship and feel who our partner really is, then that alternative will bring out the most love. There is no special magic in the mother and father simply living together. Children greatly prefer taking turns with parents who can actually speak kindly to them about the other parent, than to live with their father and mother in a tense atmosphere.

Now the couple's real fears emerged. The woman could admit to her need for her husband, her fear of loss of security, and her fear of permanent loss of her husband. The man also felt his need for his wife and admitted to his fear of loneliness. Both understood that they had to confront these fears for the sake of their marriage and family, and they left the session determined to do this.

I want to emphasize that we don't recommend separation to all couples in conflict. It's really a last resort technique, for couples who are so stuck that they are unwilling to try with each other. We all tend to equate separation with failure of our relationship. We need to let go of this judgment. The little separations can heal—and prevent the big separations from being necessary.

I mentioned earlier that Joyce and I have known quite a few couples who have divorced with great peace and harmony. One couple we know, with two children, realized on their own that they were no longer to live with one another. They share the children in the spirit of real cooperation, and are better friends now than ever before in their marriage.

We also need to know that children bring a lifetime relationship to the parents as a couple. *Once a couple has a child, there is no saying goodbye to one another.* Divorce may happen, but it means a change in the relationship rather than an end. In other words, the couple makes a lifetime commitment to one another by having a child. Some individuals try to run away from this commitment and leave a spouse and family saying, "it's my past; I need to let go of it all to be in the moment now." But that will only bring suffering, for once we allow ourselves to be channels to bring a soul to earth, we take on a sacred responsibility to oversee that soul, to physically, emotionally, mentally, and spiritually nourish that child. Even if we are divorced and living thousands of miles from our children, seeing them only a few weeks out of the year, we still have that same sacred responsibility. We can still bless our children, hold them in the Light of God, and feel our privilege to do this every day. And we can't do this unless we can also bless the other parent and be grateful for the life-long relationship we have with him or her. It doesn't work to try to parent our child while we pretend the other parent doesn't exist. This limits our parenting. As long as we hold a grudge in our heart toward the other parent, our heart is not fully available to our child.

As long as there is room in your heart for one enemy, your heart is not a safe place for a friend.

SUFI SAYING

For this and all the other unique issues that parents need to work through with one another, there is the need for support. It's wonderful when a group of parents can meet regularly to share their deepest concerns with the group. Parents often feel isolated and lack meaningful relationships with other parents. There never seems to be enough time for this, yet it's so important to make time for support. It always amazes us how parents feel they're the only ones in the world with certain problems. It's so encouraging to realize that every one of our problems as parents is shared by other parents who may have very surprising insights. We are not alone!

Yet even more important is the support we can give and receive from one another as a couple. We need to take the time to meditate or pray together, to enter into the Great Silence together, to feel the presence of the Father-Mother God coming through one another, to appreciate the beauty of our partner as a parent, and to accept ourselves as a sacred being *and* parent. Then we will discover that the flower bud of our relationship before having children has now opened to become a mature blossom, offering its fragrance to the whole world in humble service.

five

Blending Families

by Jeannine Parvati Baker

Jeannine Parvati Baker is the founder of Hygieia College and a teacher of womancraft. She is a frequent speaker at conferences and workshops throughout the continent. She has written three books, her most recent one being: CONSCIOUS CONCEPTION: ELEMENTAL JOURNEY THROUGH THE LABYRINTH OF SEXUALITY (written with her husband and Tamara Slayton).

In 1974, we met Jeannine at a yoga retreat in Northern California. At that time in our lives, we felt we didn't want to have children. We had many intellectual reasons, but now I know the main reason was fear, along with a touch of laziness. Parenting seemed like so much work!

Jeannine was at the retreat with her first husband, three-year-old daughter, and six-week-old twin girls. For one week we watched in fascination as she nursed her babies, changed diapers and clothes, and played with her little girl all in the primitive setting of the retreat. Even though it was obviously a lot of work for her, she nevertheless demonstrated to us how much joy and fulfillment there was in this work. Her face literally glowed with love for her three daughters. This contact with Jeannine began to break down our fear and open our hearts to the beauty of parenting.

Jeannine now lives in Utah with her second husband, Frederick "Rico" Baker, their two boys, and the twin girls. The oldest daughter lives with her father. Lately there has been a difficult test—her first husband is wanting custody of the twins. Jeannine wrote to us about her recent court struggle and her desire to maintain holiness in her blended family. As is her nature, she remains positive and dedicated to being a mother.

Dear Joyce and Barry,

Thank you for your supportive thoughts these last trial days. It makes a difference to have the prayers of friends when under threat, legal and otherwise. We all survived and like you said became stronger for the ordeal. I really sense our family is more loyal and committed after this last challenge.

There can be holiness in step families—and true unconditional love between families sharing children. The bonds can be psychological if not genetic, and these bonds can even be eternal. The soul as well as the spirit has special needs when blending families. Alignment psychologically can bring the bonding process the fuller blessings of integrity, efficiency in energy exchange, and harmony.

I keep returning to the fact that each of my children are one half my genes and one half their father's genes. How they feel about each of their parents is how they will feel about themselves and their future spouses. Therefore it is vital that my children love both sets of ancestry, for the metaphor extends beyond the genetic. Towards this goal I am totally committed.

As all things on this earth serve, I looked upon our custody battle as a crash course in unconditional loving. How did I create this? What can I learn about being a better mother? Whenever personal desire gets in the way of my children's best interests, I try to resolve the situation within and hear the inner message from my primal past.

Co-custody is a blending of wills and at best a healing of unfinished business, generational as well as personal. When it

Jeannine Parvati and Rico Baker with family.

works, the children thrive with two homes dear and secure in which to grow up. When it doesn't, co-custody serves to magnify the problems of the separation in the first place. How well I discover that resentment is a waste of the divorce.

Love isn't "fair" (necessarily) and children in divorce amplify this. We all know it's the children who suffer the most, but how about the inner children; trust and wonder. These also suffer during custody battles.

Knowing this, I resolve myself to not react in fear or anger and to forsake revenge. Being on the respondent side in two court custody trials to date, I have found that the best ally has been a model of "psychic akido." That is, as my soul is assaulted, to step aside and let the aggression return back upon itself. This has worked remarkably well. When I step aside of the attack (legal or otherwise), just as the earth is round, the force comes back to its source. I needn't personally try to hurt "the enemy"—the universe takes care of that well enough on its own.

Our twins are best raised here with their mother where they've lived almost continuously from conception on. The truth is, I want to live with these daughters of mine until they are grown. Their legal father likewise would like to live with (at least) one of the twins. He brought us to court to force this move. We all learned alot about attachment. My decision to keep Cheyenne (the second born twin) with her twin and me, in this blended family, along with her stepfather and two halfbrothers, was firm. From the age of three her stepfather has fully supported her. Now she is eleven. It wasn't until her legal father had a break in his career that he wanted her to live with him, at his convenience. But it wasn't convenient for us to let Cheyenne go—it was painful! And in the long run, in my heart I knew it was in her best interests to remain here. By the grace of God, the judges agreed.

Responding to the allegations and legal declarations is life under a microscope. Through this process of self-discovery I have found my relationship to the twins to be deeply loving, bonded, and guilt-free. Being asked a lot of questions has its benefits to soul-making too. It's master-warrior training for the spirit. Such deep introspection has clarified our purpose together and given me the power of integrity.

There is a great strength in the vulnerable feminine. My intelligent yet emotional motherly concern is what prevailed in our custody trial. This damsel in distress was rescued by a humanitarian lawyer, a friendly psychologist and a wise conciliator. Many friends throughout the continent prayed for our unity. Our family was supported by a larger community of friends who likewise realize the mother/daughter bond is to be honored and not torn asunder.

Above all, when I look at my twin girls I see their father still to this day and acknowledge, "that's what our love looks like," for it lives on in these beauties. There is so much healing in the blended family relationship when the parents can stay open to the changes. I can't control what the girls' father will do, but I can continue to encourage the healing dialog and respond from my truth.

Somewhere along the path, the issue of betrayal will be integrated and hopefully resolved between the parents. Then the children can keep alive the bond between "enemies" and be the obvious expression of the growth this relationship has undergone. Jesus has told us to love our enemy and, through this recent custody battle, I've realized this is not just a lofty goal but a real possibility.

It is an ordinary miracle when we transform differences into unity and the best interests of the children are truly shared.

six

Healing and the Family

A simple formula for health is to live thankfully. When a heart beats with thankfulness for its creation and for all life's experiences, a light shines from the very center of the being, which illumines the whole life.

WHITE EAGLE
HEAL THYSELF

When a child is ill, he can be helped by helpful thought. Sometimes the parents' healing thought and sympathy works with the child more successfully than any medicine that is given to the child; and in this is the proof of the power of healing...the desire of the parent becomes a healing influence for the child to recover.

HAZRAT INAYAT KHAN

Love is the strongest medicine.

NEEM KAROLI BABA

How do we face illness or injury in the family? Is it something we never think about, yet secretly dread? And when it does occur, is it some evil phenomenon to be gotten rid of as quickly as possible? Or is it something from which we and our children can learn valuable spiritual lessons?

What is our attitude about healers and healing? Is a healer or doctor someone who waves a magic wand over our head, sticks pins in our body, aligns our bones, or gives us a bottle of medicine? Does healing come from outside of us or inside us? Or both?

These are questions none of us can ignore. We hope the following thoughts and stories shed light on healing and the family.

Joyce and I gave birth to our two daughters at home. During each pregnancy we would check in several times with a local obstetrician—I think to confirm our own intuition that the pregnancies were progressing as they should. After a routine exam during the pregnancy with Mira, our second daughter, the doctor casually asked Joyce her age. She replied, "I'm thirty-four." He then added, "and when will you be thirty-five?" Joyce then revealed that she would be turning thirty-five shortly before giving birth. A sudden seriousness came into the obstetrician's face as he pronounced, "Then of course you will be having an amnio-centesis."

Joyce was shocked. She remembered from nursing school that the incidence of Down's Syndrome and other genetic problems rose more sharply after age thirty-five. And she knew that amniocentesis was looked upon as a routine procedure in women over this age. But she also knew that pregnancy is a divine gift seldom to be interfered with. She was also taken aback by the sudden change four months could make in our obstetrician's demeanor.

She answered, "Well, no, Barry and I weren't planning on having that done."

That did it! Our normally gentle and friendly obstetrician suddenly launched a tirade of arguments in favor of amniocentesis, ending with, "It's the height of stupidity for a physician and a nurse couple like you to ignore your moral responsibility." (I think he had a few other judgements—including feelings about our home birthing.)

Of course he meant well, but Joyce was shaken and confused and cried all the way home. When I heard what had happened, my first impulse was to call him on the phone and let him have it! Then I saw the foolishness of that kind of action. He was doing what he "knew" was right. Instead, I held Joyce and comforted her. Together we affirmed our trust in God, remembering how well we were being provided for. We knew in our hearts and from past experience that whatever the universe has allowed to happen in our lives has been for our own good and growth. We also remembered how deeply we had been connecting with Mira's soul all throughout this pregnancy. We had been told inwardly when and where we were to conceive her and of her mission on earth. We knew that we had to trust our intuitive, heartfelt feelings concerning the pregnancy, rather than the dictates of our obstetrician.

What a good lesson this was! We so easily forget that a physician is an advisor, not an authority. And this applies to all healers as well. If we can learn this, then our children will learn it too. A physician or healer may make a diagnosis but, in fact, this is not *our* diagnosis. It is the healer's, and it comes out of his or her training and methodology. We must make our own diagnosis. This is not to say that the healer's diagnosis is wrong, just that it must agree with our own innate awareness of what is "off" or out of balance inside us or our children. A right diagnosis, and treatment as well, will "ring true" somewhere in our being.

The responsibility we have in our own or our children's healing requires sensitivity. We must take the time to "listen within", to hear the message the body, mind, and feelings will give us.

So many times we concern ourselves with only the symptoms of illness, the visible manifestations. How do we get to the cause, which can be simple, or complex, or multiple? Sensitivity and awareness are important, true. But there is something more important: *we must ask for help.* All the sensitivity-training or meditation will not help if we do not *ourselves* ask for help. To penetrate behind the symptoms to the cause of illness requires humility, the letting go of our ego-pride and intellectual arrogance. Some of us understand this partially, and feel the need to ask the Spirit of Truth within us for healing and guidance, but not other persons or healers. This is like saying, "I only want a relationship with God, so I don't need to relate with other persons," ignoring that the deepest relationship with God is often attained through opening our heart fully in relationship with another. So, in healing, the asking of help from a healer can be a powerful way of asking our "Inner Healer" for help. If the treatment "rings true" somewhere in our being, that's our "Inner Healer" confirming the treatment.

Talking about "ego-pride and intellectual arrogance" reminds me of a rather sad story. Some years ago, when the gap between conservative and wholistic medicine was more like a chasm, a woman brought her baby to see a nutritionally-oriented medical doctor, who was also an acquaintance of mine. As I later learned, this mother was following, for some religious reasons, a very narrow and austere diet. This might have worked for her but, unfortunately, she had her baby on this diet too, and it was definitely not working for him. At the time my doctor acquaintance first saw the baby, he almost gasped in astonishment at the signs of early starvation. He spoke with the mother at great length about the baby's condition, and she finally agreed to add more nourishing food to his diet. She agreed to a follow-up visit but, once home, she found herself unable to make any of the changes the doctor suggested. Instead, she decided to be even more strict with her baby's diet. When, however, he became listless and sedate, and most of all, when a glazed, faraway look came into his eyes, she became frightened and returned to the doctor. Now he recognized not just a starving baby, but a dying baby, who had to be immediately hospitalized and was barely saved. Subsequently, the baby was taken from the mother, the mother was charged with child abuse and my acquaintance charged with malpractice for not contacting child protective services at the time of the first visit.

Although this is an extreme example, we often tend to "think" we know what's best for our child, which may be based on preconceived ideas about what's best, rather than what's "really" best at the moment. We often tend to listen to our "philosophy" rather than the guidance of the moment. Occasionally, as in the example of the starving baby, our "philosophy" becomes such a strong "head-trip" that it takes on the proportions of a delusional system. Then we become blind to what is in front of our nose, blind to what is obvious to another. In situations where we or our children are ill, we need to ask ourselves if there is any false pride or arrogance operating in us, any sense of stubbornly not wanting to seek another's help. Remember that we are not living in a vacuum. Our responsibility is first to seek help within, and then to humble ourselves to receive from one another.

All illness is nature's way of bringing the organism back into balance—into harmony. One night when Rami was eight months old, Joyce and I put her to bed as usual. She seemed fine and drifted off into a sound sleep. One hour later her cries brought us running into her room. She was burning with a high fever, the first illness of her life. The thermometer said 105 (rectal). Outwardly, the doctor and nurse did their thing. While Joyce was sponge-bathing Rami, I was busily examining for any physical signs. Nothing. Inwardly, we were frantic human beings afraid of our daughter's death. For a moment, we felt helpless in the workings of some great cosmic machine, wheels and gears ever-turning without regard for individual lives.

It was clearly time to pray, time to ask for help, which we did. I was shown, to my surprise, that this fever was not burning Rami. It was burning what was *not* Rami. My image was one of gold ore being purified, with the heat of the fire burning off the impurities, leaving pure gold. I saw how Rami, her real being, was the gold, and would be purified and strengthened by this illness no matter what the cause.

Then I had another image, one of a gasoline engine. I saw a build-up of carbon deposits in critical areas inside the motor. These were due to various reasons: impurities in the fuel, incomplete combustion, and probably others. If nothing were done these would continue to build up, eventually clogging the motor and causing damage. Then I saw a pure white-hot flame burning off the carbon deposits, leaving the inside of the engine shining.

I realized that Rami would be fine. I felt a calm inner assurance of this. I glanced at Joyce and saw her worried expression, the same expression I had on my face a moment before. I saw in that moment the effect of worry, that it slows down the process of purification, the process of healing. I shared my experience and feelings with Joyce and watched my calmness also enfold her.

Rami had by now quieted down and seemed to be sleeping peacefully. We said a prayer of gratitude and blessing and then left the room. Although the course of illness took several more days and we did all that we could for her, we were at peace and could allow Rami to pass through this needed initiation in her life.

Children being naturally close to the spirit world, respond beautifully and often dramatically to the healing power.... To heal a child is not difficult. If parents only knew how rapidly and readily their child would respond! For this is where spiritual healing finds no barriers of prejudice, preconceived opinions or sheer materialism.

IVAN COOKE
HEALING BY THE SPIRIT

However, there is sometimes another side to a child's illness. We knew a couple whose second child got sick as an infant. At first it seemed like an ordinary "flu-type" illness, and they thought little of it. However, it got worse instead of better, and the baby ended up being admitted to a local hospital. The distraught mother and father took turns so they could spend every minute close to their baby.

I received a call one evening from the mother. She was in tears as she described how seriously ill their child was. Finally she added, "Please, Barry, can you and Joyce pray for our baby?"

I was about to answer "of course" when I felt stopped. My response was instead, "No, I can't pray for your baby. I'll be praying for you and your husband, that the two of you can be healed in your marriage."

I deeply felt that the disharmony between these two parents was reflected in their child's illness. They had felt hurt by one another and had not been communicating for quite some time. The tension between them was steadily building. Something had to happen. Something had to give way.

There was a long moment's silence on the phone. Then I heard a choked-up voice, "I know you're right. Please tell that to my husband." A moment later he too was on the phone. I repeated what I said to his wife. It seemed all defensiveness was gone from these two parents. There was a deep sadness and yet at the same time a quiet acceptance of the work they needed to do with their relationship. I realized they needed to forgive one another as well as themselves for grievances which might have been imaginary as well as real.

I spoke to both of them on the phone. "Work harder than you've ever worked in your life," I urged. "Close your eyes and ask inside for the strength you need." I waited a moment, while I too asked inside for help. "Now open your eyes and look at each other." I waited another moment. "In your relationship is the relationship of the Father and Mother God, the balanced forces of all creation. I want you to feel how much you need that aspect of God in one another. Do this for your baby! He needs the healing love which flows out of the union of the Mother and Father. In my usual way I was saying more, but suddenly I realized nobody was on the phone listening. The couple were sobbing in one another's arms. They got the message. As they worked on forgiveness in their relationship, their baby's health gradually improved.

I just touched upon a delicate subject. Parents feel enough guilt without adding the responsibility of their children's health and illness. I need to make clear that this is a cooperative venture. A child is ultimately responsible for his own health—less consciously early in life, more consciously later on. It's not a simple issue.

There are choices made in previous lives which affect this current life. There are also choices made in between lifetimes where we rest and learn the lessons of our previous lifetime. Then, under the loving guidance of a more advanced being, we see *very* clearly the ways in which we can redeem ourselves. We see the path of mastery—and make some very important choices. I have read about several persons with terminal illnesses who were able to remember their conscious decision—*before being born*—to get this exact illness at this exact time. After being born this memory submerged, only to awaken later with the open-hearted sensitivity that often comes to those nearing death.

It's hard to not feel sad when we see a baby born deformed or retarded, or born healthy only to die a short time later. One friend's toddler was run over by a truck in just one careless moment. Another friend's four-year-old died of cancer. It's hard not to sympathize with the seeming helplessness of children, or feel that they are victims of an unpredictably cruel world. Yet we cannot ignore the greatness of the wisdom contained in these small bodies, or the forces coming into play which we barely understand with our practical minds.

After a while you learn the subtle difference
Between holding a hand and chaining a soul,
And you learn that love doesn't mean leaning
And company doesn't mean security,
And begin to learn that kisses aren't contracts
And presents aren't promises
And you begin to accept your defeats
With your head up and your eyes open
With the grace of a woman,
Not the grief of a child.

And learn to build all your roads
On today because tomorrow's ground
Is too uncertain for plans, and futures have
A way of falling down in mid-flight.

After a while you learn that even sunshine
Burns if you get too much.
So you plant your own garden and decorate
Your own soul, instead of waiting
For someone to bring you flowers,
Then you learn that you really can endure...

That you really are strong
And you really do have worth,
And you learn and learn...
With every goodbye you learn.

12-YEAR-OLD DUTCH GIRL
CONFINED TO A WHEELCHAIR

At the same time, we must recognize our influence as parents. There may be conditions in our children over which we have no control, but there are others for which we are very much responsible. Disharmony in the family is a stress which can contribute to an illness in a child. Children's bodies are more sensitive than an adult's and cannot contain the stress without producing symptoms. An ulcer or heart disease in an adult is usually a result of many years. A child can develop a fever in five minutes. Our choice as parents is either to wallow in feelings of guilt ... or to thank our child for being a teacher of love, for bodily reflecting the condition of the family, for showing us the work we're needing to do.

The Lessons of Illness

As parents, we would naturally like to protect our children from all of life's pain. It is a deep parental instinct to try to provide a perfect environment for each of our children. Yet try as we will, it is inevitable that they will experience some degree of pain in their body and emotions. When this does occur, parents have the golden opportunity to open their hearts to their child's suffering and, by doing so, learn as well as teach one of life's greatest lessons.

As I sit to write this, tears come to my eyes, for I am currently involved in a difficult period in my mothering. Our three-year-old Mira has a severe case of whooping cough. She has been sick now for over a month. Her cough comes in spasmodic waves, sometimes causing her to turn blue. She vomits about ten times a day, after one of her coughing spells. Since she is up half the night coughing, she now sleeps in bed with Barry and me and is my constant shadow during the day.

Barry gave me this time to write since I feel compelled to share what I am learning through her illness. Having this time seems like such a luxury, a real gift.

When we first realized that Mira had whooping cough we felt very guilty. This illness has become quite rare as a result of widespread immunization programs. Rami was immunized. However, we both felt to spare Mira the pertussis part of the DPT. After Mira was born, we read from several sources that childhood illnesses are teachers for children, coming to strengthen them and to develop their inner being. At the time of our decision, we felt that Mira's strong, healthy body could handle the childhood illnesses and thus she would develop a strong immune system within her body. The decision felt right at the time for her.

Now in the midst of the severity of the illness, we first had to handle our feelings of guilt. We hadn't fully realized how sick she would become. We needed to go back and hold to our initial inspiration. Once we could do that, we could then forgive ourselves and honor our decision. We were then free to turn our attention to helping Mira and learning as much together with her as possible. (The decision to immunize a child is very individual. Parents must search earnestly within their own heart for the right decision for each child.)

Having freed myself from the guilt of not immunizing Mira, her illness has served as my main teacher these past four weeks. Fatigue has been my constant companion as I embarked on a new spiritual practice of staying up most of the night with my sick girl, endlessly mopping up the floor from when she would suddenly vomit, changing sheets over and over again. I was basically tied to the house. Barry was away more than usual, as he needed to shoulder all of my outside responsibilities as well as his own.

At first I felt a slight degree of self-pity, which slowly grew as each day wore on. I found it hard to give up my precious meditation time. I've been so attached to my time alone. But harder by far was observing Mira's physical and emotional pain and being unable to provide much comfort.

After five days of stormy, rainy weather, the sun burst through the clouds illuminating the surrounding grassy hillsides in exquisite splendor. I told Mira we were going outside to sit in the sun. I bundled her up, brought comfortable blankets to sit on, some of her favorite books, and we ventured out. Mira happily looked at her books and I knew from experience that I might have ten minutes of uninterrupted time. I closed my eyes and gratefully received the sun's warmth, then said a very earnest prayer, "Beloved God, I only have a very short while to be with you. Please help me for I am suffering so much inside."

I felt on the verge of breaking. I couldn't see good coming out of this difficult period in my life. Perhaps because my prayer was so earnest, I received a reply almost instantly. A light opened within me as I felt divine assurance that I was not alone. Each moment God's Presence and love were there to be felt, only I had chosen to put my attention upon Mira's pain and the difficulty of the situation. I was shown in those brief moments that by keeping my heart continually open to the entire process she and I were involved in, we would both receive a spiritual gift which we could not receive in any other way. She received this illness not only to learn lessons herself but as a gift for me as well. By opening my heart to her pain, by staying grateful for this opportunity for us both to grow, I would be showing her a way to relate with all of life's pain. In the midst of a severe cough attack, to hold her and assure her of God's love and protection would provide a healing presence around her, as well as establish a healing pattern within her. An earnest prayer for help and ten minutes of quiet to receive simple guidance changed the course of her illness and my reaction to it.

I realized that providing a healing presence based on gratefulness and assurance of the omnipresence of divine love was the greatest gift I could give to Mira and to myself. Until then I was very much in my head, trying to give the perfect herb at the right time, using homeopathic and anthroposophic medicines, and watching her diet. All of those things are important, but not as important as providing a healing atmosphere and keeping my heart open and sensitive to Mira's real experience and needs.

Throughout these four weeks I have seen a deepening within Mira. Her eyes seem to have filled with compassion for both her own and other's suffering. She seems much wiser and more rooted upon the earth. When she is not coughing or vomiting, she plays with an ever- deepening sense of exuberance, seemingly thankful for the joy that life affords as well as the pain.

I feel differently as well. Mira has been teaching me not to hold on to life's pain. One minute she is coughing and vomiting and crying. Then she is finished and runs to play with her puppy, sitting on him and giggling at the silly clumsy things he does. Sometimes I just hold on to the bowl she threw up in and feel like crying over the suffering she just experienced. But then she calls out, "Mama, look how cute puppy is." Mira has moved on to joy and calls me to do the same. Children suffer and are quick to let go of it. We adults suffer and can hang on for years while we think about it from every conceivable angle.

By opening to Mira's illness I feel open to my own suffering as well as the suffering of all human beings. I can see the hand of God behind it all, gently moving us toward healing, love, and beauty. Thank you God and Mira for teaching me this valuable lesson.

Children as Healers

All can be servers, healers. To be a servant of God is the most lovely opportunity given to humanity. The practical servants are those who walk closely with God, who are ever aware of His Presence.

WHITE EAGLE
HEAL THYSELF

I once heard Richard Gordon, the author of *YOUR HEALING HANDS*, talk about the "accidental" discovery of the "polarity circle". As a polarity therapist, he was once treating a woman with a uterine problem. It was on a ranch and some children happened to come into the room asking if they could help. Richard decided to take them up on their offer. He gave each child a specific "hold" to do. The woman later described feeling surrounded by a beautiful light and immediately started to feel better.

Children are natural healers. Sometimes little four-year-old Mira will gently place her hand on my forehead, and when I close my eyes I feel touched by an ancient motherly healer. Her touch can be so pure because there's not a thought in her head that would interfere with that purity. A child's gift of healing can be encouraged and developed from an early age. If ignored, this natural ability may become buried under the doubts and feelings of unworthiness that can plague the older child and adult.

One Christmas season, when Mira was an infant and Rami almost six years old, Joyce's mother came for a visit. She came to help and we were certainly glad about that. She did help ... the first week that is. Then she got *very* sick with the flu. Days went by without any improvement and Joyce and I were left with three to care for instead of two. The worst part for Joyce's mom was the disappointment she felt in not being able to help. She felt she was a burden upon us, even though we assured her she wasn't. We did everything we could to nurse her back to health, but nothing seemed to be working.

Then one afternoon while Grandma was napping in Mira's room, Rami quietly entered the room and crept up to her. She raised her hands over Grandma's head in blessing while she closed her eyes to concentrate. In her heart she felt sure she could help heal Grandma by asking the angels of healing to help her. She was determined to remain standing there as long as was needed.

After some time, Joyce's mom started to wake up. With her eyes still closed she began to feel peaceful for the first time since she got sick. She lay there totally unaware of Rami's presence above her, enjoying this moment of peace. Suddenly she felt surrounded by a wonderful light which soothed her and seemed to warm her from within. The experience was so lovely she longed to preserve this moment forever, but something also caused her to open her eyes. There above her was Rami, with her hands still raised in blessing. It seemed to Grandma that she had never seen Rami look so beautiful, like a radiant angelic being pouring a blessing down upon her. In that moment she knew without a doubt that she was being healed. With overflowing gratitude she hugged her granddaughter close to her heart. And when the sun rose the next morning, Grandma was on her way to health once again.

Honoring the Body Temple

Children can be shown from an early age that our bodies are our beloved friends and should be treated with respect. Proper nutrition, sleep, and exercise are not only our sacred responsibilities, but can be fun as well. From the age of two or even younger, children can begin to learn healthful eating. Rami always received carrot sticks as a treat and used to devour them as another child would candy. With each food I gave her, I would explain the special way that particular food helped her body, how it was a gift from Mother-Earth.

When Rami started pre-school and kindergarten, she discovered that the foods she received as treats (carrot sticks, apple pieces, raisins and almonds) weren't considered treats by most of her friends. She began to object a little, so we added natural cookies and candy sweetened with honey. We insisted, however, that she eat well-balanced meals before receiving these treats.

I remember one incident very well. Barry had promised to take five-year-old Rami to a special movie. He also promised her a large box of popcorn. We all sat to eat lunch before their big "date". I served a special salad that Rami was usually very fond of. However, this day she picked at the salad and refused to eat. Barry happily ate his salad reminding Rami throughout the course of lunch that she couldn't have the popcorn until she ate her salad. I could tell she didn't believe him. For you see, Barry has a very soft spot in his heart for popcorn.

It came time to go to the movie. Barry casually picked up the salad bowl and walked out the door with Rami. He told me later that once inside the movie theater he set the salad bowl down on her lap. Then he went off to buy *his* popcorn. As he silently sat munching, she finally believed him. She quickly ate up the salad and received the promised big box of popcorn. To this day Rami eagerly eats her salads.

Not long ago, a Los Angeles County Supervisor suspected that poor diet contributed to the problem behavior of juvenile delinquents. He hired an expert in sociology and criminal justice to study how changing their diets affected the institutionalized youths. A group of these youths was studied before and then after removal of refined carbohydrates and chemical additives, plus the addition of vitamins and minerals. Antisocial behavior, such as assaultive and suicidal incidents, was cut by almost half. As a result of this study, permanent dietary improvements were established in all the juvenile institutions of Los Angeles.

We as parents have something to learn from this. Children are highly sensitive to diet. We don't have to be fanatics about diet. Good judgement will guide us in most cases. A healthy diet should include foods in their natural state as much as possible. Cooked or processed foods should always be balanced with raw foods, such as vegetables, fruits, nuts, and seeds. All of us should learn the basics of food combining; which food groups go well together at the same meal.

Although we have been vegetarians since 1972, we do it because we feel it's right for us. It's almost as if our bodies simply say yes to this way of life. We don't advocate that people become vegetarians. We advocate that people take the time to listen carefully to their bodies.

Our children have never had meat in their lives. Rami, now nine years old, has her own way of understanding this. Someone asked her a few years ago, "Why don't you eat meat?" She pondered the question a moment, then answered, "I feel like all the animals are my dear friends. I could never eat a dear friend!"

Exercising our bodies to keep them strong and healthy can be a tremendous source of enjoyment. It's so much fun to go on a family exercise adventure. Hikes in the woods, bike rides, cross country skiing and swimming are wonderful family sports. Baby packs and bike seats help the little ones along and allow them to enjoy the outdoors too. As often as possible families should enjoy together the bountiful gifts of nature; sunshine, wind, the natural smells of trees and flowers, wading in a sunlit stream, the clear singing of birds, and gentle rain upon the face. This beauty in combination with physical exertion brings a feeling of wholeness and well-being to each member of the family. When adults are asked to remember a favorite memory from childhood, they will often relate a family hike, fishing trip or other outdoors excursion.

Eating wholesome meals, obtaining adequate sleep, and exercising in the beauty of nature builds a momentum of health and strength for children and parents, helping each to radiate their full potential.

The Magnifying Game

God is the creator.

SARA, AGE 8

There is a story about Mother Mary that is especially dear to us. We imagine it to be quite true. It has to do with the famous "Magnificat", Mary's statement: "My soul doth magnify the Lord..." In the story, Mary wanted to convey this principle to Jesus as a small child, to awaken him to the great destiny she knew he had. She saw the soul as a great magnifying lens, that whatever its attention rested upon , would be magnified, or empowered. She knew that each of us, by our attention or awareness, had the ability to magnify either good or evil. Even more, what our attention is upon, we become. We have the power to mold and reshape our molecular structure by our continued attention. We all know this just by seeing what chronic worry does to a person's face and body, or how youthful thoughts create a continually youthful face and body.

Mary made all this into a delightful game with her little Jesus. When he would fall down and scrape his knee, she knew he had the choice to magnify either the appearance world, the physical reality of bleeding and pain, or the deeper reality of a divine being wearing a coat of flesh that had been temporarily damaged. She would skillfully help him to magnify the latter, at which point he would laugh with delight at how the sensation of pain would become a tickle instead.

They would play this game throughout the day whenever an opportunity arose. Another time, Jesus brought his mother a dead bird he had found. Instead of focusing on the dead body and giving power to that appearance, they would visualize the spirit of the bird soaring unencumbered by the weight of a body. All the while, this "game" was a very powerful training to prepare him for his work in manifesting the inner Christ.

So you can see, this game is only limited by your creativity from situation to situation. And it's not for mothers only. Joseph was equally adept at this "transformation game". So fathers can play too. And are not all children Christs in the making? Can we not help them "magnify the Lord" in even the smallest daily happenings?

Healing through Parenthood

Children can bring to their parents great opportunity for healing. Parents can be raised to a higher level of maturity through the process of raising their own children. Through loving, caring and guiding their child through the various stages of growth, they have the marvelous opportunity to inwardly heal the hurts they experienced at each of these levels in their own childhoods.

We once saw a man in counseling who as a child had been badly abused by his father. An important step in the healing of his childhood wounds was to forgive and feel compassion for his father. We asked the man to see his father's sincerity and love buried under the abusive behavior. After some initial resistance, our client was able to make an important transition in consciousness. He could now reverse the father-son relationship. He realized he was now father, and his father was now son. We then guided him to feel how his Heavenly Father had always been present throughout his childhood, invisibly guiding him in silent ways. Through meditation he was able to feel how loved and protected he had been all along. He was well on his way to healing, yet there still were deep wounds that needed further healing. We sat together and prayed, feeling an inner assurance that a complete healing would take place, but not knowing the form it would take.

Two years later we again saw this man. His face was radiant as he shared that his wife had become pregnant very shortly after we had all prayed for his healing. Nine months later their first child was born. The man was so in love with his son that he gave him all the love and tenderness that he failed to receive as a child. By doing so, he was also healing the deep wounds and hurtful memories of his own childhood. His healing came by giving away to another what he himself needed. Giving to his son was also giving to the little boy within himself.

If we look at a particular stage of development in our child and say, "I don't like what he is going through. I sure wish he'd get over that one quickly!", perhaps that is an area from our own childhood memory that is needing healing. Giving our child extra compassion, guidance, and tenderness in these difficult periods can actually be giving a great gift to ourselves, helping us to become more whole. If we as parents can remember that our children are also here to heal us, then we can also remember to be grateful for the many ways we are called upon to give to them.

Surrendering Our Children

Lord I love these children
Help me come closer to your light
Strengthen me to serve them
Heal me and cleanse my sight

Lord you are my Shepherd
I stand in the shadow of Love
Help me as a mother to turn to you
To reach ever higher above

I know I am forgiven
Help me be forgiving as well
Take away my pride that I may hear you
Help us in your Kingdom to dwell

Lord you have made me a strong woman
You've given me strong children to raise
Help me everyday to remember
To listen to serve and to praise

A MOTHER'S PRAYER
SONG BY NANCY WALLACE

When Rami was seven years old she became very sick with an unidentified illness. Her fever soared to 105 each evening, and was normal by morning. This went on for two weeks. She was barely able to eat and became very weak. Her ears were also affected, resulting in her hearing being much reduced. Neither traditional medicine, homeopathy, herbs, nor the Indian Ayurvedic system seemed to be helping. After two weeks there was still no improvement. I sat by her bed each morning and evening and prayed that she would get better.

Our friends, Maitreya and Maloah Stillwater came to town to host an evening of "Miracle Singing". Barry and I decided to bundle Rami up and take her. It seemed as if a miracle were needed to heal her. At first I regretted bringing Rami for the noise seemed to cause great pain to her ears. She looked miserable. I decided to take her home after one more song. That next song used the words, "Master come to me. Teach me how to see. You know who I am so well." I closed by eyes and saw the beautiful form of Mother Mary. I immediately began praying to her to heal Rami. Her response to me was so beautiful, "You have been praying and praying to me to heal Rami, always with the fear that I won't. Remember, Rami is my child too. Surrender her to me and ask that God's will be done in her body... and then trust."

Gradually I was able to let go of the fear and surrender my precious daughter, trusting in God's will.

I opened my eyes to behold Rami's smile. "I love you Mama. Could I have a cookie from the refreshment table?" I felt so happy inside to see Rami's lovely smile and to hear her ask for food for the first time in two weeks. By the next day she was outside playing. Her hearing returned and the fever was gone.

The spiritual attitude of a parent during a child's illness is very important. With acceptance and serenity a parent can be used as a powerful healing channel. As the parent helped give birth to the physical body of their child, so also can they help to restore that body to health. I had a very meaningful experience of this truth with my mother. The Wednesday after Thanksgiving 1966 my mother picked up the phone in Buffalo, New York, "Mrs. Wollenberg", the voice said, "if you wish to see your daughter alive, please come at once to New York City. She is very close to death."

The call came as a sudden shock to my parents for I had just been with them for Thanksgiving vacation. I had needed the rest with them as my studies at the Columbia Presbyterian Nursing School were very difficult for me. I had walked and bicycled in the crisp autumn air and felt somewhat better, though not completely healthy, by the time they put me on the plane back to New York City. Three days later I developed a high fever. Within thirty-six hours I lay in critical condition in the intensive care unit. My fever was raging and could not be brought down. My blood pressure was slipping and I had been unconscious for over twenty-four hours.

"Mrs. Wollenberg, come as soon as you can. We all feel it is very important that you be here."

My mother put down the phone and called my father. They prayed together and decided that my mother should go as soon as possible. Buffalo was having a snow storm that day and the earliest flight was eight hours later in the evening. My mother remembers a calm feeling which came over her. As a good church secretary, she did the bulletin for Sunday service then quickly hurried home. She went to my room and prayed that I would recover.

By the time my mother boarded the plane for New York City the reality that she might not see me alive finally hit her. She prayed very deeply and asked that God's will be done in my body. With gratefulness and humility she accepted God's love in this situation ... even if I were to die. With her perfect acceptance came the loving and comforting presence of Jesus. She felt as if He sat by her side for the rest of the plane ride. This was one of the deepest spiritual experiences of my mother's life. By the time she arrived in New York City she felt very raised in consciousness.

As it was late and snowing by the time the plane landed, the taxi drivers didn't want to take her to the hospital. Finally she met an elderly black man who, upon learning that her daughter was near death, eagerly went out of his way to give her a ride in his taxi. He prayed with her and sang spiritual songs the whole ride. When they arrived at the hospital he took her hands and kissed them. Then with tears in his eyes he blessed her and refused to take money for the ride.

My mother later said she felt as if she were walking in a ray of golden light. The nurses who met her at the door were very concerned and immediately brought her to my hospital room. Outside the room fifteen medical doctors were gathered, specialists, residents and interns. My illness had become the interest of this teaching hospital. One of its own nurses or doctors are always given top priority care.

The doctors drew my mother into their solemn little circle. "Mrs. Wollenberg," the chief attending physician spoke in a low, grave voice, "everything possible has been done to save your daughter. We are afraid she won't survive. The fever is still uncontrolled and she has not responded to stimulation of any kind in over twenty-four hours." Then in a more fatherly voice he added, "Would you like me to walk you into her room? She doesn't look very good and I don't want you to be frightened."

My mother observed the sad and worried faces on the doctors. Inside, she still felt uplifted from the experience on the plane in which she had accepted God's will. "I want to enter by myself," was her calm reply.

I lay in a cooling tent, not responding to anyone or anything. My last memory was of a doctor slapping my feet demanding that I count to ten. "It's very important that you stay alert," he ordered. I remember looking with love as well as pity at him and all the other doctors bustling about doing procedures on my body. I also felt how hard my life had been recently, living in New York City and attending such a prestigious nursing school. My last thought was, "This is nonsense, I'm leaving." They could not get me to respond in any way after that.

The moment my mother put her hand on the door, it was as if a bright light were turned on within me. I became conscious. I saw the door open and what appeared like a radiant angel entered my room. I felt the presence of my Heavenly Mother as my physical mother approached my bed side. "Hi Sis, (my childhood name), I am here with you." "Oh mother," I responded. "I need you so much. I'm so sick." "You'll get better now," she said confidently, her hands finding mine under the tent. "Thank you for coming mom." I felt my body relax.

Within hours after her arrival my fever broke, my vital signs stabilized and I was able to communicate in a limited way with others. I was recovering! The next morning, though still very sick, I was taken off the critical list. The doctors were amazed! Each one thought his or her own particular drug or therapy had produced this miraculous recovery. I knew different. It had been my mother's acceptance of divine will and her uplifting assurance of God's love and presence in our lives that supplied the missing ingredient needed for my healing.

My mother, as she had done at my birth, served as a powerful channel for my heavenly mother. Just her presence in the room brought healing and remembrance of my purpose, thus restoring life to a dying body. I believe that if my mother had entered my room in a fearful or negative way she could not have been used in such a powerful way to heal me.

All the next week my mother continued to nurse me back to health. The high fever seemed to have damaged part of my memory, so she had to help me learn to walk and talk and write all over again. As long as she was there, my progress was very fast.

After one week I was told I would be leaving the hospital to spend one more week recovering in the dormitory infirmary. I felt

Joyce and Mother.

strong inside and well on my way to health. My mother planned to spend one more week with me. I suddenly realized how much I had needed her. I had been like a little child again dependent upon her. This discovery scared me. I so much wanted to "grow-up" and be independent. In a false front of being totally independent, I firmly told her to leave. Fortunately, my mother understood and did not take my attack personally.

Perhaps many of the problems between young women and their mothers stem from the fact that the daughters still need their mothers very much and react by pushing them away. Wise is the mother who can understand the pushing as an attempt to be independent rather than as a rejection. At age thirty-nine I have come to peace with the feeling that I will always need my mother. I may not need her advice, her physical care or even her approval for the way I live, but I will always need her love, for at different phases of my life she has served as such a pure and blessed instrument of my heavenly mother. She gave birth to my physical body and brought life to my dying body.

The older I become,
the more I think about my mother.

INGMAR BERGMAN

seven

The Healing of Parents

The Healing of Mothers

God could not be everywhere,
so he created mothers.

JEWISH PROVERB

My mother was the making of me. She was so true and so sure of
me, I felt I had someone to life for, someone I must not disappoint.
The memory of my mother will always be a blessing to me.

THOMAS A. EDISON

My mother's love was so great
that I have worked hard to justify it.

ARTIST MARC CHAGALL
JUST BEFORE HIS 90TH BIRTHDAY

"How can I heal the deep resentment I feel towards my new baby?"
    "I feel as if there isn't enough time for me anymore. I grow angry
at how much time the children take up."

"Since I've become a mother, life doesn't really seem worth living anymore."

"I feel like my children are driving me crazy . . . I'm on the brink of a nervous breakdown."

These comments and others were heard at a recent workshop entitled, "The Healing of Mothers", where a group of fifty mothers shared their deepest needs for healing. Each woman's story was so moving. I co-led the workshop with my friend Jeannine Parvati Baker, who through her books and workshops has done much to help parents. Though we had not seen each other in over five years and lived a thousand miles apart, we had always felt a mutual respect for one another. After a short phone call we had decided we would each pick one area in which we felt mothers most needed healing, and that we felt would help prevent burnout. We would each then focus on this area in the workshop.

We were surprised to discover that, despite our different concentrations of work and different locations, we had each picked exactly the same area: healing the relationship with one's physical mother, which in turn opens the door to a deeper relationship with the heavenly mother, the Source of Mothering.

Earlier this year my mother suffered another heart attack and a major stroke. It centered in the speech and writing areas of her brain. At first, we didn't know if she would be paralyzed or even live through the night. She regained movement slowly and her walking, talking, and writing to this day are impaired. Throughout those crisis weeks, we fasted, prayed and released her into the hands of God.

As soon as my sister called me with the devastating news of the stroke, I began praying for MY MOMMY to live. I felt very humble and vulnerable to the spirit. With the exception of giving birth, I have never felt as close to the spirit.

I held my mother as she lay in the coronary intensive care unit of the hospital. Her skin was gray and scaled, dried by drugs being pumped continuously into her veins. I massaged herb infused oils into her arms, hands, feet and legs. I annointed her with healing and sweet-smelling lotions. Her skin became like a baby's and I felt like her mother holding her and rubbing her down. For an exquisite moment, I was my mother's mother cradling her, my baby. We were healed and forgiveness flooded our hearts. We knew instantly that we both loved one another forever and were doing the best we could to take care of one another during our brief sojourn upon this earth.

Consciously I've been trying to be the mother I have always wanted my mother to be, in an effort to heal both ends of the continuum at once—both my primal imprint of mothering and my present culture's current limited support of natural/ transformative mothering. Being the kind of mother I always wanted for my self, bold and honest with my own children, has mothered me also along the way.

When I forgive my mother, I release more space for me to be that ideal mother myself with my own children. How? By not tying up my emotion-backed responses to how NOT to do it. Instead I can more creatively and positively be the mother my children need in the moment. Resolution of past grievances frees present creative response. I needn't react from a backlog of unfelt pain or unconscious revenge. One of the hardest challenges mothers have is to love their own mothers the way they are and not repeat their mother's mistakes with their own children. Forgiveness opens my heart to the mothering process and allows me to be receptive to the mothering of our Divine Mother, our Lord and God.

JEANNINE PARVATI BAKER

It is almost impossible to have a deep relationship with the heavenly mother when there is an inherent grudge against one's own mother. The mother is the first channel for the heavenly mother's love to reach the infant. One cannot expect to by-pass the important relationship with one's mother. If a woman resents the way her mother raised her, she will on some level also resent herself for the way she is raising her children. If a woman cannot forgive her mother, then she will be unable to fully forgive herself and her mothering.

The link between mother and daughter is so strong. We can only glimpse at the magnitude of this connection. Much is imparted from mother to daughter on an unconscious level, which is then passed on to her children in turn. Through the daughter's act of forgiveness towards her mother, she is allowing the purity of the relationship to flow on to her children. Through lack of forgiveness, through holding onto grudges and resentments, she is preventing this flow of purity and allowing all that was unclear to flow on to her children.

Joyce and Mother (1946).

Several years ago Barry and I were guest teachers at a retreat conference. I was asked to give one of the women's classes. The women had been meeting regularly, meditating, singing and dancing together. For my class I announced that we would all work on our relationship with our mothers. I explained that a woman can go just so far on her journey of life and then she must make peace with her physical mother if she wishes to advance further.

Several of the women became negative and, as they angrily left the room, said that this was a spiritual class, not a psychological one. Other women groaned, or shifted around nervously, but stayed out of politeness to me. A few friends tried to support me as best they could, but I could tell they were doubting my wisdom. However, I felt so strongly about this that I plunged ahead. I feel that clearing our relationships with our mothers, whether alive in the body or in the spirit world, is a very high spiritual practice.

I had all of the women take turns and describe their mother's most beautiful quality. For most of the women in that circle, this was a very hard task. They were so used to seeing their mother in negative terms and feeling all the ways that their mother had failed them. I pressed each woman until she truly *felt* something beautiful about her mother.

Then we closed our eyes and imagined ourselves sitting in silence before our mothers. I had each woman feel how long she had been together with this soul—as mother/daughter in one life and the reverse in another; sisters; teacher/student etc. As a group we felt, each in our own ways, the depth of this connection. We then forgave our mothers, feeling how hard they had tried to serve us. Finally, we imaged a great master blessing and healing our relationship. There was a beautiful feeling in the room as we ended and sang a song of blessing to one another. There were no words spoken.

In the course of a year, three of the women either wrote or visited me. They were the ones that had complained but stayed out of politeness. They each described a healing that had taken place between themselves and their mothers which had brought much joy into their lives. One middle-aged woman from England was so happy as she exclaimed, "It works—it really works. I feel so much more peace."

All mothers, no matter how many mistakes they may have made, have tried. Their deepest intention and ideal was pure and beautiful. They just may not have been able to express their ideal in the most perfect way—or in the way we would have wanted. It is our job as daughters to see beyond the mistakes, to feel the pure intention within their hearts and thus receive their "behind the scenes" love. If we get caught in seeing the "on-stage" mistakes, then we miss out on the love and blessing for our spiritual journey.

While holding our first born, minutes after her birth, I resolved to be a perfect mother to her. My ideals were very high. Two days later I sat saddened. Already I had made so many mistakes. I was unable to fully manifest my high ideals. I thought of my mother and felt her beautiful, noble ideals for my brother and me, and how she too was unable to fully bring those ideals into her mothering. As I thought of her many little mistakes over the years, I suddenly felt so much compassion and admiration for how hard she tried. Then I hoped that Rami would also remember me as a mother who tried, rather than a mother who made a lot of mistakes. I was able to forgive myself and my joy in motherhood returned.

In counseling, I have discovered that women who have had difficult childhoods often found it most helpful to think upon their mother the way one would their beloved child. Some parents, though pure in heart and intention, lack the understanding and tools needed to practice their ideals. Rather than blaming them, we might see this as a result of having had a difficult childhood themselves. When the women looked upon their parents with the same compassion that they looked upon their mistake-making child, their hearts were able to open in love to that parent.

It is equally important for a woman to clear up her relationship with her father, since it affects her relationship with all men. We wrote a chapter in THE SHARED HEART entitled, "Getting Straight With Parents", which goes into more depth about this relationship as well as a man's relationship with both his father and mother. In the process of fathering, it is crucial that a man "get straight" with his father, which is described later in this chapter.

It is never too late to begin the process of healing your relationship with your mother. During one of our workshops in England I witnessed a 65-year-old woman finally forgive her mother who had died twenty years earlier. All of us in the room were in awe as we felt the presence of the woman's mother yearning to give her daughter a blessing. As the woman was able to fully forgive, we experienced light filling her being, making her very radiant. She wrote to me later that by forgiving her mother she had felt a deeper connection with her daughter and grandchildren, and that her profession as a healer had become more meaningful.

Once a woman feels love and forgiveness for her mother, the door opens for contact with her heavenly mother. Some call this a cosmic mother; others the Blessed Mother Mary, and others the Divine Mother or other women saints. All are one in the same, the Presence of our Mother-God.

The Mother-God is an infinite source of strength, compassion, understanding, love and support for every human mother. We are all blessed with the gift of Her Presence if we choose to feel Her. Her Presence in our lives allows us to feel the tender child we really are. As mothers, the responsibility we feel towards our children can at times feel like a burden. If we take time in silence to feel the loving arms of our True Mother, then we realize that we are Her humble servant, and that "our" children are really Hers. Her wisdom is ever available as we seek to guide, nourish, and inspire our little ones.

I was talking to a close friend recently whose nine-year-old daughter had been diagnosed as having childhood diabetes. The girl had been very sick and had been hospitalized for one week. Now the mother, a single parent, was having to change her life to accommodate the daughter's strict diet, sleep and exercise program, and her need for a relatively stress-free environment.

One evening the daughter had eaten an inadequate supper after her insulin injection and had fallen asleep. Her mother tired to wake her as it was important that the girl have a high protein snack for the long night time. The girl started convulsing, and continued until she was rushed to the hospital and received intravenous glucose.

The mother described feeling totally drained of energy each day. She felt overwhelmed by the stress of her daughter's illness and her responsibility to care for her each day. We talked about the Heavenly Mother and how her daughter was really Her child and responsibility. My friend gasped and said, "You mean I'm not the only mother she has!" Then the tension drained from her face and body as reassurance and love filled her being. She saw that her main work was to attune herself to the Mother-God and listen for guidance, rather than only being concerned with what the girl ate. She shared with me later that concentrating on her Mother-God's love surrounding her and her daughter had given her the proper energy and serenity she needed to care for her child.

Mother's often feel resentment for their child, or feel as if their child is driving them crazy, because they do not realize that the child as well as they themselves have a truly great Mother. Imagine the joy of having a "Master Mother" to turn to with all of our problems and concerns about our child, One who loves and knows the child much better than we do. Setting aside quiet time each day to go to our "Master Mother" and receive her blessing and guidance for the care of our children is the most important thing a mother can do each day. This Being of Love understands how busy mothers are. We don't need to sit in meditation for hours. Even a few minutes of asking for help, trusting, and sending love will do. Even if you feel nothing special happens during your quiet time, trust that you are creating a momentum of blessing which will affect you and your children your entire lives. This quiet time can provide the support and the space so many mothers are seeking.

It helps to remind ourselves every day that to be a mother, to care for and guide one of God's precious children, is one of the highest ways to serve. Motherhood is one of the most valuable professions a woman can enter into. Motherhood can also be the least glamorous and least appreciated profession as well. Yet in the overall view of our entire life, there is no more noble use of our time and talents than to give to the world the gift of a loving, spiritually aware human being.

In the summer of 1985, we had the great privilege of doing workshops and giving talks nationally and internationally. In thirty days, we had conducted over twenty days of workshops. It was our big travel tour for the year. Barry and I both love the workshops so much. They are really like a joyous vacation for us. Because of the growth and healings that take place, people treat us so beautifully.

Once back home the girls needed our attention. I was faced with all of the down-to-earth tasks of mothering. I drove Rami to a friend's house to play and picked her up again. I took both girls to the dentist, and then to buy new shoes. We cleaned out the toy chest. I felt great joy as the two girls loved one another and I tried to stay calm as they fought.

One night after folding five loads of their laundry, I began to grumble inside, "in the workshops I'm doing much more valuable work than I am right now," as I hunted in the pile for the matching little red sock. "The children don't appreciate all I do for them," I thought as I folded the tenth little undershirt. "All these mundane chores make me feel like I'm stagnating," I thought as I finally found the other red sock. (You can see I had become quite spoiled.)

I grumbled inwardly for another day. The children sensed my attitude and pulled out all of their worst behaviors. That night I prayed for help and understanding before going to sleep. I had a beautiful vision just upon awakening. I saw the Master Jesus washing the feet of His disciples, saying, "The greatest of you shall be the humble servant of others." I woke up very inspired. In our jobs as mothers, in serving and caring for our children, we are really in training, learning to be a Perfect Servant of God. Through this training, God is bringing forth our true greatness. I saw so clearly that mothering is bringing me true understanding of God. The workshops, lectures, and writing almost seemed a by-product of mothering. I felt so thankful for the privilege to be a mother, thankful for Barry and the girls and for all parents, and thankful for each undershirt and sock I have the privilege to fold. The girls sensed the inner change in me and had such a joyous day.

> *Doing little things with a strong desire to please*
> *God makes these things really great.*
>
> SAINT FRANCIS DE SALES

Motherhood involves an immense training and initiation. Loving and guiding our children opens our hearts to all the children

"Song of the Angels," by William Bouguereau

of the earth. Serving our children brings us into the consciousness of The Mother of the World. We have so much to be grateful for. We need to remember this each time we change a dirty diaper, mop up little mud tracks on the floor, or drive a car-load of giggly teenagers to a party. Each time we serve with joy and gratitude we are receiving a hundred-fold and coming a step closer to universal mother love.

The Mother was the stepping stone of Jesus to Christhood.

HAZRAT INAYAT KHAN

Cuddle your soft bundle and tuck your little ones close to your heart, embrace your husband tenderly and rest assured there is no more real spiritual path than motherhood. You are a highly privileged child of God to have been given such a blessing.

QAHIRA QALBI

The Healing of Fathers

In man I recognize Thy loving protection.

HAZRAT INAYAT KHAN

Fathers—bless us all—we often need healing! We often forget about what's important. We easily get sidetracked into a preoccupation with "jobs". Our "provider" instinct is often misdirected as we get ourselves stressed out by overworking, all with the original intention of providing a secure nest for our family. After all our "providing", we find ourselves too burned-out to be really available to our family.

Many of us swear we'll never be like our fathers, who we often remember as being "workaholics." Then to our surprise we find ourselves doing the same thing. We selectively don't remember all the good parts of our fathers and the ways they sincerely tried. The fathers of the people attending our workshops always seem to get the worst publicity. They get described as "spaced out", intellectual, un-caring, intoxicated, and abusive, not to mention workaholic.

I sincerely feel that it's just as hard to be a conscious father as mother. I feel this partly stems from the more remote way we become fathers. While the transition into motherhood is intimate and physical, fathers come into being through the mother. We don't have the preparation of pregnancy, childbirth, and nursing, with its bonding and deep imprinting on the body itself. This is changing now that men are showing more interest and taking a more active part in pregnancy and birth. Now there are more and more fathers who recognize the importance of their role in the family.

Before a man can fully realize himself as a father, he must clear his relationship with his own father. One of my favorite stories I told in *THE SHARED HEART* was about a man "getting straight" with his father:

As a little boy, this man had worshiped his father as most little boys do. Then, entering the years of late childhood and adolescence, a disenchantment set in. He saw his father as weak, self-centered, and ignorant. He no longer respected him and grew to despise him as well. All communication broke down. At the age of eighteen he went away to college and had not lived at home since. He learned to adapt himself to a superficial relationship with his father which prevailed whenever he visited.

Later during marriage his aloofness and distancing techniques finally manifested into the present crisis. A pending separation had caused him to seek counseling. Feeling the connection between his marital difficulties and his relationship with his father, I asked him to share his father's strengths with me. He told me his father had none. I insisted, sharing how I felt his marriage depended on it…that he needed to go beyond the stubbornness and rebelliousness he was projecting onto me as well as his father. That shook him a bit. He started by revealing some of his father's minor positive qualities, such as providing an income, being responsible, honest, and so on. This gave momentum to the process, however, which allowed him to go deeper. He began to see that although his father lacked education and verbal ability, he was a feeling-oriented man with a deep sensitivity who understood and related to the world in that way. Suddenly, eyes brimming with tears, he saw how lonely his father was, and how much pain he had to endure.

Not long afterwards, this man had the opportunity to visit his parents. Remembering the session, he tried to be warmer toward his father, but years of habit patterns seemed to interfere. Finally he gave up and went out to visit friends. When he returned home late that night, he was surprised to see his father sitting all alone reading. A strange sensation seemed to pull him toward his father. Yielding to this, he went over and sat next to him. The older man started talking, a little about the book, but more just to make conversation. The young man listened, but he began to look at his father. For the first time in his life, he saw this man not as his father, but as a human being with joys and pains, happiness as well as sadness, victory as well as failure. He saw a man who loved him deeply but did not know how to show it. His father continued talking, but now the son was exploring new feelings. A great love was welling up in his heart for this unsophisticated, simple, and beautiful old man.

The father noticed the moist brightness in his son's eyes and stopped talking. He fumbled over a few more words, then stopped again.

"I love you, dad." The son was surprised at the strength and courage in his words.

"I love you too, son." Now the old man's eyes were moist too.

The young man leaned over and embraced his father. They sat there in silence while a healing took place between two souls.

As with a woman and her mother, a man needs to revision his relationship with his father, or his own fathering will suffer. We think negatively about our fathers because we were so disillusioned with them. We forget that disillusionment is the removal of illusions and, thus, is always a blessing. Our illusion as men was that our fathers were perfect and therefore should act that way. We came into our bodies bringing recent experience of the Father-God, the experience of the brilliant Light of the sun behind the sun. Then we were were entrusted into the care of a human (and divine) being called "father". It is only natural that we expect the same wisdom, love, and power to come through this person. It is natural, but it is certainly not fair. The revisioning comes about when we realize that our father is not our Father—that the Great Light which we remember as Father, had used this person at important moments, but this person was not our Father. When we recognize that this individual may need our love more than we need his, we can let go of him as Father, and we can stop expecting him to act like our Father.

Although our Father is Spirit without form, that Spirit, that Light, that Consciousness uses wonderful channels for our

Barry and Dad.

expression. The Spirit of the Father is expressed perfectly through those known as Masters—men who have become One with the eternal Father, and thus become eternal themselves. One day, with faith and persistence in our loving, we will walk and talk with these Great Ones. We will receive our training from them face to face.

What is asked of us now, however, is to believe in their Presence, and have faith that they are there for us.

To fully accept our own fatherhood, we must accept our need for help from these messengers of the Father. It's not important that we call them by name, or belong to specific religions that worship specific messengers. It's only important that we believe they are there, ask for their loving guidance, and then be grateful. That is enough.

I recently saw a man who was struggling to "find himself". He was traveling around with a girlfriend, her four-year-old and their two- year-old. Although he had been meditating for twelve years, he felt that his meditations were like momentary lifts in his life, and nothing more. He felt he was missing out on the real purpose of meditation. I asked him how he meditated. He described various techniques he had learned over the years. I looked at him and saw a man who was desperate, but who was too proud to really break down and ask for help. I told him he was needing to humble himself and recognize his need for help. I mentioned the Great Ones who longed to be of service to him, but only if he sincerely asked. One part of him was skeptical, while the other part was *very* interested. The interested part sensed my own firm belief in the presence of these Beings of Light. The skeptical part wanted proof, wanted a "technique" to contact them, perhaps some magical mantra or breathing exercise. His soul was desperate, his mind was arrogant, and I told him that. I told him his "technique" was to identify more with the need of his soul than the intellectual pride of his keen mind.

He heard this more deeply than he ever had before, but the real test awaited him in implementing what he now knew. I saw him later with his two-year-old, and knew how much his fathering depended on this humbling process. I foresaw how great a father he would become as he truly asked for help from those more advanced than he in the ways of Spirit.

Many times I feel far away from the the ideal of fathering. I seem to waste so much time lost in material living, forgetting my need for God as Mother and Father. But the Illumined Beings watching over me have such perfect patience. They never seem to mind however many times I run away, trip, fall down and hurt myself. In moments of pure remembrance, I can also imagine and feel myself to contain this pure, forgiving, all-wise love of the Father. Then I look at Rami and Mira through those Eyes, talk with them through those Lips, and touch them with that Heart and those Hands. Then I see Joyce also embraced by the Father of me, as well as little Barry embraced by the Mother of her. Little Barry, you're so forgiven for all your craziness and forgetfulness. Little Barry, your Father and Mother are devoted to you for all eternity.

The heart of man is Thy sacred shrine.

HAZRAT INAYAT KHAN

eight

Children as Teachers of Peace

by Gerald G. Jampolsky, M.D.

Jerry Jampolsky is a psychiatrist and author of the bestselling book LOVE IS LETTING GO OF FEAR. He is the founder of the Center for Attitudinal Healing in Tiburon, California. He has spoken worldwide before medical and lay audiences and has appeared on several TV programs.

Barry and I had the privilege of visiting with Jerry one cold winter day in 1985. By "coincidence", we all had one free hour before our separate scheduled talks. We had a delightful time and deeply felt our soul connection. A nice way to describe Jerry is from one of his favorite quotations:

> *Teach only love, for that is what you are.*

A COURSE IN MIRACLES

The following article is excerpted from Success Magazine.

Is it possible to give children positive attitudes and a sense of self-esteem? The answer is yes. But first we may have to change some of our own attitudes about ourselves and others. We must learn to demonstrate love rather than fear, peace rather than conflict. We must convey the understanding that each moment of life can be lived with optimism and enthusiasm. We must show our children how blessings flow from giving and forgiving. We must help them grow up in a world in which they know they are responsible for what they experience, in which they are self-reliant, in which inner peace is their only goal.

To have peace we must teach peace, for we teach what we want to learn. Perhaps the greatest gift we have been given is the power to choose what thoughts we put into our minds and the freedom that results from knowing that it is our own thoughts that determine what we experience. We must make use of this gift if we wish to exert a positive influence on our children's lives. Instead of adhering to the thought system of the world, which is limited to physical reality with its core of fears and opposites, we must choose the thought system of love, which transcends the physical universe, where love is the all- inclusive reality, and where there is no fear.

These days, more and more people are becoming convinced that the thought system of the world is not working, and that there must be another way of looking at the world, another way of looking at parenting, another way of looking at what is true and what is illusory. That other way, I believe, is to let our children become our teachers of peace and love. If we can see life as children do, with their clarity and simplicity of thought, their trust, and their innate capacity for joy and laughter, we can find very practical solutions to every problem we face.

The Thought System of the World

Unfortunately, a great many people see the world as a place that is filled with confusion, conflict, fear, anger, chaos, destruction, war, and despair, with a future that looks bleak and hopeless. They are convinced that we have created a situation in which the pressing of one button could immediately wipe out all life on this planet.

Of course, most of us say that we want to live in a peaceful world and that we want to have peace within ourselves, but how many of us truly believe this can happen? Certainly, if we allow ourselves to accept the thought system of the world, the past will continue to predict the future, and consistent peace in this world will seem impossible. This thought system states that, sooner, or later, we are going to be attacked, and if we want to survive, we've got to learn to defend ourselves or to attack first. It is a system that says fear is real and the world is not a loving world, but a hostile one.

Such ideas encourage us to give only in order to get, and to put great value on the material things of life; how much money we have in the bank, the size of our house, or the make of our car. They foster a creed by which success is determined according to what we own rather than what we are.

In this kind of world, we learn to be preoccupied with the pains and pleasures of the body, and thus we develop insatiable physical desires. We can never be satisfied in a world that teaches us that our personality-self, and not God, is the director of our life, and that happiness can come from manipulating and controlling others.

In this thought system, children are brought up to be seen and not heard, and to "Do as I say, not as I do." They learn, from our example, that guilt and fear are "real"; that life and the body are the same; that life, as well as death, is to be feared; and that it is normal to be ambiguous and ambivalent about everything in life.

Despite our best intentions, most of us continue to teach our children fear, conflict, and negative thinking as often as we teach them love, peace, and positive thinking. This is because we are trapped in a thought system which implies that maturity means becoming more efficient and wiser at making judgments about other people, so that we may better determine who our friends are and who our enemies are.

The majority of us continue to establish guilt feelings in children as a way of manipulating and changing their behavior into a form that adults approve of. If the children fit our prescribed form, we love them; if they don't, we withdraw our love.

This is the thought system of the world in action. It teaches that love is conditional, that receiving love depends on performance. And that, perhaps, is the greatest error we have made in parenting. We have measured and evaluated our children, each other, and ourselves to death.

If we persist in following this futile pattern, with its underlying fears, hostilities, and dissatisfactions, it is doubtful—if not impossible—that the world will ever see permanent peace. How much better it could be if, instead of teaching our children, we let them teach us.

The Thought System of Love

Most people tend to believe that the child's world is one of make-believe and fantasy, and that the adult world is "real." We teach our children that adults know more and are wiser than they, and that they are here to learn from us. But maybe the opposite is what it's all about.

Let me suggest that, in reading what follows, you suspend judgement. Try to accept what may seem like an incongruous idea—that children can be our teachers and can lead us out of the mental prison and the bondage of fear that we have accepted. Let us, through our children, recognize that our purpose in being here on earth is to experience oneness through extending our own love and peace to others. Let us learn from children that peace begins from within, not from without. And most of all, let us learn from children how once again we can learn to trust.

To look at the world differently requires a willingness to let go of the belief that age and experience determine who our teachers are. We need to stop thinking that because we adults have been on this planet longer than our children, we have more truths to teach them than they have to teach us.

A few years ago, a friend asked me the following question, knowing that I, like he, had once been a militant atheist: "Can you think of any time in your life when you felt the complete presence of love, the complete presence of God?" This example occurred to me:

When I was a third-year student at Stanford Medical School. I delivered my first child, and in that delivery room a light went on that was beyond any words I can articulate. There was a complete wonderment in me about the love that this newborn child radiated to everyone. For a moment I felt complete oneness with that innocent child, his mother, the nurse, the universe, and everyone and everything in it. I knew that I was experiencing something completely beyond any kind of intellectual understanding of mine. And, yes, for that moment I knew that I was experiencing complete love and the presence of God. The next day, when I was back in class, analyzing and evaluating fragmented facts, the presence of God and love seemed to disappear.

As I look back on that event, I now recognize, more than ever before, the full impact of the symbolic meaning of the newborn infant as teacher. I would like to suggest that we can take a leap in faith and look at the newborn infant in another way—through a spiritual lens that sees only love.

Six week old Rami.

Use your imagination and climb with me inside the mind of a newborn infant. What we see is a mind completely full of unconditional loving thoughts. The infant is not concerned with the size or shape of his parents' bodies, what his parents' performance record has been in the past, what they look like or what they might say, or whether the parents are worthy of love. That child, I am convinced, sees the parents as perfectly joined with him in love, and perceives no separation.

The infant symbolizes knowledge, not as an accumulation of fragmented facts, but as love, which is true knowledge. Love is the essence of his being, and the light he reflects can only be a reflection of God's love. His spiritual being is real and everlasting, and he innately knows that his body is only a temporary costume.

The newborn infant does not know about death, is not afraid of death. He simply knows that his true identity is love and that love never dies. He knows that in his "real" world there is nothing but love. He doesn't understand past or future, and he knows that this instant is the only time there is, an eternal instant for extending and expanding love. He feels completely loved by God, and his natural state is a combination of love, joy, and peace.

The newborn infant knows innately that you don't have a mind—you are your mind—and all minds are joined. He knows that there are no separate thoughts, no separate minds, that there is no separation, only oneness. In no way does he see himself as separate from anything else in the universe.

He knows only one kind of love, his response of love is always total and complete, and he excludes no one. He cannot move even his little finger without moving his whole body. He does not limit his reality to his physical senses—to what he sees with his eyes and hears with his ears.

Recognizing his identity as love, he knows that love asks no questions. It simply is. The infant speaks no words, but the highest form of love needs no words. He knows not of jealousy or possessiveness because he experiences complete union with all, and he knows that as love, he is everything and is everywhere. He knows that love is complete absence of fear.

In February 1982, my son Lee and I had the unusual opportunity of traveling with Mother Teresa for 20 hours as she lectured and prayed in different cities in India. She shared with us a story that went right to my heart. It concerned a South American woman who, Mother Teresa said, obviously knew what life and love were all about because she gave her newborn infant the legal name "Professor of Love." This mother knew with all her heart that her child was her teacher and would continue to remind her that her true reality was the child of love, the child of trust, the child of God.

Do we parents interfere with the trust that the infant child comes into the world symbolizing? Is not lack of trust one of the major problems facing the world today, and is it not lack of trust that seems to be destroying the universe?

Small children express tremendous trust. If a 2-year-old falls and hurts her knee, she comes running to Mommy. Mommy kisses her hurt and the hurt goes away. It is my opinion that pain goes away because the child experiences joining with her mother through love.

As children become older they are taught by their parents that they are separate: that is, they have separate bodies and separate minds; kissing the hurt will no longer make it go away. Pain appears when we feel separate; pain disappears when there is love and joining.

Let us let the innocent newborn child be our mirror and teach us what we are—love. Let us allow the innocent child in all of us to be awakened, and let us let go of the fearful child that we have been harboring inside of us right now and forever. Let us choose to see only the innocent, loving child in everyone we meet, and let us know that whatever we see is but a reflection of ourselves. Let us let a little child lead us into a world of oneness and union, into the only reality there is, a reality of truth that never changes, a reality of only love. Let us learn from the newborn infant to teach only love.

At the time of this writing, I am 57 years old, and I am doing my best to devote all my energies to unlearning the so-called "realities" of the world I have accepted. I am attempting to learn that there is an innocent child within me and within everyone else, and that the infant's reality is the only true reality. I would like to share with you a little of my past and something about the transformation process with which I am now struggling. Hopefully you will find that you can identify with some of these experiences . . .

I was raised in the Jewish faith. However, when I was 16 years old, a close friend of mine was killed in an automobile accident and whatever faith I previously had in God seemed to completely disappear. I no longer believed that there was a loving God, and I became a militant atheist for most of my life.

In general, I have not only found it difficult to be loving to all those I met on my pathway, but I have found it very hard to love myself. So I have spent enormous amounts of time immobilized by guilt and self-criticism, feeling unlovable and unloving. I became an expert at punishing myself. I not only lost all trust in God, but had great difficulty in trusting others, and particular difficulty in trusting myself.

I had just as many problems and difficulties being a parent to two sons (Greg, now 26, and Lee, 25) as any of the fathers and mothers who came to me for counseling during the 26 years I have been in practice. I remember being concerned about wanting to be a good parent, and I think I did what many people do: I attempted to copy from my parents the most positive values I learned from them, and I put a lot of energy into not repeating the mistakes I felt my parents made with me, mistakes for which I had not totally forgiven them. I was quite concerned about how my children performed and whether their behavior would make me look good or bad in the eyes of my colleagues and friends. Unfortunately, I frequently used guilt and manipulation as a way of modifying my sons' behavior.

As I look back on my parenting experiences, I am dismayed at how often, under the guise of loving my children, I was extending only conditional love, love that was dependent on their performances and behavior. Much of their childhood was spent with my being both a workaholic and an alcoholic. When I failed to live up to my composite image of being a good parent, I judged myself harshly and negatively.

By 1975, although the world saw me as a success and I had all the material things I ever thought I could want, my personal life was in chaos and I was desperately unhappy. My 20-year marriage had ended in a painful divorce; I had developed incapacitating back pain and, although I continued to deny it, I had become an alcoholic. I was convinced that I lived in a world that attacked me, that I was a victim of the world I saw, and that I would never be able to experience peace or love.

It has taken me a long time to recognize that I didn't have a monopoly on these emotions, (everyone has these feelings to some degree) and I was not put on this earth to change others (my primary function in this world was not to be critic or judge my children or anyone else, as I formerly thought it was).

It was also in 1975 that I came across a set of books called *A COURSE IN MIRACLES* (published by the Foundation for Inner Peace in Tiburon, California) that began to drastically change the thoughts in my mind and my life. When I first read these books, which are used as a tool for personal spiritual transformation, to my utter astonishment I heard an inner voice which said, "Physician, heal thyself. This is your way home."

The teachings in these books not only allowed me to experience periods of peace of mind and love beyond anything I had previously thought possible, but they also gave me a different way of looking at parenting. Since I believe that we teach what we want to learn, I wrote a small booklet based on the principles of the course (TO GIVE IS TO RECEIVE—AN 18-DAY COURSE IN HEALING RELATIONSHIPS AND BRINGING ABOUT PEACE OF MIND), as well as a book titled LOVE IS LETTING GO OF FEAR.

The basic principles in these teachings are simple. We have only two emotions: Love, which is our natural inheritance; and fear, which our mind has invented. In other words, instead of seeing others as attacking me, I can choose to change my perception and see them as either loving or fearful and giving a call of help for love. I found that I could love a fearful person, but I could not love someone I perceived as attacking me.

These three cardinal principles had tremendous practical application in bringing more peace to me:

1. Having peace of mind, peace of God as my only goal.
2. Having forgiveness be my only function
3. Not making any decisions until I have listened to my inner voice (this also goes by the name of intuition, gut sense, inner teacher, and voice of God).

When I began to change my belief system and to apply these principles to my life, positive and dramatic changes began to occur in my relationships with my sons—changes which go far beyond the simple explanation that we have become older and more accepting of each other in the past seven years . . .

In 1975, I helped start the Center for Attitudinal Healing, based on the concepts in A COURSE IN MIRACLES. In attitudinal healing, the basic tenet is that it is not people or conditions that cause us to be upset; it is our own thoughts and attitudes that need to be healed and changed. This tenet, in total opposition to the world's belief system, states that we are responsible for our feelings and our experiences. We don't have to be robots who allow others to press our buttons and determine whether we will be happy or sad, or whether we will be at peace or conflict. We can take full responsibility for ourselves; and by changing our attitudes and thoughts, our perception of reality will change.

Letting go of negative, judgmental thoughts, so that there will be only loving ones, allows our minds to be completely free, completely full of love, at peace, and joined. This is the purpose of attitudinal healing.

The world's belief system holds that everything in our external world is the cause, and that we are the effects. So when we are unhappy or in distress, we believe it is caused by something or someone in our external environment. When something goes wrong with our lives, when we are feeling a lack of love or having trouble with teaching love and being a loving parent, we are tempted to feel like a victim, so we want to find someone to blame. A part of our mind wants to blame our parents, the world, or those in it.

Forgiveness is the key to seeing the world differently. It is letting go of the past and is therefore the means of correcting our misperceptions. Forgiveness is letting go of whatever we think other people, the world, or God, have done to us, or whatever we think we did to them. Forgiveness is celestial amnesia; that is, it is letting go of all the memories of the past except the love we have given and received. Through forgiveness, we can stop the endless recycling of guilt and look upon ourselves, our children, our parents, everyone else—and God—with love.

Children are beautiful teachers of forgiveness. Take, for example, two 5-year-olds who are playing outside. Billy comes running in to his mother and says, "I am never going to play with Johnny again. He took my car away." Three minutes later, the mother sees her son outside with Johnny, perfectly happy. Billy had let go of the incident and had forgiven. Yet adults will often carry grudges and unforgiving thoughts for years. Whose reality is correct, and whose reality is more peaceful?

Not long ago, I was hired as a consultant for a large transportation company. When I went to a meeting there, I took along a 12-year-old boy, Tony Bottarini, who had been coming to the Center because he had cancer. At the meeting, one of the regional managers was angry because a competitor's company had hired away one of his key employees and it was going to be difficult to replace him. I asked Tony what he might say that could be helpful.

Tony asked the man if he felt upset, and the manager said, "Yes." Then Tony asked, "If you could be anyplace in the world that you wanted to be, where you could be relaxed and feel peaceful, where would you want to be?" The answer was, "Hawaii." Tony suggested to the man that he close his eyes and imagine that he was in Hawaii feeling relaxed, at one with the warm sand and the sky and the water. He went on to say, "You know, mister, you can't be relaxed or feel peaceful as long as you are angry. You won't be able to make wise decisions until you forgive, not just your competitor, but the guy he took away. Forgiveness is just letting go—letting the incident float away."

Later, the regional manager came up to me and said, "You know, if you had told me the same thing. I wouldn't have been receptive, but with Tony, a 12-year-boy, telling me these things, they seem so simple and right on." Yes, children have a way of making seemingly complex things clear and simple.

We cannot consistently teach love until all blame for everything and anything has disappeared. We cannot while still blaming someone else or ourselves. We cannot demonstrate total love to our children until we have healed all our relationships. Forgiveness is the key to happiness because it removes all blocks to love, and forgiveness allows us to live in a world of all-inclusive love.

Last February, when I was visiting Mother Teresa with my son, I told her that I was writing this article and asked her what comments she might make about parenting. She said, "Let your children see that there is love for them. Children must see how their parents love them. Especially let the children see how their parents love one another."

In order to do this, we must gain control of our undisciplined, unreined thoughts. We must see value in quieting the mind and at the same time have faith in knowing that this is possible. We can start by taking a few minutes a day and gradually increasing the time we spend in silence. Whether you call this meditation, prayer, or simply stilling the mind, is of no importance. What is important is to go in the direction of peace. As your mind becomes still, you can learn to listen to that inner voice of love, telling you what to do.

When we choose to be in the consciousness of love and to experience only the consciousness of love, there are no rules. All we need is to still our minds and know and trust that we are love, that God is within us, loves us totally, and will never leave us comfortless. We can then acknowledge the fact that we are the innocent children of God, and that our own children are our teachers of peace and love.

We must keep reminding ourselves that our children are our true mirrors. Let us keep the sparkle in our eyes ignited, and the effervescence of laughter continuous and everlasting in our hearts. Let us make each instant one in which there is a newborn celebration of love.

Let us allow each instant to be one in which time and space disappear and the splendor of love is experienced. Let us be witnesses to each other that peace begins with us; therefore, let us have only loving and peaceful thoughts in our hearts and our minds. And then let us extend that peace to our family and to all those in the world so that we and our children can enjoy a peace that is everlasting.

nine

Beginning Life

Each newborn child brings the message that
God has not lost his trust in man.

TAGORE

Before I came to earth my angel blessed me.
She told me I would be having a good mother and father and then a
sister too.

She said I would do something special on earth, but she didn't say
what it was.

I felt happy and excited to come to earth.

I felt a drop sad to leave my heaven friends, but I knew I could come
back in my sleep to visit.

My angel hugged me and gave me a lot of love, and told me to give the
love to lots of people to make them happy.

She said she would stay close to me and I could pray to her if I needed
help.

RAMI, AGE 8

Pregnancy

I remember so well a bright sunny day in August when Barry and I were camping with Rami, then four years old. This was the first year we had actually enjoyed camping since before Rami was born. Barry and I are both enthusiastic outdoor people who take to the woods and mountains as often as possible. Right before we conceived Rami, we had been traveling and camping throughout the U.S., Mexico and Europe for over one year. It was quite a shock to discover that, as a baby and toddler, Rami didn't enjoy camping at all. She hated to have her secure little environment disrupted in any way. Many were the sleepless nights in our tent while Rami cried.

At the age of four she accepted her fate as having joined a camping family and was enjoying herself immensely. Now that she had left behind her difficult two-year-old behavior and a darling but confusing three-year-old stage we were really enjoying the emergence of our little four-year-old girl. From our 6,000 foot perch in the mountains, sitting together with Barry watching Rami pick wild flowers, life seemed absolutely perfect. Having come through some difficult stages in parenting, we both had the secret wish that nothing would change, and that life would stay as simple and sweet as it seemed in that moment.

I closed my eyes and immediately felt the presence of another being. I quickly opened my eyes wondering who had come, only to discover Rami and Barry in the same scene as before. Closing my eyes once again, I felt another presence in an even stronger way. I felt this being to be a very dear and special friend, and heard deep within my heart, "You are ready now. I am coming to you and Barry. My presence will bring more depth to your relationship, as well as bringing more balance and harmony into the family. I would like to be conceived soon."

I then felt myself being surrounded by a peaceful warmth. I rested and nourished myself in the joy of that experience.

After a while I turned to tell Barry that we were going to have another child. I was bursting with joy of my recent experience and so was quite unprepared for the pained expression that came over his face. In a loving but firm voice he said, "I really don't want any more children right now. Let's just enjoy Rami." I dropped the subject.

Several weeks later I had a similar experience and felt within that it was time to conceive. When I again shared this with Barry, he merely gave me the same pained expression and no more was said.

One month later the being again visited me in a very powerful way. This time I simply talked the way one would talk to a dear

Pregnant with Mira.

friend on the phone. I explained that I was open to having another child only if Barry were too. If it wanted to come, Barry would have to feel the desire as well. Then, with a smile on my face I said, "Get to work on Barry."

Three weeks later Barry woke up one morning so filled with the desire for another child he could hardly talk about anything else. For several days in a row he had vivid dreams of holding an infant, seeing it being born, and caring for it. Meanwhile, I had become preoccupied with a project and had forgotten all my desire for another child. It was Barry's enthusiasm that helped me to regain the desire. We eventually journeyed to Mt. Shasta and conceived Mira.

These little babies coming to us are actually very conscious, expanded beings. Before birth they are not limited by their bodies and therefore have great power, insight and ability to help their dear struggling parents. They know us well and have deep compassion and love for our human condition. All we need to do is ask for their help. They are drawn to us because of our inherent love for God and our deep desire for growth. They come to help us as well as to fulfill their own destiny.

A couple I knew tried for several years to conceive a child. With each passing month of infertility they became more and more upset and depressed. They consulted doctors and tried every possible physical way to conceive. Finally, they were told they might never conceive a child. They were heartbroken.

I suggested to the couple that they begin to talk to the soul of a child in the spirit world and tell it how much they loved it without any thought or pressure of wanting to conceive. I then suggested they actually take pre-cautions to not conceive for one month, concentrating only on sending love to this child.

Four months later the couple called very excited. They were pregnant! When the expectation and tension involved with conceiving a child were lifted, the couple was free to contact a being and draw it to them by their love and devotion.

Along with the communication with the soul of the baby before pregnancy, there is also the need to keep this communication alive during pregnancy. In his book, THE SECRET LIFE OF THE UNBORN CHILD, Thomas Varney has done extensive research to validate that the fetus in-utero does indeed respond to the mother's thoughts and feelings. Not only do most pregnant women well understand that, but they also feel that their baby is pouring forth much wisdom and love to help them along.

Well into our pregnancy with Rami, we discovered that her head was nestled very close to my heart. As the weeks passed she grew in size and stayed in the same location. If she did not turn her body soon she would need to be born breech. I grieved over this, for I had so hoped for a homebirth with only Barry attending me. Since he had not delivered a breech baby before, we knew we would have to go to the hospital.

Barry tried manually to shift Rami's position within me. I tried difference postures and exercises hoping that she would turn. Rami's head remained stationary, close to my heart (I could hardly blame her!). We were told that in several days her body would be too large to turn and that we should accept a breech delivery.

That evening before going to sleep we both put our hands on my abdomen over Rami's head. We talked out loud to her and told her how much it meant to us to do a homebirth. We carefully explained that this would be impossible as long as she kept her head so close to my heart. We lovingly asked if she would consider turning her body. By the next morning she had turned and was in perfect position for birth.

From our own experiences and from talking to other women and men, I firmly believe that the pregnant fetus is conscious and aware of what the parents are feeling and thinking. The soul of the baby is coming from a vibration of light and God-consciousness into the world of physical matter. While in the womb, the soul is aware of both, the world of light and the world of physical matter. We parents can help bridge the two worlds for our baby by bringing the light of God into the physical realm through our thoughts and feelings. Any thought or feeling of love will be deeply felt by the soul of our baby.

A certain amount of retreat from the fast pace of the world is so beneficial for a pregnant couple. I have counseled many pregnant women who claim with pride to have been able to keep up fully with all of their outer activities, that it hasn't even seemed that they were pregnant. I feel somewhat sorry for these women, for in failing to slow down a little they may have missed out on so much. Pregnancy is an initiation and great spiritual training for women. In almost no other time in a woman's life do the two worlds of heaven and earth come so close together, except during her own birth and death. In helping to bridge the gap for her baby, the mother is being trained to bring the wisdom of the higher spheres to earth. Pregnancy can be a time of developing receptivity so that the mother can absorb the vastness of spiritual understanding that the soul of her baby has gathered over its many lives. The soul of the baby in its unencumbered spirit body can be such a powerful teacher to its mother. The mother in turn helps to bring the vastness of this soul being into a physical body. What a powerful team!

Any amount of time that a pregnant woman can be alone in a receptive peaceful way is so valuable. The time we spend being pregnant is so small compared to our entire life span. Each pregnancy is a golden opportunity to grow spiritually ourselves as well as helping our baby. There is usually much time and space afforded a woman who is pregnant for the first time. With each consecutive pregnancy, the mother needs a certain amount of creativity and will-power to have this much-needed time alone. A friend of mine who had three small children at home, rose each morning at five so she could have time alone during her fourth pregnancy.

Pregnancy, almost more than any time in a woman's life, is a time to trust. Having a baby, especially for the first time, is like taking a leap into the unknown. So much changes for a woman and she needs to trust that the changes will be positive and growthful. During my first pregnancy I had the distinct feeling that I was going

Rami

to die. I had dreams about death at night and intuitive feelings during the day. In my last month of pregnancy I suddenly panicked, as I knew without a doubt that death was close.

No one around me believed this, including Barry. He thought this was a manifestation of my fear of giving birth, yet I knew I was going to die. I felt very lonely.

Impending death and grief were my constant companions in the last month. Finally, in meditation it was revealed to me that a part of my ego was dying and would be replaced by something much greater. When I could fully trust in God, I was filled with an unbelievable joy and sense of expectancy. When the thought came, "I don't want to change," then grief and loneliness would prevail.

As I look back upon that experience I realize thankfully that a part of me *did* die when I gave birth to Rami—a self-centered little girl died and a mother was born. As Barry and I held our new born Rami, I experienced the deepest fulfillment I had known in my twenty- nine years of life.

Pregnancy is scary and totally wonderful at the same time. Besides being a channel of light for her unborn baby, a woman must practice mothering by mothering and caring for herself. Pregnancy is a vulnerable time and therefore constant self-forgiveness is needed. Women have come to me afraid that they have ruined their unborn child's life because of their negative thoughts, angry feelings, fears and doubts. Our babies do not expect perfection from us. Any thought of love or attempt at prayer is so healing and so much more powerful than the other thoughts and feelings.

When I was pregnant I tried to do two things each day. First, I set aside a time to just love myself and give myself alot of mothering: "I love you, Joyce, you sweet soul. You made a few mistakes today. Its alright. Keep on trying. I love you." Almost more than any other time in her life, a pregnant woman needs to give herself love.

The second thing I attempted each day was to receive guidance and inspiration from the soul of the baby I was pregnant with. I wasn't always successful, yet all that is asked is that we try. As wisdom would come through I would quickly write it down in a special book. These two "books" of short inspirations have helped me greatly to remember who it really is that came to me in the form of my two babies.

With my hands on my abdomen feeling a little kicking body, I would talk to my baby, telling her that she is coming to earth to learn more deeply the lesson of love; telling her that the gift of a human body is very precious. She will use this life to love fully and grow closer to God. Her path will be one of service to others while remembering love. As I talked to her I could feel her respond. But more importantly, as I talked to her my own memory of why *I* came to earth was rekindled. As I felt her inspiration to begin this life, my own inspiration to live was felt as well. In striving to give to my unborn child, I was the one given to. In desiring to create an open channel of light for my baby to come to earth, a door was opened to the heavenly spheres and I was allowed to peek in.

September 21, 1981 (Journal entry written ten hours before I unexpectedly went into labor with Mira Naomi)

As I sit alone I reflect on the pregnancy and all it has meant to me. I feel at one with all pregnant women, and feel the specialness of this sacred time in our lives. Pregnancy is both joy and pain, sweetness and sorrow. If you invite a spiritual being into your life, then there is no such thing as a smooth, completely joyful pregnancy. This being is coming from a higher plane of consciousness, and we as women must be strengthened and raised to meet our child. The strengthening and purifying process is sometimes difficult; the rewards are always great, always worthwhile. I often feel that there is no faster way to grow spiritually than to invite one of these beacons of light into your life.

The contractions come and go now. Sweet baby, you are pushing down upon me so gently and asking me to surrender to love and open the door. I feel your head opening my body. I feel your spirit opening my soul to more light. How can I ever thank you for all you have taught me in these nine months. You showed me where I am selfish, and quietly asked me to give that up. You helped me experience not only my Mother-God, but also my Father-God. Then you insisted with all the strength of your being that I call upon them more and dwell more in their Presence. You scolded me gently (and not so gently) when I strayed. My body went through all kinds of physical pains and joys as you grew within me, and you reminded me constantly to see it all as purification, and to be grateful. You helped me feel my beauty, and experience God in such a deep, inner way. And now you push upon me and ask me to open and set you free. I feel your joy and excitement to begin your work upon the earth. I thank you for all you have given me in these nine months that we have lived as one. As I surrender to the love that you are, I pray that you continue to teach me and help me to grow.

THE SHARED HEART

Childbirth

When I was born my Heavenly Mother and Father were there and my Guardian Angel.

I felt peaceful and happy to be on earth. The angels sang to me.

My mama and daddy seemed like my brother and sister and were real special to me.

RAMI, AGE 8

Childbirth, besides being a deep and meaningful experience for all involved, comes in a variety of ways. If we can prepare ourselves during pregnancy to be grateful for whatever way our birth experience turns out, we will be preparing ourselves to also accept the experience of parenting. No two births are alike. No two children are alike. No two parenting experiences are alike. When we compare our birth experience in a judgmental way, we will be missing the lesson the birth was meant to give.

In *THE SHARED HEART,* I wrote in detail about the birth experiences of each of our girls. Each experience was different than I had envisioned and yet, in their own way, each was perfect, teaching me valuable lessons. Now nine and four years later each birth serves as a powerful reminder of a great opening in my being. Each experience continues to teach me.

Having delivered both children in the warmth of our home, I feel very partial to home births. Each girl was born in a different room and for each their birth spot has become very sacred. When Mira was a baby, sometimes the only way we could console her was to bring her to her birth spot. The energy of that sacred spot seemed to comfort and calm her. At age two and three, I noticed that she often went there, sucked her little thumb, and seemed absorbed in deep contemplation.

Many of my friends have had births in a hospital and have reported beautiful experiences. The energy of birth can transform any setting into a holy temple, depending upon the attitude of the parents.

During the moments of birth, time seems to stand still as the room is filled with light and angelic beings. It is the parents' responsibility to make this moment as sacred for the child as possible. The impressions of the first few minutes are permanently recorded upon the baby's being. I have been at births where everyone was screaming and shouting. I have also seen a birth were someone yelled out to the mother, "Oh no, you have another boy!" Imagine disappointing someone at the triumphant moment of your birth! It's important that the parents carefully choose the people who will be with them during the birth, communicating with them very clearly their vision of the baby's first few moments of life. Sometimes in the hospital it is not possible to know who will be at your birth. Through appreciation and love, the best will be brought out of the hospital personnel. They are usually happy to honor any requests the parents might have.

With both children I found that quiet was the best way to honor these sacred moments. Besides, the angels are always present at a birth and it takes real quiet to hear their singing.

The important thing is to be thankful for whatever birth experience you are given. A friend of mine became pregnant eleven years after the birth of her first son. The woman dreamed of having a beautiful, natural birth. I was asked to help her by saying prayers at the appropriate time. Another friend was going to sing birth songs. A third friend would be concentrating on massage. Her husband was prepared to help her with the breathing. Her son would be included also. She had picked out sacred music to play, had grown her favorite flowers so they could be near at the birth, and had selected pictures of holy women. Everything seem so perfect and ideal.

Then the doctor discovered a problem with the baby's heartbeat. My friend suddenly found herself two weeks before the baby's due date driving to the hospital for a caesarian section. The couple had only twenty-four hours to adjust to this change. The baby was soon lifted from the mother's uterus and she caught a quick glimpse of him as he was wheeled off to the newborn nursery. There he was attached to various machines which would monitor his heartbeat. The mother was taken to a hospital room where she was unable to see her baby for twenty-four hours.

I have seen women dwell in self-pity in a similar situation. The agony of missing a natural birth or being unable to bond immediately with their baby overwhelms them. My friend overcame these things by concentrating all of her attention upon gratefulness that her baby was alive. This gratefulness sustained her through the five hectic days in the hospital until she could go home and properly bond with her baby. Her birth experience, though different from how she would have liked, has proved very strengthening for her.

Infancy

The heart which is not struck by the sweet smiles
of an infant is still asleep.

HAZRAT INAYAT KHAN

If we weren't here, God wouldn't be here.

KALEB, AGE 4

The days and weeks after a baby is born are very sacred. Every effort should be made to keep the mother and child quiet and secure at home during this time. Once, while shopping in a big department store, I saw a two day old baby lying in an infant seat on a counter top while the mother shopped for new clothes. Many people were coming up to the infant, touching her and commenting on how tiny she was. My heart felt like crying. The poor child, so new to the earth, was being exposed so quickly to earth's vibrations without even the time to integrate the experiences of her birth and new home.

The transition from the heavenly spheres to earth is a big one for infants. In many ways this is the greatest transition a human being has to experience. In death a person leaves the body to return to their original heavenly condition, their true home. In birth the soul leaves the lightness of its soul body to incarnate into a helpless body, it leaves the finer vibrations of heaven to come into the coarser vibrations of earth. For this reason alone, all effort should be made to aid and respect this transition.

One custom is for the mother and child to spend the first forty days of the infant's life within the surroundings of the home and garden. Some people end the forty days with a baby blessing. One doctor we know who has delivered thousands of babies in the home insists that the mother stay home with the infant, for at least ten days, and has seen problems with those who didn't. Any amount of sheltering and protecting of an infant in the beginning is valuable. Many friends will love to help during this time by bringing meals, shopping, and cleaning.

The days and weeks after a baby is born is also a powerful experience for both mother and father. For the first two or three weeks after birth an infant dwells as much in the heavenly spheres as on earth. They can be looking while you make a funny face at them and really be seeing your eternal soul qualities. During this brief moment in time a mother and father are truly blessed with an absolutely pure being of light. It is a golden opportunity for both parents to re- experience what heaven is truly like and to learn of God's love first hand from their little "messenger". After several weeks the soul gradually comes more and more into its body and earth consciousness.

Having had the experience only twice in this life, we suggest so strongly to all parents of a newborn to take full advantage of this special time. It's all right to devote many hours to just holding and rocking the baby and letting all the cares and concerns of worldly life wait for later. It's all right to unplug the phone, ask people to hold off on visiting, and leave a loving note on your door asking not to be disturbed. It's also all right to ask those very special people, the grandparents, to please wait a short while before coming to visit. (When they do finally come their presence can be such a blessing!) The time a mother needs help the most is in the baby's fourth, fifth and sixth weeks of life, when the soul more fully enters the body. Let the first few weeks be such a special time in which mother, father and siblings all bond together as a family, welcoming and learning from the new arrival.

The father's presence these first few weeks is also very important. Any amount of time taken off from work will bring deep rewards in the bonding between father and child. When Rami was born, Barry and I took off one week and then we both went back to work seeing a full schedule of clients in counseling. That proved to be a big mistake, especially my returning to work so early.

Time and place for everything in life. Fulfill your duties as a householder, and you will not be pulled back later in life to fulfill them.

MURSHIDA BHAKTI

When Mira was born I took off one year, my only work being writing and an occasional women's group. Barry decided to take off one month. His fellow doctors at the hospital were in disbelief that he would take off so much time just because of a new-born baby. We used up much of our meager savings during that month he stayed home, but it was completely worth it. Our family harmonized in a very special way during that month and we learned invaluable lessons. We look back upon that time as the greatest spiritual retreat we've ever had.

Rami nurses dolly while Mama nurses Mira.

Most siblings do not want to sit around while mommy and daddy rock and walk their new brother or sister. After a few days, they want to get on with more activity. Barry was able to give Rami extra attention and helped to include her in the activities of a new born. Whenever my friends called and asked if they could help, I always responded in the same way, "Plan a special adventure to go on with Rami." Rami thrived on all of the extra attention and activity, and Barry and I enjoyed the quiet with newborn Mira.

> *Quiet down dishes and laundry; be still cob-webs and dirt. I'm nursing my baby and babies don't keep.*
>
> ANONYMOUS SAYING

The precious time of a new born life is no time to worry about a clean house. There will be plenty of days ahead for cleaning and organization. I remember so vividly that I would have to walk through the kitchen, using my hands as blinders so I wouldn't see all that was calling for my attention. Each time that Mira slept I knew my greatest gift to her would be resting and meditating in the sun or relaxing with Rami and Barry, rather than cleaning. When she awoke, *I also* was refreshed and eager to have her nurse. I always held in my memory a time when I had cleaned our house while seven-day-old Rami napped. I had become so exhausted from the cleaning that when she awoke my milk hardly flowed, I felt irritable, and Rami cried for a long time. I knew after that experience that taking care of my body and filling my mind with peaceful thoughts was the greatest gift I could give my baby.

The experience of nursing a baby is truly one of the crowning glories of motherhood. The occasional difficulties of baby and mother adjusting to nursing in the first several weeks or months are wonderfully forgotten as they settle into a happy rhythm of nursing. It was during the times of nursing my babies in peace and stillness that God seemed to nurse me as well with heavenly nectar.

From the hearts of mothers comes the natural flow of love for the precious life placed in their care. Each look at the rosebud mouth and fingers assures the mother that her only place is with her baby. Baby smiles, cups her breast in soft, reaching hands and the fountain of milk nourishes a bond almost unbreakable.

QAHIRA QALBI

From the time babies are born they learn and grow through sensitive communication with their environment. Physical touch transmits the whole world from parent to baby, as well as providing deep healing and nourishment. It is an art which men and women learn by becoming parents.

Bodily connectedness is the basis of that interconnectedness with others that we call society, and this is brought about by the closeness of mother and child in infancy. Such a close bodily relationship is the basis of good feelings about oneself.

ASHLEY MONTAGU
TOUCHING

What a mother communicates to her baby when she holds him with a good firm touch is that he can relax—she's not going to drop him—its all covered.

INA MAY GASKIN
SPIRITUAL MIDWIFERY

As they slowly make the transition to this world, massage is a gentle loving way to welcome our newborns to their bodies.

ROBIN SALE WITH SON EHRIN

Mira's nineteenth day of life was her first really hard day. It seemed as though she cried the entire day. Nothing seemed to please her. Shortly before dinner, Barry brought out crying Mira from her five minute nap. Handing her to me he lamented, "Life was sure easier before this little gal came along." I felt totally weary. I held crying Mira. The thought of doubt insidiously crept into my mind, "Maybe we made a mistake to have another child." I dismissed the thought and went on trying to comfort Mira. Though the thought did not come again, I had not taken the time to clear and bring light to that doubt. It continued to act in my subconsciousness.

The next day I awoke with a sense of depression. Rami went off with a friend to make Halloween costumes and Mira slept most of the day. Barry went for needed groceries. In my aloneness my depression was all the more obvious. "Well, maybe this is just postpartum depression," I thought, but I didn't believe it. I felt so lost I didn't even have the desire to meditate or pray.

Finally, I picked up one of my spiritual books and randomly opened it to a section on doubt. I read that doubt can rob us of so much energy, enthusiasm and vitality. I put the book down and remembered my thought of doubt about the rightness of having another child. My tears flowed and I prayed for forgiveness and felt God's healing love wash me clean. Of course I wanted Mira, and so did Barry and Rami. It was just in a moment of weakness that I had allowed my mind to dwell on the negative. I felt so happy inside that I tip-toed in to see my sleeping baby, my heart bursting with love.

Through that experience, I realized the danger of allowing doubt to enter my mind when things are difficult with a new born. The mother after birth is in such an open and vulnerable place. Doubt can sneak in much more quickly and perhaps causes much of what is described as post natal depression. There are so many opportunities to doubt in infancy as it is a period of so much change and adjustment. An attitude of gratefulness for all the many moods of baby and mother herself will be a great companion in these first few weeks.

I recommend that all pregnant women keep a little journal on their impressions, feelings, and inspirations about the baby they are carrying within. My book on each girl served as a great strength whenever weakness threatened to overwhelm me. A strong impression that came to me with Mira was to try always to remember who it really is that came to us. This often helped me to not get lost in caring for her little body and forget what a great soul resides therein.

Quiet time is so important for a parent caring for a baby (and really for any age child). As Mira grew to be several months old, I found I could no longer spend most of her nap time in meditation. Soon, outside responsibilities and the needed extra time alone with Rami took up most of my time. It became obvious to me that I needed to find a way to meditate that included Mira. I tried lying her down next to me and closing my eyes, but she fussed for attention. Then I discovered that she loved when I read or talked to her about God. I don't know if she understood the words, but she certainly was receiving their vibrations. Sometimes she would sit still for an hour intently listening as I read to her from my favorite spiritual books. I watched her eyes and saw the beautiful way that she received the truth of the words. As she felt the vibrations within her, she began teaching me to do likewise. We usually ended our spiritual time together by singing. I would sing my songs, and she would loudly sing in her way. Those times with Mira are indeed precious to remember.

My favorite memory is how tenderly Rami used to hold new-born Mira. Rami's face glowed with motherly love for Mira.

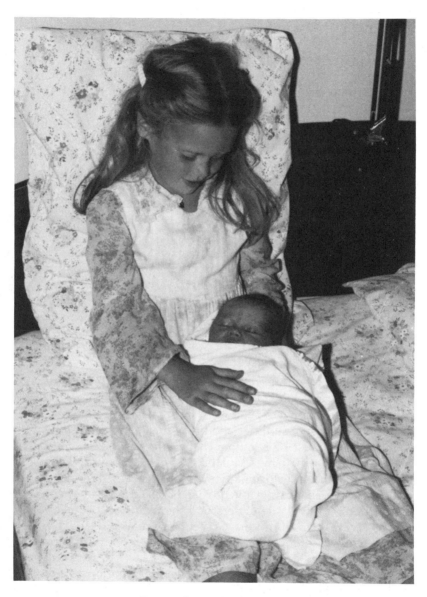

Rami and Mira (one hour old).

They have grown to be so close. They yell and scream at each other occasionally as siblings do, but their love is so evident. With Mira's arrival, Rami lost her place as the only little princess in the house and, as a result, she did receive less individual attention. But she gained far more than she lost. We often hear about sibling rivalry, but the more predominant feeling is sibling love and devotion. From the moment Mira was born, Rami began to learn about true giving and sharing and she became a much happier and fulfilled child.

For those of you who are holding a newborn as you read this, or are expecting your little one to come, you are truly blessed. The birth of your own baby is perhaps one of the greatest wonders and treasures of life. No matter how many children a couple has, deep in their heart will always be the desire to return to that newborn sense of angelic beauty. A newborn baby is a beautiful reminder of how deeply we are all loved and cherished by God.

The infant that is born on earth brings with it the air of heaven. In its expression, in its smiles, even in its cry you hear the melody of the heavens.

HAZRAT INAYAT KHAN

Lessons of Pregnancy and Childbirth
by Safiya Williams

Safiya Williams is a wife and mother of four, an exquisitely sensitive poet, and an incurable mystic. She and her husband, Isaiah, live in Santa Cruz and have been wonderful friends to Joyce and me. When I originally read the following piece, almost indecipherably scribbled on fourteen sheets of paper, I would have been totally carried away except for the need to frequently decode her handwriting, which kept me on the ground. It is the story of four pregnancies and four births, but it is much more than that. It is such a beautiful description of soul communication, of the inter-relatedness of life in and out of the body, and of the unique destinies we and our children have on this planet.

Our children make themselves known to us long before their first cry on earth. I think of the woman whose adopted baby inspired her to start a journal for him on the same day that his natural mother conceived him.

I am often asked how I chose my childrens' rather unusual names. But I did not choose. I listened.

Our children are communicating with us all the time, of course... and how much they have to tell and teach us! The lessons can well begin before pregnancy, but certainly the moment of conception is not too early to tune in to the unique and valuable messages these new beings have to share about themselves and their life-path on earth.

I am sure that many pregnant mothers have experienced the phenomenon of not only mood changes, but taste and thought-patterns and any number of other inclinations that normally make up their personality. For me this was always an intense experience. I also discovered during the births of each of my children that my labor was one of the strongest indicators of the nature of the child; a kind of last minute crash course on essentials I might have missed during the precious months of pregnancy.

Aram

The outward changes surrounding the pregnancy of my first child were so many and so dramatic that at first I did not notice the inward ones. I had shifted quite suddenly from being separated to becoming re-married, from employed to unemployed, city-dweller to country- dweller, private to community existence. However all this was nothing compared to the inner transformation. Now I began to read the Old Testament avidly. Familiar fairy-tales tempted me less than nature books, especially on the mysteries of the universe. No more mild pastels! From now on I wore *red*; the brighter the better! I craved meat, after being a vegetarian for years and was hungry as well for this new and challenging experience of group living. Strong, powerful Eastern chanting comforted me...only that or the gentle, inspired folk music of my husband. My dreams were mythical, sometimes terrifying, full of archetypal imagery, awesome with the presence of prophetic figures. I felt passionate, intense with everyone and everything and at the same time, vulnerable. I was getting to know my son.

My labor started on the birthday of one of his best friends. It progressed cautiously, tentatively, with a secret, deep-down smile. At last, at last! The birth of my first child. There was an almost overwhelming naivete about it. Nothing could go wrong. We were

Aram.

protected. We were "on course." The purposefulness of the situation was obvious; what else mattered? Then—crash!—we encountered the world. Although I had hoped for a home-delivery, it was impossible; we attended a clinic regularly and appeared on schedule at the hospital. Not without some show of independence and impishness, we sneaked in a back-way to avoid the repugnant wheel-chair and its connotation of helplessness and announced our presence somewhat grandly in the obstetric ward. At first we were refused admittance (I couldn't be in labor and not in a wheel-chair!), but once admitted the dream became a nightmare. Everything in me resisted being told what to do or how to do it. We were commandeered in the most vigorous and obnoxious way. The nurse literally told me that I was "doing everything wrong" and that "it" would get "much worse". Of course, then, it did. Resisting and encountering resistance, my contractions slowed down; labor became a battle: attack, clash, retreat, summon up forces, advance, clash, withdraw again, while meanwhile my husband staunchly by, gently playing his guitar and creating beautiful music. A doctor appeared at one interval threatening dire consequences (a Caesarian) if I did not deliver in 45 minutes. We rallied. I did. After pushing for 10 minutes the baby was hauled out, tossed around and after a brief interlude of grateful cuddling, whisked away for 12 hours. But the fierce lights in the delivery room that had concerned us were dimmed and nearly extinguished by the blast of light and power as our son came into the world.

And so, after 9 months and 14 hours I was introduced to the being with whom I had shared identities for so long: passionate, heroic, encountering and engendering turmoil at every turn (a Wednesday's child!) and paradoxically tender to the point of pain, innovative, creative, with a purpose and a determination so clear that his infant gaze intimidated would-be baby cuddlers and encouraged one hesitant admirer to exclaim, "Oh-my-what a-a-an OLD-looking baby!"

A note from Isaiah (Safiya's husband):

The purpose in sharing this story, perhaps not unlike many others, is to show how the pregnancy and birth were indicative of, even created by, the character of our child. For example, our son loves the natural sciences, so my wife intuitively, even against her natural inclinations, chose nature books over fairy-tales. Our son is a kind of warrior or knight; he cannot tolerate helplessness or imperialism; he suffers terribly when the atmosphere is inharmonious or unbalanced—so there we were battling the whole institution and personnel of the hospital. He is also sensitive, poetic, deep and we were touched, hurt, wounded and healed by his birth. It all leads me to think that there is already knowledge, personality and purpose to the child before the age of six, before infancy, before the birth, before the womb, before conception, before time and space. They bring it all with them and we as parents can tap the source of that information through our intuitions to aid in the unfoldment of our children.

As I thanked God for my Mother's Day cards which I said I loved more than anything, Aram said, "You can't love them more than God, Mama—you can't love anything more than God."

ARAM, AGE 5

Joachim

My next pregnancy, following a rather intense miscarriage, could not have been more different. Everyone *knew* that we were having a girl except my first son who told his father severely and with conviction "Boy, Abba (father) boy!" and me, although I gave the sex of the baby less thought than I did the intriguing possibility of joining a convent. This I considered seriously while listening (exclusively) to Gregorian chants and reading (devoutly) stories about Christian mysticism and the Middle Ages (an era I had always particularly abhorred in "my studies"). Nevertheless I emerged from my meditations long enough to participate in a community production of "Blessed Among Women", a beautiful book that we transposed into a play about the life of Mary as seen through her eyes, in which everyone in the community took part. Mary was enacted by all the ladies, at different stages of her life. I, conveniently pregnant, dressed as usual in sky blue, played Mary en-route to Bethlehem, just prior to the birth.

During my real journey to the hospital, if there were difficulties, we did not notice them. My husband, our friend and breathing-coach, and I were hilarious with joy. Unlike our first son, born on his due date, this baby was "late". Even so, there were no complications. On the contrary, the labor was straight-forward; text-book perfect. Should I have been anxious after my last hospital experience? Oh! What was anxiety? I was in bliss and everyone around me smiled with harmonious intent. Did I want to know what time my baby would be born? "3:44am said a small voice within and at 3:44am to the words "Oh my God, it's a boy!" our second son slipped peacefully and affirmatively into the world.

Evidently, our second child is a joyous being whose nature has always seemed oblivious to the idea of separation—that is, separation of man from God. So it was he who evoked the divine qualities of Mary and Joseph latent in us. As our first son reminded us of power—our inner strength and purposefulness—this child showed us the path of harmony and bliss. In his simplicity of being he offered us love incarnate.

(On a camping trip with his father, the site was messed up with trash): "doesn't matter if it's beautiful—we can make it more beautiful by being here."

JOACHIM, AGE 5

Joachim and Fleur.

Fleur

With my third pregnancy my husband wondered who I would "become" next. But in the beginning it was difficult for me to remember that a soul was incarnating through me or even that I *was* at all. Instead my whole being felt swept up and intoxicated by...I can only describe it as a frequency of sound, a vibration that was so ethereal, so exquisite that I wanted no part at all of the earth plane. I have no idea what I wore, I had no desire to eat, I could tolerate only the most refined, angelic music. Gradually my direction changed...a new form...oh! Yes! I was having a baby. A water baby (Pices). And how this baby craved water. I became seriously dehydrated after a prolonged illness. And suddenly it became obvious that the entire structure of our lives must change instantaneously! We moved to California, away from rustic communal living in the woods to a luxurious house overlooking the ocean, shared with a few friends. Now everything seemed in flux, challenged and challenging. Who was I? One moment ethereal, the next wildly romantic. One moment enterprising and bold, the next so timid I had to hold my husband's hand to enter a roomful of people. In religious gatherings I felt awkward and uncomfortable. Alone, in meditation, at the breakfast table, I heard angels singing and thought everyone else did too. I had to read, constantly; novels of devotion and duty, of the joy of being alive, of romance—and poetry—reams of lush and passion-filled poems, plays, Shakespeare above all...insatiable for insight, for the perfection of knowing!

Bizarre is one word for that labor. Unfathomable, dramatic, impulsive, unique. A whole new method of labor introduced into the world. Impossible to analyze or categorize. And it went on and on and on. The sun rose and set. I watched the sky and the ocean and breathed the scent of jasmine, surrounded only by dear, supportive friends and my husband in the seclusion of our home.

And then, when we had grown perplexed and weary, somehow unexpectedly, but with vehement aplomb our daughter burst into the world...burst, but elegantly. She lay there quietly for a minute and then said distinctly, "Ehh!" It could have been translated as "Oh—is this it? Oh, well..."

And there you have her. She left no stone unturned, as it were..she wanted to be quite sure that we knew her by then, because she is unknowable. She wears an overwhelming, irresistible disguise. She is not easy. But she is as unforgettable as she is unforgetting of her purpose in entering this plane. However she fulfills, it will be *her* way, no one else's, and an entirely *new* way which she will not hesitate make known—with charm, with delight and with a subtle but superb conviction.

I'm on a special diet...daffodils and roses
and something else too...love!"

FLEUR, AGE 4

Caitalin Claire

The next time I became pregnant was not the right time for us. In meditation together we explained this to the incarnating soul: "But please come back, because we do want you and love you." And she obliged. Not for some time. And not at *our* timing either. "Was this pregnancy planned?," I was frequently asked. (A fourth child is a little unusual these days).

Ah! Was ever a pregnancy *more* planned. And was ever divine planning made more apparent in our individual lives! Yes I knew about this child; for seven years I had known her name, that she was coming—but how could I know that the date of her conception

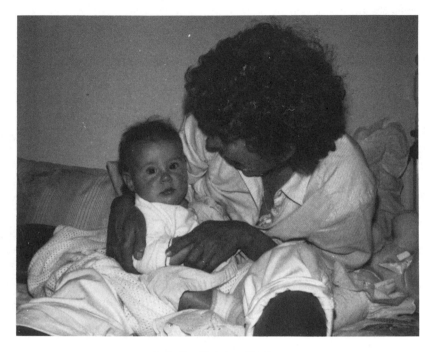

Caitalin Claire and Safiya.

marked the death of the Saint whose name she bore? A saint who
had been gradually taking possession of my heart, whose being
seemed to absorb me during the pregnancy so that the soul within,
the saint and I merged, in pain and in love. Every glance showed me
a mirror, I saw myself reflected, I could not evade the truth of
myself. And beauty was above, below, all around me. But it was
agony to be seen, to be touched. I yearned to be alone; to
contemplate this call; to marvel in this wonder of translucent
beingness. The "Kyrie Eleison" became almost an obsession; but it
was the song of birds I loved most. If I could have always worn
white and carried aloft the Holy Grail, I would have been perfectly
happy—but I did have to read; about the Holy Grail, the Franciscan
path, and always, lives of the Saints. Then, towards the end, I felt
radiant, full of laughter. At Christmas, everything I gave my
husband was Irish—from music to soap. The Celtic influence was
clearly and forcefully felt.

If I could have given birth alone with my mid-wife, away in the
hills, in a cave perhaps, in the moonlight, I would have. As it was we

entered that cave together in my room, a deep abyss in the center of the earth and an earthquake took us there. The power and the clear intention of my body, of this soul, catapulted us both into the most intense and somehow satisfying birth experience yet. So this was labor! No night, no day, no husband, no friends; only this one other woman carved from ancient rock, and whatever I was and this soul made of crystal, giving birth together, as it had been before time began, as it would always be. This one I touched first, I put her over my heart and we clung together in victory—we had come through, we had been born again—together.

And I can only describe my little earth baby as a crystal; clear, radiant, reflective; a self-contained and luminous being whose purpose is less to do than to be; who smiles and laughs willingly at loved ones but gurgles contentedly alone watching the patterns of leaves or nestled quietly in my arms, heart-beat to heart-beat.

I am not alone in these experiences. Many, perhaps all women, share them. Yet I know how quickly we forget the revelation of pregnancy and childbirth in relating to our children. Is this adorable three-month-old baby one who truly bears the light of the Grail into the world? Will I rebuke her, ignore her perhaps, in crucial moments when the force of her being clashes with mine? Will I forget the Christ-light that shines through her and give vent to my irritation, my tiredness, my preoccupation with all the pressing "consequential" details of life? Well, I have before. I have slapped my passionate warrior for being too intense. I have shaken my blissful Cupid for being too silly and vague. I have argued with my daughter for having her own point of view. But now and then I remember. I remember what they asked me to learn and who they asked me to become when the eyes of my heart were open, when I allowed myself to see. I remember who they truly are in their origin of being. I remember their dignity, their purpose and I feel humbled and grateful beyond any words that we are treading this path together; even though we may stumble and fall and get in each other's way. But I know also through their confidence in sharing so much of themselves with me during the pregnancy and birth that the potential is there to be friends. Our pact together is sacred and, in remembering, a great part of our purpose is served.

Hi bird!

CAITALIN CLAIRE, AGE 9 MONTHS

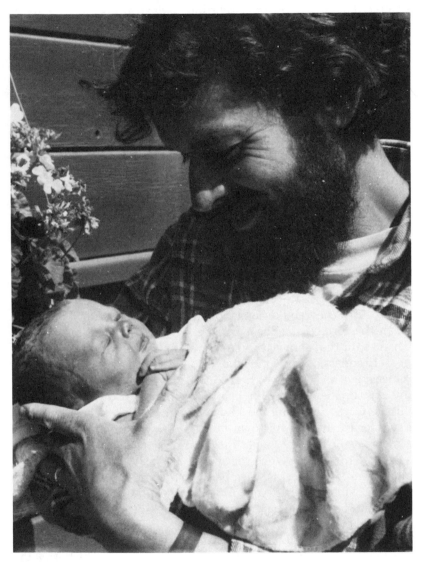

Barry and newborn Mira.

A Letter to Fathers-to-be

Dear Beloved Fathers:

Please remember that your wife is not the only one pregnant. You too are pregnant, and will go through changes and growth which parallel your wife's. In the beginning months of Joyce's pregnancy with Rami, our first child, I noticed to my surprise that *my* belly was also growing—and I don't think I was eating more than usual.

More important than shared physical growth is the shared spiritual growth. Please, fathers, remember that pregnancy is a time of real sensitivity to finer vibrations, for you as well as your beloved. Take time—take real time—to share in this spiritual bounty which pregnancy affords.

Take time daily to remember that your child has chosen you as father with the same loving wisdom as he chose your wife to be his mother. The qualities you possess as father-to-be—loving protection, firm discipline, dispassionate wisdom, strong yet gentle hands—these and many more are so needed by your child. If these qualities are latent, they will be brought out by your child—often in the time it takes to say, "Daddy".

I feel the most important lesson I can ever pass on to you, my dear brothers, is to take time. Life will seem to test you by giving you more to do than ever before, but take time. Is what you have to do more important than the unfolding miracle-flower of pregnancy? Is it more important than sitting with your wife, silently holding hands, and praying together for the well-being of your holy family? Is it more important than lying with your ear pressed to her pregnant belly, listening and feeling new life, and thanking God?

Take time to find words to express your appreciation for this mother-to-be. Take time to be alone, to nourish your own soul in the Omnipresent Spirit. Take time with God.

Take time.

He who has no time also has no eternity.

OLD PROVERB

ten

The Baby Blessing Ceremony

Words cannot adequately describe the profound joy of a new baby's arrival. For the parents of a new born, life is almost other-worldly for the first few weeks. The infant is, after all, bringing to earth a little of the heavenly condition. The vibration of a newborn child is pure magic.

When Rami was born, her eyes and smile were so deeply bonded upon my consciousness that I could see them in everyone and everything. I was totally and helplessly in love with her. Then with Mira, I remember holding her to my heart almost every minute the first twenty days of her life. I felt I could bathe in the peace of her consciousness as long as I held her. Of course, there were low periods, including a scary bout of "child birth fever", but these did not much alter my overall elation.

It seemed to Barry and me as we held our babies and watched other newborns, that they are not yet fully incarnated upon the earth. Their consciousness is still very much in the non-physical realms. However, sometime between the third and sixth week a change takes place in infants. They become aware of their little bodies and increasingly feel their limitations.

I remember so well holding Mira when she was three weeks old. Previously while holding her, she would simply open her eyes after sleep and smile at me. I knew in these times she was communicating to me something of the luminous condition from which she had just come. On this particular day, however, I was allowed to rise in consciousness to the plane in which she was dwelling. I felt in ecstasy! Then I experienced her feelings as she awoke into her helpless little body. She started to scream! She was fully aware of her limitations in a wet, hungry body and didn't like the feeling at all.

For the next several days Mira screamed whenever she awakened. The transition from her expanded level of consciousness into that of a human body was very difficult for her. Karen Pryer, in her book *NURSING YOUR BABY*, describes this stage as the nursing crisis. Many other parents feel that their infant isn't receiving enough breast milk and switch to a formula. My observation is that infants need to nurse more than ever in this period as it can be quite a stressful time for them. Rami handled the stress of this transition period by nursing from eight to ten hours a day. She needed me to be close. Mira reacted to the stress by screaming and fussing four or five hours a day.

After one week of this, we realized that Mira needed help to settle into her body in a peaceful way. Barry and I were exhausted and irritable with each other and Rami was misbehaving. The whole family was in need of help!! We felt like screaming out for help from anyone who could hear. Instead, the idea of the Baby Blessing Ceremony was conceived, a ceremony in which we and our friends could help Mira to feel at peace with her body and her life on earth.

The morning of her ceremony Mira screamed almost continually. I wasn't sure if we'd make it through the service. Our friends, however, were very happy to come. (All of our relatives live too far away, but they would have been a welcome addition.) We have always found that people, if given the chance, love the opportunity to help and bless others.

As it turned out, Mira sat perfectly still throughout her blessing, absorbing everything that happened. We feel as if a miracle had happened on that day, for Mira definitely settled down into a more harmonious rhythm in life and from that day on seemed more tolerant of her limited condition. Rami, in turn, seemed more accepting of her new sister and Barry and I received the strength and inspiration we were needing. Since then we have participated in several baby blessings and have seen not only the baby and family benefited, but all those who participated as well.

Although, for Joyce and me, the baby blessing ceremony was born out of an urgent need, we nevertheless received a clear vision of its form and purpose. We saw a ceremony which would symbolize the passing of a soul through the four great initiations of life: water, air, fire, and earth. Part of our inspiration came from a book we had read, *THE PATH OF THE SOUL* by White Eagle, which describes beautifully how every being must eventually pass through these four great initiations, corresponding to the four elements, before it can fulfill its destiny here on earth. We saw a ceremony which would initiate Mira and other children onto the conscious path, the journey of mastery over all the elements, the journey to divine unconditional love.

Joyce and I often refer to the term "initiation" because we feel that our own earth life is a series of initiations, or significant soul-tests, which we pass through in order to awaken our love, wisdom, and strength. It is passing through the initiations of life which teaches us our lessons in this earth-school. Of course we have a choice in the matter. We can make our lives as comfortable as possible, avoiding pain and insecurity, and not have to endure the soul-testing of initiation. But then there will be no growth. And since life is growth, there will be no life. We become imprisoned by a stagnation of our own making.

I think, however, that you who are reading this book have made the choice for life, for growth, for love. I also think that you understand what we say about the necessity of these soul-tests, and are willing to go through them—and have your children go through them. So it is to you and your children that we dedicate this baby blessing ceremony.

We love ceremonies and rituals. Unfortunately, there are too many ceremonies and rituals being done without reverence, love, or spirit. I'm not only talking about those performed in organized religion. Life is full of rituals, and they're all spiritual—if we bring spirit into them. Putting our children to bed at night (a chapter of this book) can be a glorious ceremony. Love-making can be a very sacred ritual. Yes, even cleaning the house! There is a story of a woman saint who cleaned her dwelling as an act of worship each day, filled with a feeling of expectancy for visitors—the Holy Ones of God. Sometimes they came and sometimes they didn't, but she always expected them.

I think many of us were somewhere along the way turned off by ceremonies because of the lack of love with which they were done. It is now part of our work in the new age to create new ceremonies, to enliven old ones, and to make our whole life one joyful ritual.

Ceremonies can either wake us up or put us to sleep. It depends on our intention, which is really our desire. The more consciousness focused into the intention, the desire, the more the ceremony will help in our awakening process. However, this is not always painless.

A few days ago, we officiated a wedding ceremony for a very sincere couple. The loftiness of their intention and desire caused them to go through a real period of testing before their wedding. Their high ideals of marriage set in motion a period of purification which was an initiation in itself. All their human-ness came to the surface, especially during the week before the wedding. Their fears and doubts crowded in on them. She felt all her unworthiness. He had severe diarrhea all week. It seemed crazy, but it brought them to the point of real readiness which allowed the ceremony to be a heart-opener. It's almost as if the universe has an automatic "humbling" principle which especially comes into play when very sincere people are preparing for a deeply spiritual event. Were it not for this "principle", the persons involved might be lured into a false pride which says, "look how important I am". For our groom, for example it took a week's worth of diarrhea to remind him that all good comes only from the spirit of love within him, his "Self" rather than his "self".

We love ceremonies because angels love ceremonies. Their presence is what adds the magic. A ceremony done with heart draws the attention of the angelic kingdom. At a baby blessing, these beings help to focus all the positively-directed energies to convey a powerful blessing not only upon the child, but also upon the parents, the siblings, and all those present.

Timing is also important. We had Mira's blessing on her fortieth day of life. This felt like the perfect time in general and especially for Mira's crisis. Forty is the number of the gestation. There are forty weeks in a human pregnancy. It is a universal number referring to a period of incubation or development. Jesus fasted in the wilderness for forty days while a key change was taking place within him. Lord Buddha sat under the famed bodhi tree fasting and meditating for forty days. Moses and the Israelites wandered in the desert for forty years before they could enter the promised land. Even the forty days and nights of torrential rain in the time of Noah was a gestational period for the land itself, a washing away of the old and bringing in of the new.

As we described in the "marriage ceremony" chapter in THE SHARED HEART, all ceremonies have three main elements: the invocation, the body of the ceremony, and the closing.

The invocation is the call to God. Here, the tone is set for the entire ceremony. Meditation, prayer, and singing may help participants to open their hearts. The officiants should offer a spoken prayer such as, "Father-Mother God, make Thy Presence manifest now at this ceremony. Beloved Angels and Masters, we ask your fullest blessing upon this event and upon this child which we now dedicate in divine service."

Then comes the body of the ceremony, which symbolically depicts the four great initiations of every soul. These can also be seen as purifications, or the cleansing and uplifting of the four elements within us. Water, air, fire, and earth have unevolved, dense, or gross aspects as well as evolved or spiritualized aspects. The "path of the soul" is the spiritualization or evolution of these four elements of our being.

We begin the body of the ceremony with the water initiation, or purification. This is the baptism with which most of us are familiar. In THE PATH OF THE SOUL, White Eagle says, "In the Bible and also in other mystical revelations, 'the waters' signify the psyche, the soul of man (woman)." The psyche pertains to the soul's desires, feelings, and emotions. He continues, "The waters of the soul, which can be either calm and still and so reflect the heavens, or else so rough and turbulent that they reflect nothing, must be brought under control of the Master."

Our desires, feelings, and emotions, as we all know, can easily be turned in the wrong direction, and bring us endless unrest. This is the first initiation, and desire is the key. It is very difficult to control our emotions by our own power. It can be done easily, however, by mobilizing the power of God within us. The turbulent waters are easily stilled by the Christ, as Jesus demonstrated to his disciples. And "right desire", desiring that our will be in tune with God's will, provides this power for mastery of the water element.

Before the ceremony, we fill a bowl with the purest water available and then add rose petals. The rose is a symbol of divine love. While introducing the water element and initiation, we pass the bowl around the group, asking each person to bless the water. Then we "baptize" by sprinkling a little of the water on the baby's head. We pray that his or her soul will learn to desire and feel in divine harmony and to learn stillness.

We move now to the air initiation, which concerns itself with the mind and mental nature of the individual. We need to remember that we have two aspects of our mind. The lower mind reflects our material, physical life, while the higher mind reflects spiritual truth and existence. As White Eagle puts it, "The lower mind thus becomes the tempter, doing all it can to refute, to confuse, or even to overshadow and overpower the higher mind. The higher mind receives the inspiration, the in-breathing of the »air» of God, but it needs to be continually fortified against the arguments of the lower mind. The neophyte has to train himself to be loyal and true, to resist staunchly any such arguments, knowing that they are spoken only by the mind of earth; he has to learn both to discern this fact, and put this earthly mind back in its correct place!"

As with the water initiation, a key to passing the air initiation is stillness. The thoughts of the lower mind are incessant, passing through consciousness like clouds through the sky. Although clouds are only made of water vapor, they sometimes appear very substantial. Likewise, the thoughts of our earthly mind give the illusion of solidity and importance, and lure us into identifying ourselves with them. Our thoughts are very seductive. To pass through the air initiation we have to practice stillness; stillness of body first and then stillness inside. We don't have to stop the thoughts by force. Struggling in this way only creates more turbulence which ends up increasing the thoughts. Nor does trying to think "higher" thoughts always work. Very often, our "higher thoughts" end up an assertion of our ego natures rather than a reflection of our spiritual self. The answer lies in attitude rather than method, identification rather than striving. We need to identify with the space in us which is beyond thoughts, that place of quietude at the center of our being. This is where the higher mind resides, the receiving station for inspirations and revelations. This is the "divine hook-up", out of which emerge pure thought-forms. If we desire this peace enough, it is ours to experience right now. If we can identify with our center rather than our thoughts, we will pass the air initiation. Then our lower mind becomes a channel through which our higher mind can emerge, and we become an instrument for divine wisdom.

In the ceremony, as a symbolic representation of the air

initiation, we use the spoken prayer. If the group is not too large, we all take turns offering a prayer of blessing for the soul of the child, each in his or her own way. In a large group it might be best to ask those who are inspired to share their prayers. There is something magically powerful about a group of people offering their individual prayers. The "higher mind" is always wonderfully expressed.
Here is one prayer:

> *Beloved Mother-Father God, All-Wise Spirit, teach this soul the secret of Thy wisdom. Help this child learn to enter Thy silence, to allow the perfect expression of his (her) higher mind, for the benefit of all people.*

Next comes the fire purification. White Eagle says, "We remind you again that the Water Initiation entails the control and the right use of man's emotions, and the Air Initiation the right use of the mental bodies or the mental abilities of man. Yet we find that the Air Initiation, which disciplines and trains the mind, can still leave the soul cold—let us say, as air remains chill while the sun is obscured. So we think of the mind also as being cold; for we know that intellectualism is cold and exacting, and because of this it cannot live. So the Air initiate turns to something which will bring him (her) warmth and life. However brilliant the mind, unless it become infused with the love of God, all its works will gradually fade and die. It is the Fire Initiation which brings warmth and light and beauty into life."

From White Eagle we can see how the initiations of the elements follow a natural order, one leading to the next like a dance of awakening. This is not to say that each of us works on only one element at a time. We are all moving in varying degrees through all the initiations at the same time. The order, however, is there to help us in our understanding of the process.

When we look at our own awakening process, we can see the water to air to fire progression. We can see the quickening of our emotions leading to the quickening of our minds, or the stilling of our emotions helping the stilling of our minds. Then the purifying of emotion and thought prepares the way for the fire initiation, the kindling of the flame of Divine Love. It is the fire initiation which fans the little spark in each of our hearts into the flame of God-Consciousness, so that we shine like the sun.

As with the other elements, the fire element has a lower and a higher nature. In its lower nature White Eagle says love is a "passion that sears, burns, and consumes, but on the highest plane it creates and gives life". An example that comes to mind is the way love is expressed in our sexuality and sexual relationships. We often get "burned" when sexually unconscious. And when conscious, it not only brings in "destined" children, but gives *us* life as well.

In the baby blessing, we light candles to symbolize the baby's passing the fire initiation, the kindling of Divine Love in her or his heart in this lifetime. We ask those present to concentrate on their own hearts opening, a feeling of "presence" or warmth in the center of their chests. Then we ask everyone to imagine or feel a ray of light or current of energy passing from their heart to the baby's heart.

As we have seen, the water initiation was the cleansing of our desires, feelings and emotions. Then the air initiation was the mastery of the Higher Mind over the lower mind. Finally, the fire initiation accomplished the kindling of Divine Love in the heart. Now for the fourth and last initiation, that of earth. You ask, "Why is there need for any more initiations? Isn't it enough to have Divine Love kindled in our hearts?" To this White Eagle replies, "The Earth Initiation is necessary because even after the soul has received divine illumination, even after it has been caught up in the heavens and seen the vision glorious, it has to learn *to use* the power of the Divine Fire in order to control physical matter wisely and rightly." The path of consciousness can be likened to climbing a mountain. The water initiation begins the ascent through meadows, forests, and alongside streams. The air initiation is like the steeper upper reaches of the mountain, with the windy terrain of rock and snow. The fire initiation is the summit, like Moses and the burning bush. Finally, the earth initiation is the descent from the mountain top back down into the valley. There is the temptation to stay on the summit, to bask in the Divine Sunshine. And for a time, there is certainly nothing wrong with this. We need to receive the energy of the mountain top to replenish us. But, once replenished, we must all return to the valleys and the "plains" (the plain life), to give what we have learned and gained on the summit to the rest of humanity.

The earth initiation, then, is the lesson of surrender and service. It is the letting go of *my* spiritual growth, and replacing it with »our» spiritual growth. It is putting the planet, and even the whole universe, before our little egos, thinking of the good of the whole first. It gives purpose to all aspiration. The earth initiation is reaching for the Light of God so we can illuminate the darkness. This doesn't mean we should not enjoy the Light. Far from it! Our enjoyment is multiplied with each person we share this love with.

A classic earth initiation is the story of the crucifixion and resurrection of Jesus. All of us, in some way, must pass through a kind of crucifixion and resurrection in the name of surrender and service. All of us must experience the crucifixion of our self-will to allow the Divine Will to be resurrected in and through us. This not only applies to us as individuals. We must learn this in our relationship with one other person. From there we can go on to learn the Divine Will as a community, then as a nation, as a planet, and finally as a universe.

In passing the earth initiation, Jesus was demonstrating mastery over physical matter. He *consciously* surrendered his physical body on the cross, knowing well that anything surrendered freely and lovingly is never lost. As a Master, he knew he would always retain full use of his physical body if ever he should need it, not for himself, but only in service to others. His resurrection was a training lesson for those who "have eyes to see". He was openly urging us all to see that physical matter (the "earth") is not as solid as we tend to think. Just as thought, like clouds, can appear to be solid and dense, physical matter gives the same illusion. It has taken scientists almost two thousand years since Jesus walked out of Joseph of Arimathea's tomb, to finally realize that particles may not be particles after all, that matter is also waves and energy patterns. With surrender and service as the keys, all of us can and will attain the same mastery over the elements as Jesus did. We will all learn to infuse matter with light and love, to bring the energy of the mountain-top into all life's situations, and thus pass the earth initiation.

To enact this initiation in the baby blessing, we ask the parent or parents to carry their child around the room from person to person. We ask everyone present to bless the child by placing their right hand on the child's head or heart. Through the touch of the hands, the baby can learn the secret of the earth initiation. While people are taking their turns, everyone can sing a blessing song. The one we use is as follows:

May the blessing of God rest upon you.
May God's peace abide with you.
May God's presence illuminate your heart.
Now and forever more.

The ceremony can then be closed. We ask all present to join hands while standing. Then we offer a prayer of thanksgiving; for the baby, and the wonderful oportunity of a life's experience and service; for the parent or parents, to strengthen them as models of not only giving but receiving as well; and for all of us gathered together, to be the extended family for this baby, to take responsibility to "be there" in love and support for all the initiations of this soul.

eleven

The Blessing of Emotions

To feel is for real!

JOE MILLER

God is love and care and feeling.

CHIP, AGE 6

Rami and I wrote this chapter together during her eighth and ninth years of life. We had fun working together, helping each other to remember special moments in our lives. We are both very emotional and deeply experience life through feeling. By writing this with Rami I hoped to show her and all "emotional" people that emotions, although not always easy and painless, are truly great teachers and blessings.

A wonderful gift that we can give our children is to teach them to accept and respect their emotions. Through accepting emotions, rather than repressing them, children grow in wholeness and health. Each emotion, if listened to with love and understanding, can be a tool which children can use to better understand their total nature and to develop faith and confidence in the God within.

In our counseling practice we have seen too many people who have repressed their feelings from early childhood because they were told that anger, fear, sadness, and sometimes even enthusiasm and joy, were bad or silly. All feelings are very real to children and, if discouraged by the parent, they will attempt to bury them to please their parent. However, sooner or later these will come forth, sometimes not until adulthood, and often in unhealthy ways.

We are all born into the human condition and thus are subject to the full range of human emotions. Rather than giving the message that some emotions are negative and others positive, we can teach our children to respect each one, learn from each one as a companion on the journey of life, and eventually become masters of them all. If we start this process at an early age, we may be giving our children very valuable help in times of great need and emergency, as well as teaching them a healthy way of life.

Like most children, when I was young I had a fear of the dark. By the time I was nine years old I was convinced that there was an evil person hiding under my bed every night who would attack me as soon as the lights went out. I had my father check under my bed each night and then my mother, but as soon as it was dark in the room I was sure an evil being was down there ready to kill. The fear became worse every night. Finally my mother taught me the words to the 23rd Psalm:

> The Lord is my Shepherd, I shall not want;
> He makes me lie down in green pastures.
> He leads me beside still waters;
> He restores my soul.
> Even though I walk through the valley of the shadow of death,
> I fear no evil;
> For Thou art with me
> Thy rod and thy staff, they comfort me....

She described God as a loving shepherd. She then told me that as long as I repeated the 23rd Psalm, no harm would ever come to me. In my childhood innocence I believed her and repeated the Psalm each night upon going to sleep. It worked like an affirmation or mantra. The image of God as my loving shepherd became stronger than the image of an evil being, and soon the bedtime fear was overcome. My mother had given me a spiritual tool that had enabled me to master my fear and in this process had strengthened my faith in God as a loving protector in time of need.

When I was nineteen years old, I left the secure, home-like environment of my small college town of Oneonta, New York, to travel by bus to New York City for an interview at Columbia-Presbyterian Nursing School. The interview went well and I spent one night in the college dormitory. I felt very lonely and yearned to be in Oneonta and with Barry. I had the choice of leaving in the middle of the night and catching a 4:30am bus to Oneonta, or staying to wait for a 3:00pm bus. My loneliness caused me to choose to leave at 4:30am.

The nursing school was located at West 168th St., quite some distance from the bus station. From my map I saw that I needed to travel by subway trains the entire way and change at a place called Harlem. I was very innocent to the ways and names of such a big city and did not realize the danger I was getting myself into.

I rose at 3:30am and tip-toed downstairs to the main floor of the nursing dormitory. A guard met me and asked what in the world I thought I was doing. I explained how I was leaving to go back to my college and was on my way to the subway. He became visibly shaken and didn't want to let me go, explaining that even strong men do not risk traveling the subways in that part of town at night by themselves. He told me that a young woman carrying a suitcase was bound to be in danger, especially changing trains in Harlem.

He was all set to lock the door on me when he must have noticed my determined and sad look. "All right," he said, and showed me the quickest route to travel. "I'll say a prayer for you. When you get off at Harlem, head for the nearest policeman and ask him to escort you."

At age nineteen I was still very much a young girl and had no idea of the dangerous situation I was getting myself into. I hopped the first subway and sat clutching my suitcase, not daring to look at anyone. The subway stations speeded by and finally I saw HARLEM in big letters. I got off the subway, and the train quickly left me alone on the platform. There wasn't a policeman nor another woman in sight. (I learned later that during this time in 1966 there was so much unrest in Harlem, that even policemen were refusing to work the subway stations at night.)

It didn't take long for me to sense the danger I had gotten into as two rough-looking men approached me with sticks in hand.

Adrenalin shot through my body and I almost felt paralyzed. My mind went completely blank except for one thing: the image of God as my loving shepherd and the words to the 23rd Psalm. I had not thought of that Psalm since I was nine years old. In a loud voice I began reciting the Psalm.

The men got within five feet of me and then backed off. I felt as if I had an invincible wall of protective light around me. I kept repeating the psalm in a loud voice as I walked the ten minutes to catch the train that would take me to the bus depot. During that time several other men agressively approached me only to turn back when they came within feet of me. A wine bottle was thrown at me but never reached its mark.

When I finally rested in the seat of my bus to Oneonta, I closed my eyes and let the tension drain from my body. I knew that my life had miraculously and repeatedly been saved and I thanked God for the tools of protection my mother had given me as a child.

God is u beautiful being who is always there for you.

NESHOMA, AGE 11

From the time Rami and Mira were two years old Barry and I have told them of their guardian angels. We talk to them about these protective beings much the way one would talk about a loving grandparent who was a very close and wonderful part of their family. We sing to the angels and keep up a steady flow of love to them. Small children seem to need a form for God, such as Mother or Father, Jesus, Krishna or Kwan Yin, or the lovely angelic beings. Our children have both readily accepted the idea of a guardian angel. We always tell the girls that God and the angels cannot always be seen with our eyes, but their love and help are always available and sometimes can come through other human beings.

When I was five years old I went shopping with mama to a big store. She wanted to buy a new dress because she was pregnant. I got tired and I decided to play a game on mama. I ran and hid in the pants rack. She couldn't find me. I thought it was funny. But then I couldn't find her. I got very scared. I ran behind the dress rack. I didn't know what to do. I said a prayer that my guardian angel would help me find mama.

Right then an old woman came looking for a dress and she saw me.
Her white hair was shining like a light and she looked like an angel.
She knew right away that I was lost and brought me to a desk
where they called for mama to come. I was so happy to see mama
once again. The old woman who had been an angel to me was
gone.

RAMI

A good time to present various spiritual images to chilidren is right before they go to sleep. (See Bedtime Receptivity chapter). At that time, an image such as God as protective Mother and Father can live and grow within them while they sleep.

The *COURSE IN MIRACLES* has many beautiful thoughts and images for adults which could be translated into simpler terms for children. I like the image that whenever I don't receive what I want, I need to turn up the light in my heart even stronger. The images and spiritual tools that we give to our children will be valuable only so far as we are willing to also use them ourselves.

My brother, peace and joy I offer you,
That I may have God's peace and joy as mine.

COURSE IN MIRACLES

Somewhere over the rainbow
You'll find your dream
It's only because
You and I are singing in harmony

RAMI, AGE 7

I have always told Rami whenever she is angry with someone that she sit right down and try to think of something positive about that person. (Mira, at age three, has not yet experienced the powerful force of anger.) As soon as one can see the positive in another human being, the anger can no longer live within the heart and a greater perspective can be seen.

When Rami was almost six years old, Mira was an infant. Barry at that time worked almost every Sunday as a general physician at a hospital. That winter was very severe in Santa Cruz and the storms were causing mud slides and ocean front damage. After thirty days of gray skies the sun finally broke out on a Sunday afternoon. Mira was taking her usual two hour nap, Barry was at the hospital, and I was alone with Rami. I always tried to make Sunday afternoons a special time to be together with Rami, as Mira generally took up so much of my time.

On this day we had made flour clay and were happily preparing to go out in the sun to make a teddy bear family. Suddenly I heard loud rock music drift in through our closed windows. My heart sank! Pete, our neighbor, was blasting his radio again.

We live in a very rural area, renting a home on a 120-acre ranch. Our only close neighbors are the caretakers of the ranch who live quite close, down the hill from our home. The couple are retired Texans, whose world is hard physical labor and raising cows for meat. As they catch glimpses of us meditating outside from time to time, they think our life-style is quite weird. Over the years we've learned not to cross them and usually coexist quite harmoniously. Their son, Pete, also lives with them. His world is rodeos, roping calves, and constant work. Each day as he drives his pickup past our home we wave at him if we are outside, but he has seldom waved back.

As I walked outside with Rami the sound of the loud music was painful to my ears. Pete is usually away at a rodeo, but because of all the rain he was forced to stay home. I tried to forget the music and concentrate on the warmth of the sun and the beauty of Rami's face. However, sound is very sacred to me and I am very sensitive to it. I thrive on the sounds of birds and nature or delicate, sensitive human-made music. Loud rock music is often painful for me to experience. Try as I did to feel peaceful, I was becoming uptight.

Finally I announced to Rami that I was going into the house to phone Pete and ask him to turn down his radio just a little. When I called, his mother reported that Pete was inside watching a game on TV. When he came to the phone I *very* politely explained that he left his radio on outside when he came in to watch TV. Since he wasn't listening to it I asked if he might turn it off. "No!" was his sudden response as he hung up the phone on me. Going outside to sit with Rami I watched from over the fence as he walked outside to his radio, turned it on to full volume and then walked back into the house.

Anger boiled within me!! I felt like walking down to the radio and throwing a rock at it.

Rami was fully aware of all that I was experiencing. She also felt angry. I brought her into the house from the precious sunshine to the one dark and cold room of our house where Pete's music did not reach. "Rami, I feel really angry at Pete," I admitted. "Let's both try to feel something positive about him." This was a hard assignment, so we both sat in silence for a long time. Finally Rami's eyes brightened as she said, "He loves his horse!" So we expanded on that theme, discussing how thoughtfully he brushes his horse before each rodeo, the beautiful barn he built for his horse and how clean he keeps the stalls. As we became more and more involved in talking about how much Pete loves his horse, we both saw how his horse was the closest friend he had. We began to see how lonely and scared of people he must be. "So that's why he never waves!", said Rami thoughtfully. Our hearts were now filling with compassion for Pete.

I then felt that we needed to go outside again. As we stepped out the door the only sound that greeted us was the birds happily eating at the bird feeder. Rami and I jumped up and down for joy! Pete had turned off his radio!! We felt the vibration of our love had reached him on some level and he felt moved to honor our request.

The result and lesson of that experience has had a lasting effect on both Rami and me. She is developing the good habit of naturally seeking the positive in whomever she feels angry with.

Sometimes my mother yells at me when I tease Mira. She makes me go to my room. Sometimes I feel so angry at her that I slam the door. I even yell, "I hate you Mama." I go to the window and look out. I make myself say all the things that I like about her. Soon I feel happy again. I peek my head out the door and say, "I love you mama and Mira." Mama lets me come out and we talk about why she sent me to my room. Mira and I have a little hug and we play again.

RAMI

Relatives of ours tell the story of their six-year old son's remarks in church one Sunday. A traditional part of the service was the singing of "The Lord's Prayer." This particular day, after the song was finished his response was, "I like that song, but it always makes my eyes wet."

All human beings experience sadness at different times of their lives. Little children experience the emotion several times a day. The emotion comes on very easily and usually leaves just as quickly. How marvelous if we adults could learn to let go of sadness as easily as small children.

Self-portrait by Mira.

Mira can be playing so happily with her dessert of honey animal cookies. Suddenly she bursts into tears, "Elephant's head broke!" I run to look. Sure enough, elephant's head lay in crumbles. "Now I can't finish my story." Mira's crying is now becoming deep mournful sobs.

I run to the bag of animal cookies hoping to find another elephant. No luck. The only whole cookie left is a lion. "Mira," I venture hopefully, "how about a lion cookie." "No," she wails, "I need an elephant." Handing me the elephant's body she says can you fix it mama? Please! I need to finish my story." Her eyes hold so much trust in my ability to make it somehow better. Rummaging in the bag I finally find an elephant's head. With a little scotch tape, elephant is back in the story with a new head. Mira plays happily for the remainder of the story and then eats up all the cookies when she is through.

Little children come freely to their parents in time of need and sadness. If our help is given in love, they seem to accept it so readily. The solution we offer is not always as they would like, yet out of their great trust for us they accept our offering and let go of the sadness.

Once three-year-old Mira burst through the front door crying, "Rami and her friend won't play with me. My feelings are very hurt." I looked out the window and saw Rami and Sarah at the top of a tree. "I want to be big like Rami," Mira sobbed as big tears rolled down her cheeks. "Mira, you are a very big and lucky girl today. Do you know why?" As she pondered the question, my mind raced for appropriate answers, "because Mira gets to help mommy make special cookies for tonight. And *you* can measure the raisins!" As her little face lights up I marvel at how quickly the sadness leaves and how fully she trusts.

As children grow, bandaids, quick distractions, scotch tape and little kisses don't as easily mend their hurt or sad feelings. There is a transition period when children come to mommy or daddy to make it all better but are starting to need more. It is at this point that a parent can guide their child to ask their Heavenly Parents for help, cautioning them that the solution that comes from God may not always be as they might have wanted, but will be the most helpful. (See "Kriya goes to the Heaven World")

God is the place to go when you are feeling sad and need a feeling of peace.

ALIA, AGE 13

God makes me happy when I'm sad
He talks to me and tells me wonderful things
He tells me things I could be doing rather than being sad
Sometimes I feel God's arms around me
God is my best friend.

RAMI, AGE 7

Children also experience many disappointments in childhood. Each disappointment can be used to help children trust in a higher will than their own.

When I was in the third grade my class was going to the county fair. We were studying farms in school and were going to see all the animals at the fair. We were all very excited. I was going to meet my teacher down at the bottom of our road. My mom and I waited and waited for my teacher to come. She never did! (We found out she was waiting at another road.) I was very disappointed. As we

*walked back up the road my mom suggested that we breathe out
the disappointment and breathe in God's new plan for us. She told
me that if one door is closed for me, another will open.*

*When we got home the phone was ringing. Marie, our neighbor,
was on the phone, "Is Rami home by any chance? Judy just gave
birth to her calf." Judy is my favorite cow on the ranch. I ran down
to Marie's house. I had never seen a newborn calf before. I felt so
happy and got to pet her. I helped Marie name the new calf
June-Bug.*

RAMI

*Joy has no cost.
It is your sacred right.*

COURSE IN MIRACLES

God is a good feeling.

QAYYUM, AGE 10

In joy and happiness children can also learn to experience God.
Joy is always a special gift. It provides rest, nurturing and
inspiration for the soul. Joy reminds us of our heavenly home. This
beautiful emotion can be enhanced if our thoughts turn toward God
in thankfulness. If children begin at an early age to be thankful, it
will become a way of life. Those who live and breathe thankfulness
are the most blessed of souls.

Little Mira was so happy when Barry brought home our new
puppy. She jumped up and down for joy. Barry had us all gather in a
little circle around puppy and be thankful for the blessing of this
lovely animal. Mira's joy changed from an outward jumping up and
down to a deep inner joy. She laid her hand on the puppy's head and
sweetly said, "Thank you God for our pretty puppy."

Gratitude before a meal is also very important. This simple act
can help us to remember where our food really comes from.
Thankfulness for the joy of a bright sunny morning after the gray
storm clouds have parted, reminds us of the brightness of Divine
Light. Helping our children to use every opportunity to thank God
for joys and blessings helps us to live our own lives more gratefully.

*I thank God for my handicaps for, through them,
I have found my work and my God.*

HELEN KELLER

Gratitude goes hand in hand with love, and where one is the other must be found.

COURSE IN MIRACLES

Love is a warm feeling when you like someone.
God gives us the warm feeling.

CLARE, AGE 8

Love is the most powerful force in the universe. It is the centripetal force which holds atoms together in a molecule as well as holding planets in orbit around their sun. It is an awesome power. Parents cannot teach their children to love. They must be a model of love.

True love always has an element of wanting to serve another. In loving another, we care more about their happiness than we do our own. In loving our children, we care more about their well being and their spiritual growth than we do our own. When we love them fully, they desire to model what they feel from us. While singing Mira to sleep, I feel so much love for her. Lying in her bed with thumb in mouth, she is so adorable. In those moments there isn't anything I wouldn't do for her. My heart wells up full of feeling as I say, "I love you Mira." "I love you too, mama." "This wonderful feeling, Mira, is God." "I love God," she sleepily responds.

As children grow, give them the opportunity to serve others with love and devotion. Help them to see that serving takes the feeling of love to deeper and deeper levels. In giving love to another, the love returns to the giver a thousand fold.

Recently, Barry took Rami and Mira to San Diego for a week-long reunion with his family. I was going to fly down later to join them. I hadn't had time alone in our home since before Mira was born. Five lovely days stretched before me to write.

On the second night after their departure, I was out jogging at 11:00pm when our big, clumsy, full-grown puppy suddenly darted out in front of me and stopped. I sailed over him, landed on my arm and broke my elbow.

The next day my arm was set in a cast and I decided to fly down earlier to join Barry and the girls. I was in a lot of pain and feeling very vulnerable. I was touched especially by Rami's sensitivity to me. She watched over me the entire day, carrying things, helping me on with my clothes and helping me to eat. Throughout the day she became totally immersed in her desire to care for me. In the evening she gave me a bath, tenderly washed me all over, and then shampooed my hair. She dried me off with the love of a mother for her new-born baby, brushed out my hair, and dressed me. Then she gently guided me to bed and covered me with blankets. She sat down beside me and caressed my forehead. I thanked her for helping me so much and closed my eyes. When I opened them several minutes later Rami's face was absolutely radiant. "Oh Mama," she exclaimed, "I've never felt so much love in my whole life. My heart feels as if it will burst with love. I don't know what to do I feel so happy."

At age nine Rami had discovered the precious secret of a truly joyful life. In giving love to another, she herself had received more love than she had ever known.

As I lay on the bed looking at my radiant Rami, I also glanced at my broken arm. I touched it tenderly. The beauty of this moment far surpassed the pain I was experiencing. I was grateful for the many ways God teaches us and helps us to unravel the mystery of Divine Love.

Don't worry mama, God will fix your arm real good.

MIRA, AGE 3

Ministers of God are by your side. No single detail in your life, not a thought or an action, escapes them, but they judge not. They only love, with deep compassion and wide understanding. Remember this and pray that a love such as theirs will fill your heart so that you look upon all people with the same gentle loving kindness as the Brethren of the Light regard you.

WHITE EAGLE

Beloved, let us love one another...

JESUS

twelve

From Monk to Dada

by Jack Kornfield

Jack Kornfield is a meditation teacher who trained as a Buddhist monk in monasteries of Thailand, Burma and India. He is a founder of the Insight Meditation Society, author of LIVING BUDDHIST MASTERS and A STILL FOREST POOL. He also has a PhD in clinical psychology.

When I learned that Jack and his wife Lee had given birth to a baby girl named Caroline, I was amazed. I wondered what would prompt a man whose very life had been spent in quieting his mind and simplifying his life, to choose the sometimes not-so-peaceful-and-quiet marriage and family life. Even though I did not know Jack at the time, I felt that his decision to become a father would give great hope to all parents. He knew the depth of silence and solitude, and from that knowledge chose marriage and family.

While visiting in Marin County, California, we found ourselves driving by Jack and Lee's home. Our friend stopped her car, pointed out their house, and we knocked on their door. Jack greeted us holding their baby. In the few minutes that we visited, I saw why he had made his choice for fatherhood. He revealed how much Caroline's presence in their lives had opened his heart. Parenting had now become an important part of Jack Kornfield's spiritual practice.

We later asked Jack to focus one of his weekly talks on this transition in his life. The following is an excerpt of that talk.

Parenting is one of the most rewarding and demanding practices that one will undertake in this life. It makes a very demanding guru seem like a piece of cake. Your guru or teacher says to you, "Get up at three in the morning and do your bajans, prayers, or zazen, and you usually get up. But if you don't feel that good you sleep in and say you're sick. After all, what is he or she going to say? You can get away with it. But when your child wakes up in the middle of the night sick and throwing up, you *have* to get up and care for her. It doesn't matter if you're exhausted from a very full week, or are sick yourself, or were up all day taking care of your other child.

I have looked into my own heart to figure out why I became a parent. Before becoming a parent there was some sense of a lack in my own personal life. I was successful as a teacher and certainly living a wonderful life. Being a dharma teacher is a great job to have because you get to meet really nice people who are on their best behavior in beautiful places and circumstances, and talk about love and things that are basically noble and profound. You feel like you are doing something valuable (whether it's true or not is another question).

In that way things were successful and fulfilling. But there was something else missing for me. How can I express it? It's a very personal thing, but I imagined somehow that if I continued to teach and travel, even though I might get better as a teacher of meditation, explaining clearly how to work with meditation practice and develop awareness, that in some way something else would get dry in me. This may not be so for other people but I felt that while I would be a skillful teacher, I would also lose contact with something that's more alive within me, something that has to do with the heart. So having a child came from this deep desire to keep my heart open. Certainly, being a parent is a very hot fire alot of the time. Also, I think I chose it on purpose because I like challenges.

Yet I don't want to make the decision to become a parent sound too thoughtful and conscious. It wasn't. It was really something from the guts and the heart. It came from being in love with someone and saying, "Well let's try this one." But it's really a big ride. When you take the ticket you go for twenty years. Older friends say the problem is not the empty nest syndrome, it's the empty the nest out and they come in the back door and want to live a little longer and get you to support them into their 30's.

Somehow, consciously choosen or not, having a child is mostly an expression of love. It has continued to deepen the intimacy and connection in my marriage. For me it was pretty amazing because I never had a sexual life where we tried to do what sex is actually connected with; making babies. It was a really powerful thing to make love and have the intention be to have a child; really quite extraordinary, mysterious, and wonderful.

When the baby was born it was beautiful and awesome. I was exhausted because it was a three-day labor for my wife and I tried to stay fully with her. There was this glow as the baby was born, but also I was checking her out and saying, "Are you the right one?" "Is this my child?" She looked like my child, but who is this person? What will she be like? For anyone who has had children, its very clear that they are not blank slates. They have their own personality, agenda and karma from the very beginning.

You get to know this whole new person. You cannot be at a birth and not have your heart touched in some way. The pain and the beauty is just such an amazing thing. It is a mystery to watch a baby grow. As it walks, looks around or just smiles, there is a whole sense of wanting to take care of it. It must be cellular or something; it is so ingrained in us. Who can see a baby crying or some child that's hurt and not want to respond? In some ways it speaks to the innate goodness in all beings; that there's that kind of response to children. The natural response of our hearts is to care for someone that's hurting or in need.

There is a mixture of pleasure and pain as you look at a baby and say, "I don't want them to suffer. I want to take care of them." Caroline's just learning about "hot". So she went over to a candle and said "hot", and went to touch the flame, we pulled her hand away and said "No, no hot." She put her hand in anyway and it burned her fingers—not badly—just a little bit. She cried. Then her face changed to outrage. Why should it hurt? If it's not the candle or the stove it will be the heater or something. Yet what can a parent do? Life is pleasant and painful. From the beginning you realize that you can't fully protect anybody. You can love them, but you can't protect them. Eventually everyone has to openly engage in the world that is light and dark, up and down, sweet and sour, and pleasant and painful.

In the beginning of parenting there is a tremendous sense of surrender. Once I lived with a woman who had two children. I got really jealous of the children. I wanted to be with her and have her attention. The children were jealous of me too. After a day in pre-school they wanted mommy's attention and kept pulling on her. "Stay here, read to us, play with us." It was a real struggle for a number of weeks over why we couldn't go out. I said, "Lets get more babysitters. Why do they have to get up so early and then bounce on the bed at 6 in the morning." In the end there was no contest. I finally just gave up and raised the white flag of "I surrender". They come first. There was no question about it. I was defeated. It wasn't like I didn't want what I wanted. But it was really clear who came first. There is a tremendous amount of surrender to parenting and a kind of love that most people rarely touch in their lives.

A good friend of mine had four daughters and a son. Her youngest daughter, when she was thirteen years old, had a brain tumor and had an operation. She came out of the operation as if she had had a really bad stroke: unable to walk, unable to speak, unable to feed herself. Her mother was Hawaiian and grew up in an Asian culture where, when someone's in the hospital, you go and camp in the hospital with them. She camped in the hospital for three months with her daughter, until she could bring her home. She said, "I spent every waking hour for two and and half years bringing her back so she could walk and speak and eat and read. I knew somewhere in my heart that she hadn't died and that she was still in there and she could be brought out. I would pick up her hand and put it down, pick it up again until she could learn to pick something up again; saying words again until she could speak, and help her walk." You couldn't pay somebody for that. This tremendous capacity which we have to love another person is evoked by having children.

We also have a tremendous capacity to hate, or to feel frustration. Already I have a very deep understanding about why child abuse happens. Here Caroline was a wanted baby and I consider myself someone who's got a decent amount of equanimity and awareness and still when the baby is collicky and crying, and just won't stop, what am I going to do. It's not just one night but nights and nights. And then you think of people in a poor apartment where its cold, not so comfortable, there's five kids and the latest one is just crying and screaming for two months and is collicky and won't stop.

I remember teaching at a conference one day, with a whole roomful of people. In the room there was a young child that was really fussy. He started to scream and throw a tantrum. Finally the child was quieted and taken out and then one of the women in the room (obviously a professional mother) said, "Don't you remember the time when you just wanted to take them and throw them out the window and it didn't matter how many floors down it was." And every mother in that room laughed. Every mother in the room laughed because they all knew that somehow their children had taken them to their very edge of sanity.

Parenting is a spiritual practice. It is a place of tremendous surrender and giving. You just give. You get a lot back sometimes. Sometimes you don't get anything. Then they become a teenager and they don't seem to care about you at all. All they seem to want to do is be free and leave. "But I raised you and I did this and I gave you that." And they say "See ya, so long." If you're lucky, they say "See ya," before they disappear. What did I get from my giving? What you get is what you gave.

When you look at the path of perfections in Buddhism; generosity, patience, surrender, virtue, attention, and equanimity are all major components in the practice. For a start, parenting is a tremendous field in which to cultivate giving and surrender and patience and loving. It is really a practice if you can do it in even a somewhat mindful way. Perhaps those of us who are involved in becoming more aware are also relearning certain things that are known in simpler cultures, but have been forgotten in the busyness and ambition of our Western society. We're trying to relearn what it means to be part of a village or a sangha or a community and to raise our children in a way that's more caring and less ambitious; more patient and less greedy. Still it's hard. You give up a lot of yourself. If you think that sitting meditation comes first, you really have to reorient. There's a lovely book by Zen master Thich Nhat Hanh called the MIRACLE OF MINDFULNESS and this is the first question he addresses, speaking to the parent who says they never have enough time for themselves. Until you can make a shift and see that your time with another person is also *your* time for yourself, you will be frustrated. Somehow you must learn to take that time with another person as your practice, as your own place of opening. Otherwise you will be frustrated all the time.

So in parenting there's DANA, which means giving, patience

and surrender. Next there's SILA, the step in practice which means virtue. As a parent there are all kinds of ways to work with virtue. In the beginning it's simply learning how to say no to somebody and setting appropriate boundaries; saying no an awful lot of times and learning that it's really important that you're able to say no. People don't like to say it. I feel uncomfortable saying no to anybody. It really becomes very obvious with a child. You don't have to think about it... NO, cut that out..Stop it .. Don't go in the street... Of course you can find skillful ways to do it which don't undermine their exploration and self esteem but still it must be said. Your whole sense of self changes as a guardian, a caretaker for another person, as a parent. So at first there's a kind of sila of setting boundaries. But in a much deeper way as the children grow older, life makes you have to look at your own values. What are you going to teach them? You're a daddy or you're a mommy. Are you going to teach them to play football or knit or whatever your image of what a young man or young lady is supposed to learn. You look at those parts of your values. Even more, it makes you question what kind of school they're going to go to, what are they going to learn. You see the blessings of our culture: its variety, its choices, its richness that your children will inherit. And you see as well the curses, the difficulties, the consumerism, the kind of superficiality, the shallowness. Just turn on TV. Have your children watch TV for awhile. Do you want to do that to some young person?.... have them watch TV? So what do you teach kids? and how do you educate them? It really makes you look at your values.

And of course every step of the way is a compromise. There's no perfection in this game whatsoever. If you're a bad parent then they will probably go to therapy and work it out and so forth. If you're too good then they go to the therapist because they're unable to separate. They're too connected with you. There's no way you can win at the game. And in a way that's perfect. Because the perfection is that you realize that the child's not supposed to be a certain way or that you're supposed to be a certain way. You give what you can give and maybe learn not to judge yourself so much. Fortunately for me, my wife is intuitively a wonderful mother, so I learn a lot from watching her way with children. I remember Kalu Rimpoche, an old Tibetan Llama coming to visit friends of mine with a two-year old child. They asked him "Would you please tell us about how to raise him so he will be spiritual and wise, a compassionate child, and fine person and so forth." And this 80-year old Tibetan Llama, just shook his head and said, "No, no... You have the wrong idea." He said, "He will be whoever he's going to be. If you want to raise somebody properly, raise yourself. You can do your own practice with a sincere heart and let him feel that from you." In fact this holds not just for our children, but it's really the only way we affect the world anyway. The world is overpopulated. And since we can't get rid of the extra people what we can do is to make a space of love and wisdom for them all. So even if there's not enough physical space, they will find the more important space of the heart.

Someone said that every psychologist should have a child and a dog. It's true. If your interested in psychology and want to learn about behavior and conditioning and the developmental stages of what makes us all as nutty as we are, have a child and a dog.

There is a story from *TALES OF THE MAGIC MONASTERY* by Father Theophane called "It's Very Simple". These tales are of a monk who goes to visit this magic monastery. He says:

> He looked so holy when I saw him, the Magic Monastery's teacher, that I simply asked him, "Tell me what God is really like." With feather gentleness he replied, "It's Lent now. I'm accustomed to refrain from talking during Lent. But take this book." It was the book he had been writing in. "If you read this at the right hour, it will tell you what God is like." I couldn't wait to bring it back home and share it with my wife.

> Back home, she was a little less excited than I about the book, since she hadn't been to the Magic Monastery, and because her mind was on her first child which she was carrying. She had already turned inward. "What did he mean by 'At the right hour'," she asked. I didn't know. We began to speculate...maybe at noon on Good Friday...maybe at noon on Easter...maybe at the moment when we are in deep distress. Perhaps we should wait for God to reveal to us the right hour. It might even be years from now. We decided we better wait for a sign. Two weeks later my first son was born. How can I tell you what it was like? First you worry and then there's this child. I was a father. You grow up when you become a father. It's true, and not so easy. When I looked at that child I was so proud and I knew I was somebody, yet I was humbled. I scarcely knew how to hold him, much less how to bring him up. What was I supposed to do? I used to think I had it all figured out but I got up and I reached for the book. I brought it to my wife and told her this is the right hour, we'll open it now. I opened it at random and I read, "It's very simple. God is a father." My wife opened it again and she read "It's very simple. God became a little child." "Let's open it again," I cried. "Let's open it together." So we held hands and opened it and read, "It's very simple. Every breath you breathe is the breath of God. Every child is the child of God."

Jack, Lee and baby Caroline.

Somebody said that parenting is one of the few things that's left in the world for amateurs. We get training to become drivers. We get training to be teachers. We get training to be counselors. Then there's this basically impossible task of trying to be kind and wise and helpful, set limits and teach your child how to be a fine human being and we get zero training. We're really amateurs. In some way its powerful this way, beginner's mind. Here's where wisdom grows. You don't know what your child will be like when it's born and there it is. You just get it. And you don't know what it's going to be like when it grows up or what it's going to do. You have a fifteen-year-old and you don't know what career it will take. You have a twenty-year-old and you don't know what kind of marriage it will get itself into. It's a little child and you don't know what mischief it will get into. It's really a process of learning how to deal with the unknown, holding your breath, waiting and seeing what happens.

Caroline, who likes to eat cheerios for breakfast, can really teach me how to live in the moment. She can sit down with her cheerios, and line them up or put them on top of one another or spear one with her little finger or look around... put it in her mouth...chew it... take it out and see what happened to it... then stick it in to my mouth to see if I like it...then pull it again and spend twenty minutes experimenting on all the properties of a cheerio. Then put it down and be done with it and experiment with the spoon... This tremendous capacity to be in the present moment reevokes that spirit of the child in ourselves. I love going out with a child and looking at a tree. Introducing her to it, "This is a tree." "Wow, that's tree. Look it has leaves and moves in the wind and there's lots of them all around, different kinds. They smell different." But we adults forget. We take trees for granted. Walks along the street, "Oh look. There's dry leaves. They crumble and crunch. We forget that the world is tremendously interesting. We take it for granted. We loose a certain mystery. Maybe that's the best thing about children. They keep us awake, seeing the world in some difficult and fresh way. It's not that you just get the samadhi of being very present with a child with your attention, but also you learn the other special practice called in Sanscrit, sampajanna which means to be able to do many things mindfully at once: like change a diaper, hold the child still and get some other clothes or take care of two or three children, one who's pouring things on the floor and one who's running around and the other who needs to be fed and all at the same time while you're also trying to answer the phone that's ringing and do several other tasks. For me it's been a very different kind of meditation, that, of walk when you walk, eat when you eat. Kids know how to do that. Eat when you eat and play with your cheerios when you play with your cheerios and so forth. But its more like the Koren Zen Master Sevng Sahes who was sitting at the table at the Zen Center one morning eating his breakfast and reading the morning paper. A student came up to him and was very upset and said, "How can you do this, Roshi. Here you teach us to just eat when you eat, walk when you walk and sit when you sit and now you're eating and also reading. What kind of an example is that?" He looked up and laughed, "When you eat and read, just eat and read." Keep it simple. Don't make it so complicated. You learn that alot with kids too.

A friend of mine, a woman who is a poet and was on the faculty at Naropa Institute, is a wonderful teacher and a successful business woman, having started a company which makes millions of dollars. She also spent many years in India. Right before our baby was born, I asked her "What did she think about having children and family?" And she said, " You know, it is the one thing in my life I really don't regret doing at all. It brought me the most satisfaction, the most happiness and the most joy." It connects us with the earth. It connects us not with all the things we want to do, and our busyness in our world of work, and the society around but it brings us back to the trees and to biology and our bodies and to our hearts and to our family. Mother Theresa said, "If the world is to end nuclear war, if we're to stop the arms race and its madness that we find around us, it's not just the politicians who must do it but it's each person in their own family in their own neighborhood. If you can't learn to love your own children, and your neighbors, the people who live next door to you, how do you expect the world to change in any way that will bring peace for us?"

On Becoming Earth-Worthy
by William Lonsdale

William Lonsdale is a counselor, astrologer and visionary. We have never met anyone who so fully embodies the heart of astrology as William. A long time student of Rudolf Steiner, he seeks for the deeper meaning behind the ordinary in life.

I once called him to ask if his older daughter could come over to our house and play with Rami. My mind was filled with driving arrangements and what clothing Corin should bring. Within five minutes, we were deep in thought concerning our destinies here on earth.

I wondered what it would be like for a person of such depth to become a father...

Becoming a father has been a huge transition from my being a full time visionary into becoming a person in this world, which is always involved with coming down, in the sense of grounding.

With Corin, who is now ten, her being says to me, "Come down right here and be with me; in this moment, in this place. I cannot meet you on your visionary territory. I demand to meet you on my child territory." Even though I have agreed with her, it has been such a struggle to get myself there. I have had to do it layer by layer and phase by phase. It's like descending a ladder. At each point I get off and say, "Here I am," then I realize there is more to go.

My other daughter, Audette, who is about six, is with me in

those inner spaces. She needs me to help her make the connection with the outer spaces where she has more difficulty. Her being demands that I become a bridge and that I become an "earth-worthy" person.

Both children have been endlessly calling me down in one way or another. I have found this, surprisingly, to be the best thing that has ever happened to me. My ego would have said at thirteen different points, "Ouch!; No!; This isn't it!; Why is this happening to me?!" It keeps turning out that it's just what I needed to be myself. It isn't the least bit tangential even though I had somehow gotten convinced that it was. It's like all the people of the world are speaking through these children saying, "We need you to be here. Don't stay in your secluded reverie. Make your peace with the world."

thirteen

Bedtime

The child's greatest friend is the one who helps it to go to sleep.

HAZRAT INAYAT KHAN

Bedtime can be a very rewarding experience for both you and your child. It can be a special time to look into each other's eyes, to deepen your harmony, to laugh at little happenings throughout the day and together grow closer to the source of love.

There are times in the lives of infants, babies and children when they enter into very receptive states in which they are open to absorb much from the world around them. Infants and babies go in and out of these states quite frequently. For children, one of the most receptive times is at night, just before going to sleep. The thoughts, feelings and impressions that children have upon going to sleep live and grow within them for the 10 - 12 hours that they are sleeping. We have found that bedtime is a very effective time for conveying spiritual truths to a child in a heart-to-heart way. It is also a time to communicate your love to your child. These bedtime experiences can have a profound effect on your child's whole life.

When Barry was in the psychiatry residency training program at the University of Oregon, I worked for the department of child psychiatry. We both had the marvelous opportunity to attend many workshops as part of our work and training. One of these was a five-day psychodrama workshop which lasted from nine in the morning until eleven at night. There were thirty of us that attended: psychiatry residents, social workers, psychologists and nurses. This was an intense experience that quickly wore down defenses and let people experience the joys and pains of their lives.

At one point in the process it became evident that the energy of the participants was very low, so our leader suggested we experience our bedtime as little children. Since we were in a huge room filled with couches and chairs, he instructed everyone to make a little crib or bed for themselves. He then asked for two volunteers to go around and tuck everyone into bed. Barry and I raised our hands. We had a lot of fun as we went around to everyone, giving little kisses and hugs, saying gentle words: "You were so loving today, Ivan"; "I love you Gertrude"; "Good night little Hal."

We were thoroughly enjoying ourselves as we progressed from "child" to "child" until suddenly, sobs and moans started emerging from the "cribs" around the room. Soon the room was filled with the sounds of crying and whimpering.

Afterward, the instructor asked us all to get back into a circle and share our feelings during the exercise. I had been feeling very close to my father and had been merely acting out the things he used to do for me as a little child. A few other people related happy childhood memories of their mother or father spending special time with them upon going to sleep. For the majority of the people in that room, however, it had been a very painful experience. They remembered feeling very lonely and sometimes scared when sent off to bed. "My parents were always too busy watching TV to come up to me." "My mother was always going to meetings and I was either home alone or with a babysitter." "My father seemed glad when my bedtime came. It felt as if he couldn't wait to get rid of me and just ordered me off to bed." "My parents were too busy fighting, I just had to put myself to sleep." The memory of the lack of parental love and attention at bedtime caused more pain for people than at any other set time of the day.

Children are vulnerable right before they go to sleep. In their open and receptive state they can either draw love into their being or allow themselves to dwell on their fear. When parents spend a little extra time helping that their children drift off to a sweet sleep, it can establish a valuable lifetime pattern.

When I talk about this subject in my classes for mothers, there are always several mothers who come up to me afterwards and say, "I know it's important to spend time at bedtime, but I don't have any time." If we knew how vitally important it was for our children, then we would make time. Perhaps we need to reevaluate our day to see what can be sacrificed. Spending this extra time at night with a child often involves some sacrifice for the parent. A child's bedtime can often be the busiest time of day for the parent, who might be wanting to go off to a social event, school or church meeting. The telephone or even the dinner dishes might seem more important at the time, or the parent might be exhausted from caring for the children all day or working away from home. It can be so tempting to send the children off to bed with a quick kiss in order to get all of our work done.

Sometimes parents are forced to work at night, making children's bedtime an impossibility. In such cases, if the parent committed even one night a week on a day off to being with their child, it would still be very special and meaningful to both. Keeping these commitments to our children is a way of showing them that we really care about their spiritual growth.

I am tested in my commitment over and over. Something always seems to come up and I am often tempted to say, "This is more important." Yet when I follow through on the commitment to be with the children at bedtime, I am always deeply rewarded.

We have evening groups, classes and counseling appointments at our home at least three times a week. Barry and I earnestly try to begin putting the children to sleep early to allow them each to have a special time alone with one of us. As is often the case, we do not allow enough time and there is a mad scramble to get pajamas on, find their favorite teddy bears, brush teeth, etc. One typical night I was running through the house at top speed with an arm full of clean diapers when the phone rang (which it always seems to do at these times). "I'll just get a quick message," I thought. As I picked up the phone I heard the all-too-familiar long distance sound. Since our first book has come out, we've been receiving more and more long distance calls from people in need. "Hello," then I heard muffled crying sounds, "My husband died two weeks ago and I really need help." I glanced at my watch. Thirty people were coming soon for a class. Just then Rami appeared, all ready for bed with a beaming smile, "I set up the alter and lit the candle for our prayer time together. Come on mama! You promised!"

It is at these times when our commitment is tested and we must quickly assess where we are to serve. I have found that when I put service to my children first, all else follows in harmony. I simply told the woman that I could not talk with her because I had promised to spend a special time of prayer and singing with my daughter. I assured the woman that we would say a prayer for her and then I would call her after the class.

I told Rami about the call and the woman's need. I then explained that I needed her help in sending love. We sat right down to pray for this woman and soon felt a warm glow enfold us. Our time together that night seemed especially blessed. When I later called the woman, she told me the help she needed had come during the time Rami and I were sending our love.

Other nights there are different distractions and excuses for not spending this extra time: a special friend visiting, a yoga class being given in our home or, the most difficult of all, not feeling close to the children because of an inharmonious day. But once I push past my resistance and set in motion the little rituals they and I have set up, the distractions and discord melt away and my heart opens. I realize that I was resisting because I was denying my own need to kneel as a little child and receive God's blessing and love. From kneeling together with Rami and Mira I receive as much if not more than they. When we say our last good-night, I know once again that I have been renewed as a mother *and* as a child of God.

In the later stages of pregnancy with Mira, I, like many pregnant women, was very open and sensitive. One day, two weeks before Mira's birth, I felt especially burdened by recent problems and difficulties. With some sadness I went to put Rami to sleep. I read her several stories and then snuggled together for our nightly little talk and songs. When I looked into Rami's five-year-old eyes they seemed to hold the love and compassion of an ancient sage. I put my hand on her heart and told her how much God loves her. Then a very peculiar thing happened. I had the distinct feeling of another Presence in the room reaching down to touch my heart and reassuring me how much God loves me. I felt filled with God's love. Rami's eyes continued to pour forth love and compassion.

We then spoke about how close Rami's angel is to her, always protecting her. Suddenly I felt an angelic Presence in the room protecting and loving me. I sang Rami several songs all the while feeling the nearness of God. When I finally reached down to hug Rami good-night, I felt myself being hugged and mothered by invisible comforting arms.

When I left Rami's room that night I knew that a healing had taken place within me. The anxiety, worry and fear had been replaced by a reassurance of the closeness of God. The heaviness of heart had been replaced by lightness. In mothering Rami and endeavoring to bring forth her spiritual life, I had been mothered and my own spiritual nature revealed. I knew then that I needed that time with Rami as much as she needed it with me, if not more. Today I am not as psychically sensitive as I was just before giving birth, yet I am aware of the same process going on, including the same opportunity to be mothered and nurtured while giving that to my child. What a marvelous blessing awaits us each evening at our child's bedtime, if we but open to it.

Tuesday evening! Lately this has been my time to recuperate after twenty hours between Monday and Tuesday of running a county medical clinic and seeing patients. This particular Tuesday evening I was feeling more "burned out" than usual—my mind reeling with problem patients, my body numb and tired, and my soul pleading for peace and quiet. With a little bit of luck perhaps my evening could be free of responsibilities.

Maybe it was a little sneaky, but I did it anyway. As I approached our house, I turned off the motor and glided noiselessly into my parking place. That way the children wouldn't notice me and I could slip out of the car for a "cooling out" walk in the woods—by myself!

As I opened the car door, the living room curtain flew open and two bouncing, smiling little people were enthusiastically pointing at me, wildly screaming "Daddy's home, daddy's home!" My cover obviously blown, a sheepish smile on my face, I pretended as best I could to be happy to see my eight-year-old and two-year-old girls.

A moment later in the house, the bouncing children became hugging-each-of-my-legs-children, and Joyce greeted me warmly with a kiss. Then, before I could say anything, she announced there was an "urgent" meeting at Rami's school—and she would be late if she didn't leave immediately—and could I please bathe the girls, read them a story, and put them to bed. However, one look at the expression on my face, and she slowed down a bit to apologize for being caught in a bind like this. She really meant it.

It didn't help much. Of course I understood, but that didn't help much either. Then I looked down at the eager faces at each leg. "Let's play rough-house," begged the bigger face, and an immediate echo came from my other leg. So before I had time for any serious indulgence in self-pity, I found myself romping on the rug amid a chorus of squeals.

"Rough-house," naturally, consists of everyone jumping on daddy for as long as daddy can take it. Five minutes later daddy decided that "chase" would be more humane (for him). So "chase" it was. This is one of those gentle, loving games: daddy plays the mean old ogre who tries to catch and viciously devour the fleeing children. But alas, every time he catches one and is about to munch, the other miraculously rescues the captive child right out from under the open jaws of the ogre. This goes on until at last, Rami, out of tender-hearted pity for her daddy the ogre, submits herself open-arms as a willing sacrifice. This transforms the ogre back into daddy, who then tenderly holds his two daughters in a loving embrace.

I'm feeling better. Bath time! Two little kids and one big kid in the tub, rugs moved aside and towels placed in position "just in case" we splash. By the end of the bath the three of us put our heads together in counsel to decide if there's more water in the tub or outside. Mira surveys the situation very thoughtfully before giving her two-year-old assessment: "inside" (usually).

I'm feeling better still.

Next, the bathroom clean-up committee is formed (three persons), and then the diapering-Mira-for-night-time committee (one person). Pajamas are donned (two persons), and we're ready for story-time. We cuddle together on the couch and I open a carefully chosen book. I read the text, but there's always something very interesting to be said about the illustration that isn't quite said in the text.

After the story, I send Rami out to her bed and lift Mira into her crib. I lean over the rail to give her a good-night kiss but a muffled voice leaks out around her thumb, "daddy, sing me a song." So I sing her a song I used to sing to Rami when she was Mira's age and it brings back sweet memories. Mira stops me in the middle of the song to say, "I love you, daddy." I look at her as if for the first time. Her eyes are no longer the eyes of a two-year-old. She is on the border of sleep and her eyes have taken on that fathomless depth of the real being inhabiting that little body. I relax into her gaze; "I love you too, Mira. Go now and be with the angels." As I watch, her eyes slowly close and within seconds she is asleep. I touch her gently in the middle of her chest and ask God to bless her through me. I ask the great Father-Presence to use me as His instrument in guiding Mira to adulthood and the emergence of her true nature. I give her a kiss on the forehead and tiptoe out of the room feeling uplifted and grateful.

I find Rami in her bed, her face lit up with a smile at my approach. She is still tucking in her teddy bear and dolls, each with their own pillow and blanket. I sit on the edge of the bed and sing her favorite songs. As I sing, I watch her shift into that sweet, peaceful, pre-sleep state. Suddenly she looks questioningly into my eyes and asks, "Daddy, you weren't in such a good mood when you got home, were you?"

"Right," I reply.

"You feel better now?", she asks.

"Ten thousand percent!"

"Daddy, why do people get sad?"

I have to smile at the pensive look on Rami's face, and at my own day's predicament.

"We get sad, Rami, because we make things important that aren't really that important."

"What should be important?", she probes.

"Love!", is the first word that comes to me. "Everything else in life, everything else we fill our days with, is less important."

Rami looks like she is hovering right on the border of sleep, yet she is more with me than when wide awake. While I marvel at this, she speaks again:

"Love is what God is made of."

I smile at her, nodding yes. Then I feel my heart welling up with love and tears come to my eyes.

"Rami, thank you for coming to live with mama and me. You've blessed our lives more than you'll ever know."

All she says is "daddy", but with such sweetness and love that I know she has heard my deepest feelings. She has taken my whole being into her and has given me back the fullness of her own love and gratitude. Her arms reach up to me and we embrace for a brief eternity, then she lays back down.

She now is moving through the transition into sleep. Her eyes are still open, but her breathing is taking on that relaxed, sleep rhythm. I am amazed at how similar this is to dying. It is as if I've been with a dying person all this time, preparing her to leave her body so that her last moment on earth is one of love—that this is the greatest gift I could give her. I feel how similar sleep is to death, and how important conscious preparation is. I remember often reading about the "halls of learning or wisdom", or the "temple of healing" — places where a soul abides for learning or healing, whether in sleep or after death of the body. I have dreamed about these places and sometimes have glimpsed them in meditations. I am convinced of their reality. I also sense the conscious preparation required before a soul is able to enter these sacred places, these levels of awareness.

Rami's eyes are closed. She's gone! And I know by the way she left that she has made it to her special temple, where she may be reviewing this past day, or looking ahead, seeing the overview of her life, or studying with one of her guides, or perhaps a great master, who, with infinite wisdom and love, reveals her destiny on earth.

I sit a long time on the edge of Rami's bed, trying to follow her soul's travels in my imagination. I am grateful beyond words for this privilege to serve as an earthly guide for these two beings, who will then go on to add their blessing to others in an ever-widening circle—until love and peace fill this world.

And all this happened to a "burned-out" father who was reluctant to put his girls to bed.

There is a special place in the heaven world that I go when I'm sleeping. Sometimes I call it the Healing Temple and sometimes the Angel Temple. People can go there when they feel sad or hurt and it makes them feel better and brings back the joy.

I go there because it is my heavenly home, and makes me feel so happy. Sometimes I tell the little children there special things so they will be happy too.

Every time I come, the angels welcome me and we sing and dance and play together. When it is time for me to go, they give me a wish that I might have a happy day on earth.

I just love my heaven home.

RAMI, AGE 8

Bedtime Rituals

"Help! Help! Get me out of here!"

Those cries of anguish were familiar to my parents. My father would awaken in the middle of the night and rush to the side of his four-year-old girl, finding her very upset and pleading for help.

Awakening suddenly in the middle of the night or occasionally upon going to sleep, I would experience the sensation of being trapped within a prison. All that I knew myself to be—free and expansive—was suddenly confined to a little body, which seemed heavy, awkward, and terribly confining. I wanted to get out as quickly as possible. I tried to explain to my dad that I wanted to get out of a heavy box that was closed all around me. He could only understand my predicament as a nightmare. I tried to explain that it wasn't a dream. My experience was real. He did understand my fright, though, and lovingly picked me up and brought me to bed with my mother and him. They laughed and told me to pick a better dream next time. I wished I could. Next to their warm, loving bodies I felt secure, and while they slept I would gradually grow accustomed to my human condition.

These experiences would happen at least once a week as a small child. As I grew older they became less frequent, and I learned to handle them by myself. The last such experience came when I was eighteen. I decided to surrender to the feeling of being trapped and to experience it for what it was. I had the beautiful experience of discovering my inner self, which was an important catalyst that started my spiritual search.

For children, the entry into and out of the body upon going to sleep and awakening is a very delicate time. With some understanding of the process, the parent can use this time to greatly further the child's spiritual growth, as well as to transform this sometimes frightening experience into a positive one for the child. Children sometimes report feeling trapped or in a box (like I did). Some children feel that they just don't want to be where they are at the moment. Some children, especially infants, will just cry or be frustrated and agitated.

When Mira was two weeks old I was given an inner gift: the direct experience of her state of consciousness while she was sleeping. I was holding her one evening as she drifted into sleep. I felt in a state of ecstasy. Then I experienced her re-entry into her body. She went from a very high, light, expanded consciousness rapidly into her helpless, wet, hungry body. The shock of such an abrupt change was almost more than she could bear and she burst out screaming. No amount of comforting would soothe her. Finally, I held her very tightly and, with the best of my ability, I began communicating to her through my words, feeling and body. I told her she came into her little body to learn more love, to grow closer to God, and to help others. On some level I felt she heard me for she stopped crying. I needed to repeat this process many times in the early months until she became accustomed to her new body. Since then the entries into and exits out of her body have been easier.

One woman reported that her three-year-old son was having a

very hard time waking up in the morning. He would cry and kick and have tantrums. She tried many things until she finally discovered how to help her boy. When she heard him waking she went into his room and started telling him beautiful things about his life on earth, the wonderful things he would learn to do with his body, and the many people he would be helping. His wakening process took a noticeable change for the better.

Perhaps the best way for the parent to work with the child's re-entry into the body is to concentrate on making their last thought before drifting off to sleep as peaceful as possible. Then they will awaken with the same feeling.

Bringing a child into a receptive state at night isn't something that just happens. Sometimes it takes real, but gentle, persistence on the part of the parent, and a patience to go through various rituals to bring your child into a more quiet, open state of consciousness. If a child has just watched a wild and active television program right before bedtime, it will be hard for him to turn off the impressions of that television show and come into the receptivity needed to feel his higher nature. The child most likely will go to sleep with the events of the television program playing in his mind. Those impressions will live and grow within him while he sleeps.

Even if a child has not watched television, he will need a certain amount of calming and quieting from the day's activities before he can enter into an inward, receptive state.

Using candles instead of lights may add a magical atmosphere. The flickering of the soft candle-light almost demands quiet. Another very helpful ritual, which I use every night, is reading or telling a story. So much can happen during the story time. The parent can hold the child or gently rub his back. (Even a child who doesn't normally like to be held will usually enjoy it at story time.) The parents touch can communicate so much to the child.

A good story will cause the child to step into another world and feel the feelings of others; the little frog prince, or the princess in the woods, or the lonely little horse. The stories can cause the child to begin to think of others and develop compassion.

In telling or reading a story to a child, you have a rich opportunity to make the story come alive for your child. You can also quiet and soften your child's energy by talking in a quiet, gentle way with a voice that soothes and caresses her into a peaceful relaxed state. The way you speak as you are telling or reading a story can convey your love and devotion to your child.

There are many good children's stories with simple yet profound messages. To the extent that you love and feel inspired by these stories yourself, they will grow within your child throughout his sleep to become a deep part of his being.

As long as a child is not needing to recover from violent impressions or some traumatic event at home (which requires special attention) most children will respond to a bedtime story. They will feel the love of their parent and thus will be helped to come into a quiet receptive place. When Mira was two, she could come bouncing into her bedroom full of punchy, giggly energy after a bath and tickle time with daddy. All she wanted to do was jump on the couch. It is at those times that I read the story with a very quiet voice going very slowly. Within five minutes she leaned her head against me and was relaxed and calm.

Older children also respond to a special time at night. I once worked with a group of ten to fourteen-year-old boys with behavior problems. These boys were unable to stay in their homes because of their behavior and were housed in a ranch setting with a loving, caring staff. Our experimental group consisted of eight boys, most of whom had already been in the juvenile jail at least once. They were tough boys who were hard to get close to. I was the supervising nurse in charge of the staff and program.

Though I worked only in the day, I decided to stay once in the evening to see their bedtime routine. Since television was not allowed on the premises, the evening staff played games with the boys, helped them with their homework, or talked quietly with them.

When it was time for bed, the staff just ordered them off to bed and that was that. "But they need a story," I protested. Everyone looked at me like I was crazy, including the boys. "Big boys don't need a story," was their taunting reply. "Well I'm going to tell you one anyway," and I went in search of a book and candles. When I arrived at their room, the boys shouted at me in no uncertain terms, "Go Away! You *@!#!." I always considered the swear words to be a secret message that they needed love. I lit the candles, turned off the lights, and began to tell them a story. There was not one bedtime story to be found so I made one up. I began talking in a very soft voice, telling them about a group of boys who had a wonderful adventure in the mountains. Through this adventure they learned to love and trust one another. (The plot was obviously aimed at them.) I had only just begun the story when the oldest boy shouted, "You *@!#!, shut up!" I persisted in an even softer voice. First the youngest boy crept out of his bed and sat very close. His excuse was that he wanted to hear better. Soon seven boys were crowded around, some leaning against me, all close enough so I could alternately reach out and touch each one. Finally the oldest and toughest of the boys came and sat in the shadows. They all sat spell-bound through the adventurous part of the story, and listened attentively as I told how the boys in the story grew to realize how much they need and love one another. We sat in silence for a moment and then I asked them to quietly return to their beds. I went to each boy and whispered how much I loved them and told them each how special they were. Half of the boys covered themselves with their blankets when they saw me coming, so I just whispered into the blankets. (One cannot be put off or hurt by whatever behavior these children show. All children need love, especially those that push it away the most.)

My heart felt so full of love as I closed the door to the boys room. Their tough and totally self-sufficient image had been broken down for a brief moment. I could see them as the sweet children they really were.

The next day was markedly better for the boys. They had gone to sleep with love and thoughts of caring, and thus it reflected in their behavior towards one another. Of course they all had to put on a little act of pretending they didn't like me, just in case I might get the "wrong" impression of them. It didn't bother me. I could see past their actions.

Once the story is finished, the child will usually feel sleepy, relaxed, and receptive. As they snuggle into bed, the next few minutes before they drift off to sleep can be the most important of the entire day. A few words of love and appreciation will be deeply felt. The parent can use this opportunity to draw out a wealth of goodness from the child.

After Mira passed from the infant stage into the baby and crawling stage, Rami suddenly became very rough with her. I would catch her tripping Mira as she crawled around the corner, or giving her a little shove as she was proudly sitting up by herself. I knew Rami was acting out jealousy towards this new family-member who was taking up so much attention. I used her bed time to assure Rami how special and precious she was to us, how much we needed her, and how proud we were of her. Rather than dwelling on the negative, how rough she was with Mira, I looked over the day and tried to recall even one moment when she was gentle and loving to Mira. Even if I had already reinforced her behavior at the time it happened, I used this very receptive time to again reinforce her positive qualities. "Remember when you gave Mira her toy that dropped, and then you gently gave her a kiss. Each day you become more giving and loving." She would then go to sleep with the thought "I am loving. I am gentle. I am *loved.*" In time, the rough acting out was replaced by a genuine love and helpfulness toward her sister.

Next I usually sing a song while I rub their back. (These are meant only as suggestions. It's fun to make up your own rituals with your child.) When I was in the fourth grade, my teacher insisted that each one in our class come up individually and sing "America, The Beautiful." I was so afraid when it was my turn that I could barely make it to the front of the class. I was shaking all over and could hardly get out any words at all. All the children laughed at me. I was deeply humiliated and vowed to never sing again.

As I grew, singing became a bigger and bigger phobia for me. One night when Rami was quite small, she became sick and I needed to stay up and rock her. Since no one else was around, I timidly began to sing to her. She responded so beautifully to my singing voice that I ended up singing all night.

The quality of the singing voice is totally unimportant. Children respond to the feeling and love from the parent while they are singing, not to the technical quality of the voice.

Children are especially open and sensitive to simple, devotional songs. Before Mira was two and a half she knew all my little songs by heart and would wake each morning singing the last one I had sung to her the night before. During the day I could hear her singing in her play about God's love to her dolls and stuffed animals. She doesn't seem particularly conscious of the words she is singing. But on a deeper level the words and sweetness of the tune are molding and strengthening her inner life. Singing devotional songs to children is perhaps one of the most powerful ways of awakening their inner being.

If Rami has had an extra-stimulating day or is expecting some special event the next day, she often needs a little extra time at bedtime. Children may want to stay awake just to be sure they don't miss anything. If you find your child still isn't ready to go to sleep after a quiet talk, a guided meditation often will work. These meditations can be totally creative and suited just for your child, or read from a book. I like to read meditations to Rami while she is lying down with her eyes closed. Some nights I like to make up my own meditations to suit her mood.

The minutes before a child sleeps is also a perfect time to introduce a simple truth. When Rami was four I started introducing the idea that she had a Heavenly Mother as well as me, her earthly mother. I simply explained to her that she and I each have a very special mommy in the heaven world who is always protecting and loving us. I further explained that I, her earthly mother, would not always be able to be with her to help her if perhaps she was off by herself somewhere. Her heavenly mother would always be there. I wanted Rami to grasp the idea of God's ever-present love and protection. I also wanted her to begin to expand her innocent, loving devotion (that was almost exclusively directed to Barry and me) to also include her Heavenly Parents.

The physical mother is the first channel for the Mother God to raise and nourish the child. As I have seen in my counseling experience, when the child's only inner devotion is to the physical parent, this can be turned off when the child learns that the parent is human with weaknesses and shortcomings. Then, in the turning off of their devotion to their parent, they are in effect closing the door to the experience of the Mother-Father-God. Men and women have confided in me that they just can't grasp the concept of God as mother. I feel that these individuals, while little children, probably worshipped their mother as God, then later found out her weaknesses and in disillusionment turned off to their Divine Mother as well. The same holds true in the relationship with the father. The child, young adult, or even middle-aged adult, then has to go through a process of tremendous inner growth and forgiveness so that the energy of Mother-God or Father-God can come through clearly. I feel that this devotion need not be turned off at all in a child, but simply expanded. Then when the child realizes that their parent is not perfect, they already have the awareness of a higher, heavenly parent who is the perfection of that which they seek. The child then feels more compassion for their human parent as well as for their own human condition.

When Rami was six years old we traveled to our favorite camping place in the Sierra mountains. Mira was just seven months old and required much of our attention. At one point, while Barry and I were struggling to change Mira's messy diaper, Rami wandered off by herself with our dog Kriya. She was happily picking flowers and came upon a little stream. Rami jumped over it and continued on her way. She came to a forest and wandered in farther and farther. Suddenly she realized that she did not know her way back to camp. She immediately started to yell and scream for us to come to her. This behavior had always worked for her in the past. However, the noise of the stream prevented us from hearing her screams, so she sat down and started to cry. Our faithful dog, Kriya, sat down and shared her sadness but seemed unable to understand that they were lost and she could lead them back.

Rami told me afterwards that she cried for a long time, "until there were no more tears left." Then she remembered what I told her about her Heavenly Mother who was always with her and ready to help whenever she asked. So she sat down, closed her eyes, and prayed to her Heavenly Mother for help in finding her way back to us. She then just sat quietly trusting and waiting. When she opened her eyes she saw a golden path leading out of the woods. She followed it all the way back to our camping spot! That experience has had a profound effect upon Rami.

I was lost.
All of a sudden a bright, shining,
sparkling road was in front of me.
I walked along towards camp
As happy as a dove.

RAMI, AGE 9

God is a guiding light with every step we take.

JENNY, AGE 10

Thy word is a lamp unto my feet,
and a light unto my path.

PSALM 119:105

In talking with your child in the moments before sleep, let your heart guide you. These talks usually can't be planned. The child's open and receptive state will draw the perfect words from you, if you simply remain open.

We try to end bedtime with a thought of gratitude, "What would you like to thank God for?" The answers are always so lovely and the parent can gain an understanding of what their child is deeply appreciating.

"I'm grateful for the egg I found in the bird nest."
"I'm grateful that daddy came home early tonight."
"I'm grateful for the picnic we had today."
"Thank you God for my family."

Children also love prayer. Some like their parent to say a prayer. My mother always said the same prayer, "May God bless you and keep you and may God cause the sun to rise and shine upon you forever more." To this day, whenever I hear those words, sweet tears come to my eyes. Other children like to make up their own prayer and repeat it every night. Others like to make up a different prayer each night. Mira, at age three, refuses to have anything to do with praying. She has very strong feelings against spoken bedtime prayers. If I make up a special tune and sing the prayer, she responds with great delight. In guiding our children, we cannot be attached to how they will respond. We need to be sensitive and listen to them.

Prayer is the mortar that holds our house together.

SAINT TERESA

My final words to my children are always to thank them for coming into our family. I let them know how much they have given me and how much they are helping me on my journey to God. Perhaps one last song is sung, and one last kiss and hug given.

No matter what my state of consciousness before being with them at bedtime, I always feel more love, and a sense of fulfillment and purpose in my life. I feel deeply grateful to God for the privilege of being a parent. These moments of sweetness as they drift off to sleep, carry me through the harder times of parenthood. I think all parents need times like this.

God is everything and he is everywhere and he loves everyone.

JULIE, AGE 5

Meditating with Children

Meditating with children can be a very powerful and wonderful experience. Many times children experience more in five minutes of guided meditation than adults do in an hour. Children of all ages love to use their imaginations and have great ability to visualize. If meditation is introduced as a wonderful game and adventure, children will respond with joy. A child should never be forced to meditate.

If a parent feels insecure in the beginning about how to meditate with a child, they might try reading a few of the meditations included here or from another book. In Jenny Dent's book series for children (see back of book) there are many excellent meditations to read to your child. One is as follows:

> Picture a light, like the flame of a candle. Don't think of anything else except the little flame of light. Every time you breathe in, picture it getting brighter and brighter. Then imagine you are right inside the flame and it becomes a beam of light carrying you up and up, until you reach the sun. Now you bathe in the sunlight, and your body gets lighter and lighter as you are filled with sunlight and become a part of the sun. All crossness, unhappiness, coughs and colds melt away in this healing sunlight and you feel full of love for everything. Picture the light going from your heart and the centre of the sun to help and heal people all over the world who are all part of our great family.

Rami and Mira enjoy meditating with me during the day, but they especially enjoy it just before they go to sleep. Here is one of Rami's favorite bedtime meditations, which usually puts her into a very sweet sleep:

> You are walking in a beautiful meadow with lovely flowers growing everywhere. You pick a fragrant bunch of flowers and continue walking. Suddenly you see a very beautiful angel. She is shining with a wondrous light. You know that this is your guardian angel. She takes you to a special spot in the meadow and gently asks you to lie down on a bed made of flower petals. You lie down on the sweet smelling bed and feel so good and so happy. The angel sings a sweet song and you drift off to sleep. The angel watches over you while you sleep and surrounds you in love and protection.

If the children are feeling sick or are worried about something, we do a meditation of going to the healing temple:

> As you are lying peacefully in your bed, an angel comes and gently picks you up and takes you to a very special place. She tells you that this is the healing temple, the place where children can come while they sleep and the angels will help them to be healthy and strong. The healing temple is so beautiful and you sit on a soft golden chair while the angels sing to you and help you to feel all better. A golden light from their hearts goes out to your body and helps to heal you. (Or parent can mention specific body part that hurts.) Then they lead you to a lovely little bed, where you lie down and fall into a sweet peaceful sleep.

Parents can use familiar scenes for the children in these meditations; or favorite colors or a special friend or teacher. The possibilities are unlimited; having them start from one place, then moving on to greater beauty and light. The following meditation (one of Barry's) uses the imagery of a favorite camping place in Mt. Shasta:

Imagine yourself walking on a beautiful path, following a joyful, gurgling brook upstream. Smell the sweet scents of the trees and the flowers. Listen to the sounds of the stream, with its little waterfalls. See the sunlight reflected on the water, like thousands of sparkling diamonds, and a butterfly fluttering from flower to flower.

Now look ahead and see the path go into a brightly lit area. As you walk, everything around you becomes brighter and brighter. There are angels and other great shining beings who greet you with love. Your whole family is there, your friends Bokie and Kriya (our dogs that passed on) come wiggling up to greet you. Everyone you love is there. Feel how much we all love you. Feel how much the light itself loves you!

Children often have great fun making up the meditations and having the adults follow them. Rami made up this meditation for a teacher at her school.

Close your eyes and imagine a tiny crystal in front of you and see it grow and grow. First it is white, then it turns gold, and suddenly it turns into a castle. When it is big enough you step inside and there sits the Master of the land of nature spirits. And all around fly angels. You hold out your hand and slowly go out of the castle with the Master. You watch the castle turn back into a crystal, then you take the hand of the Master. You open your eyes in love and the Master is before you. You then fall asleep with the Master.

Good night.

Some older children respond more readily to a more "modern" approach to meditation, using the images of rocket ships and outer space. Jenny Dent, our friend in England, wrote the following meditation for her nine-year-old son when she found he was not responding as well to her usual meditations of angels and gardens of light.

A Space Mission with a Difference

(Meditation for Space-Age Children)

TIME: Dawning of the New Age

PLACE: Any quiet corner of the earth.

MISSION: To reach the brightest six-pointed STAR.

PURPOSE: To bring back to earth magic Christ healing Light found in the STAR.

PREPARATION FOR THE SPACE TRIP:
Weeks and days of patient work...teaching the earth-body what it finds the hardest of all—discipline!...to sit still; to concentrate on one thing at a time (programme computer to find "destination brightest six-pointed STAR").

PUTTING ON SPACE SUIT (Body of Light):
Sit in quiet corner...relax earth-body, but sit up straight so life-line to space craft is direct and clear. (higher self)

CONNECT BREATHING EQUIPMENT:
Start slow, deep breathing, concentrating on breathing in Christ Light—God's magic fuel (pictured as a little flame in the heart).

ENTER SPACE CRAFT (golden cone of light):
Flame grows bigger and brighter—go right inside it, safe and strong.

COUNTDOWN TO BLAST OFF...
Set computer on course—destination: BRIGHTEST STAR...

> (picture the great Star overhead, see a ray reaching down to touch the little flame...)
> 6....5....4....3....2....1....BLAST OFF

Music plays as you zoom up into heavenly space.

THE JOURNEY:
With computer programmed to take the quickest flight to the brightest STAR, no time is wasted on the journey. Space craft does

not go wandering off course to strange dark planets or get caught in orbit in the earth's atmosphere! (No danger from alien astral forces or psychic meanders along the milky way!)

DESTINATION:
VROOOOOM...up...up...up into the light...
nothing but light now...
all is Light...VROOOOOM...AUM...
Landing now...
all is Light...LOVE...JOY...AUM...
no time...eternal now...AUM...

CALL TO SERVICE:
Bleep...bleep...bleep...divine computer reminds the purpose of mission...Light not for self alone...but for all earth.

Switch on great laser ray...
Direct it down to earth...
Watch the bright beam dissolve the darkness...
It lights a light of love and hope in the hearts of many...
Mission accomplished...mission accomplished...

HOMEWARD JOURNEY:
Opportunity to visit heavenly places before returning to earth—a planet of great beauty (the infinite and eternal garden of the spirit). Greeted by friendly inhabitants (friends and loved ones in the spirit world).

Enjoy the beauty together, feeling the peace and joy of this land.

One inhabitant is special—
a teacher, your "space instructor". Your task is explained—
Your computer is re-programmed back to earth now—STAR shining in heart.
New supply of magic fuel on board.
STAR MISSION handbook before you.

TOUCH DOWN:
Before leaving space-craft, check all controls.
Seal with protective light...
Read and memorize handbook while memory of mission clear.

Star Mission Handbook

(for Aquarian Age Astronauts)

A star astronaut (child of the light)
Follows this code of conduct in daily life—
He/she is STRONG IN THE LIGHT
(The magic force of the Star is with him/her at all times and
beams from the heart to all companions)
He/she THINKS OF OTHERS BEFORE HIMSELF
He/she is LOVING AND KIND TO ALL (including animals)
He/she is QUIET AND CALM WHATEVER HAPPENS
(knowing the divine computer makes no mistakes)
He/she THINKS WELL BEFORE SPEAKING

It is fun after meditating with children to ask them to describe
their experiences or to draw a picture of what they experienced.
Meditation can be something the whole family can participate in
together to feel more clearly the depth and love of the family bond.

fourteen

The Home Atmosphere

by Jenny Dent

In the summer of of 1985 Barry and I fulfilled a long-held dream, to visit the White Eagle Temple in England. The Temple, surrounding gardens, walks, chapel and buildings are all lovingly called New Lands. It was wonderful to be a part of the high spiritual vibration of New Lands. While there, we met with Jenny Dent, granddaughter of Grace and Ivan Cooke, founders of the White Eagle Lodge and Temple. Jenny has written a series of four excellent books for helping small children understand spiritual truth and beginning meditation. They have been a wonderful part of our family. While meeting Jenny, I was struck by her deep love and devotion to the spiritual unfoldment of children. She herself has always lived in the beautiful setting of New Lands. Her parents and grandparents began her spiritual training from birth. I asked her to write some of her experiences while growing up in such a wonderful spiritual atmosphere.

My grandparents are Grace and Ivan Cooke, who were guided to found a church and spiritual centre, called the White Eagle Lodge. Their guidance came from a teacher in the spirit life named simply 'White Eagle', who was able to use my grandmother as a channel to bring through much spiritual teaching—a re-statement of the truths of the ancient wisdom for our modern age—which has subsequently been published in many books including the little best-selling pocket book *THE QUIET MIND*.

Family love is the keynote upon which the White Eagle work has been built. The founding family has remained at the centre of the work, and now there is a large White Eagle family of members and groups extending all over the world. The new country retreat centre at New Lands became the family home of my grandparents. My parents (John and Joan Hodgson) moved into a small bungalow (a converted pig-sty) which they named 'Wide Horizons' because of the glorious view of the western horizon and the setting sun. My aunt (Ylana Hayward, Grace Cooke's younger daughter) lived in the gardener's cottage.

I was born at "Wide Horizons" in April 1947, after one of the longest, coldest English winters of the century. My elder sister Rose (now Rose Elliot, the vegetarian cookery writer and astrologer) was born just before my parents came to New Lands and my cousins, Colum and Jeremy Hayward, five years after me. Some of my earliest childhood memories are of the happy times Rose and I had with our baby cousins. As the years went by our closeness continued, and we spent most of our free time all together as a foursome.

It was during our early childhood that my mother started the White Eagle children's services (as well as writing in the White Eagle Lodge magazine, "Stella Polaris", about teaching spiritual truths to children). Before she left her career to devote her life to helping my grandparents establish the White Eagle work, she completed her teacher course and had some years teaching experience, which was to prove extremely useful in her future work.

My mother is one of those people who has a natural love of children and children love her. There could be no *more* popular grandmother in the world. She never has been (and never will be, in spite of ever increasing responsibility) too busy to play with her grandchildren, and gives them freely her time and attention. I remember the hours she has spent with all of them, creating lifelong bonds of friendship and happiness as she joined in imaginary games with dolls and teddy bears, or played football with Michael (her only grandson). Then as they have grown older, there have been happy walks around the New Lands estate and surrounding countryside, enjoying the beauty of "mother earth", and learning to say "thank you God" for all the blessings of life. My daughter Sara often says, "Granny is someone I can really talk to", which I reckon is one of the biggest compliments a young teenager could pay her grandmother.

Returning to my own childhood, I can remember loving the monthly children's service my mother started in the little chapel in the New Lands house. We always started with a hymn, "Praise Him, Praise Him, all His Children Praise Him. He is Love, He is Love" and then we stood in a circle and closed our eyes to think about the spiritual sun shining down on us all and then send its light out to the world. We were always taught to think of God as being like the sun, the giver of life on earth, never as an old man somewhere far above the clouds! I can't remember ever questioning whether there was such a thing as God. Complete faith in the Creator of life, from the smallest flower and insect to the largest animal, has always been a basic part of my life.

Teaching us how to send out the healing light to all parts of the world in need, has always been a central part of our work in the White Eagle children's services. My mother taught us, first of all, to picture the shining sun and then to "see" it taking the form of a blazing six-pointed star. (This is the symbol White Eagle has given to help us to concentrate and focalize our thoughts. It is a powerful symbol for the new age of brotherhood, depicting as it does mankind working in full co-operation with God to co-create the new Golden Age.) We learnt how to breathe in the light of the Star, and then project it out to the world.

Another important part of the children's service was always the story. My mother has the gift of making any story she tells really come alive. I will always remember the stories of St. Francis, St. Columba, of Jesus and of Gopala and Krishna, as told by her. Then we had great fun acting the stories. There was one which was a special favourite; it was a legend about a little milkmaid who had to cross a lake in order to deliver her milk. She was very worried because the ferryboat man kept oversleeping and was very grumpy when she tried to wake him up, so she could deliver her milk on time. One day she confided her trouble to the wise old hermit who lived at the edge of the lake. He gave her a piece of paper on which he said was written a magic word, which would enable her to walk across the lake without the need of the ferry. The little girl took the paper gladly and was indeed able to walk on the water. She did this every day and delivered the milk on time. Then one day the grumpy ferryman got so curious he insisted on looking at the paper and found the word was "GOD". "That's not a magic word, it's all a trick" he said. "But it *is* a magic word" said the little girl, and her faith continued to allow her to walk on the water, even though holding the magic paper didn't work for the grumpy man! (When we acted the story we really enjoyed being the water sprites swamping the poor old man!)

We ended the services with a short meditation, usually a creative meditation led by my mother during which she would take us into the heavenly garden to learn to open our "inside eyes" and other spiritual senses to gradually become aware of all the beauty there.

This learning to use our inner eyes and senses was an everyday part of our upbringing. At the time I did not think there was anything different or unusual in this; it seemed quite natural to look out for fairies in flowers, to be aware of angels, and our own special guardian angel who was always close to watch over us, and we even had our friendly gnome called Bup, who lived in New Lands garden. I do remember though being rather upset when I confessed to friends at school that I believed in fairies and was teased so much that I decided to keep quiet about my beliefs in future. But perhaps my biggest embarrassment, and the question I most dreaded was, "What does your father do?" I found it difficult to explain that he was the Treasurer of an obscure religious organization called 'The White Eagle Lodge'.

The faith in God my mother gave us was one of the greatest gifts she could have passed on to us. In her recent book, *THE WHITE EAGLE LODGE BOOK OF HEALTH AND HEALING*, she says, "Faith is caught, not taught", and I am sure this is true. We certainly "caught" our faith from her. Childhood can be fraught with fears, and I was a very nervous and sensitive child. I can remember being greatly comforted by my knowledge of the protective power of the light and particularly of the power of the symbol of the equal-sided cross of light encircled by light. My mother often reminded us of the poster showing this symbol with the words, "The forces of darkness halt before the cross of light"—which White Eagle had us display as widely as possible in London during the blitz bombing of the second world war. Many people had testified to the miraculous way they (or their homes) were protected when the poster was displayed. I found for myself it really DID work and often surrounded myself or people I was worried about in this "magic shield" of protective light.

Joan Hodgson with her two daughters: Rose (left) and Jenny (right).

Another area in which White Eagle's teaching helped us greatly as we grew up at New Lands, was our absolute conviction and knowledge that death was not an end, merely a change from one state of being to another far more beautiful and harmonious one. I was fortunate not to "lose" a close relative during the growing-up years, but death was of course never a taboo subject and we accepted the death of loved pets with tranquillity and the happy awareness of their continuing love and life with us. I remember when our much loved dog, Sally, died; my mother told us how she had clairvoyently seen our grandfather (my father's father in spirit who was a farmer with a great rapport with dogs) come and collect her. He gave a whistle and she got up out of her dying physical coat and went happily into the sunshine of the spirit life with him. Of course, we were greatly comforted by this and were quite often aware of Sally joining in our family life for sometime afterwards. I cannot remember ever doubting the reality of the life of spirit, nor our own individual ability to feel (and even see) the presence of loved people and pets living in this inner world. My own children have this same belief and are often aware of their great grandmother (my mother-in-law).

I think my upbringing in the light of White Eagle's teaching was also very helpful in relationship problems. For example, the belief in karma ("as you sow, so you will surely reap") and the ideal of brotherly love and forgiveness do have a marked effect on the way one conducts relationships, even while quite young. I can remember incidents of karma working out in my early life and recognizing these as such, has made a very strong impression on me. I remember one incident when I was involved in a 'three-some' and I behaved very selfishly. The third girl in our triangle was the 'odd one out' and I deliberately made her feel that way until eventually she left us alone. Several years later I was involved in a similar situation with two other girls but this time I was the one who was made to feel the odd one out, and I suffered a lot of pain as a result. But I will never forget the lessons it has taught me, both in the swift outworking of karma and the necessity for tolerance and kindness in all relationships. My daughter has been involved in a similar situation and hopefully, through sharing my experiences with her, I have been able to help her cope with it in a more loving and sympathetic way.

One of the happiest of all my childhood memories is of our family Christmases. Almost every year we have all moved into New Lands for four days from Christmas Eve to the twenty eighth, and so much enjoyed being together for this time of celebration. The highlight is always the twelve noon meditation on Christmas Day when we meditate on the blazing Star and the symbolism of the Christ birth, and link in spirit with all White Eagle's famiy of members and friends throughout the world.

So, in conclusion, looking back I feel very blessed to have had such a secure and happy childhood, surrounded by a loving family, all working together for a common purpose. This purpose, I know to be my purpose too, so it was not difficult to make the decision to work full time in the White Eagle Lodge after a brief secretarial course in spite of the pressures on me to go to university. My favourite subjects at school were English, Latin and ancient Greek, but looking back, had I taken a degree in English or the Classics, as my teachers wanted, I should have spent at university those very years which I now realise were some of the most precious and valuable of my life! For those were the years I worked daily with my grandmother as her secretary and personal assistant, helping her with the manuscripts of her books *THE ILLUMINED ONES, THE JEWEL IN THE LOTUS, SUNMEN OF THE AMERICAS*, and *THE LIGHT IN BRITAIN*. I also helped her with correspondence when again and again I saw the way in which she was able to work with White Eagle to bring comfort and illumination to those who were bereaved or in great trouble. This time with my grandmother has proved invaluable training for my work now as General Secretary. I am so often aware of her continued help and inspiration in the letters I now have to write. The first time I felt her presence was just a week or two after her passing to the spirit life at the beginning of September 1979. I was working in New Lands garden, enjoying the sunshine and beauty, and feeling so happy and at peace, knowing that I was in the place I was meant to be, doing the work I was meant to be doing. I sat on a seat at the far end of the garden, looking down the lawn to the beautiful red-brick house. Suddenly I realised I was not alone. I realised my gandmother had joined me on the seat. I said, "Oh Nanna" and she said, "don't call me that, call me Minesta", and I could see her in her young body of light, as Minesta, the daughter of Hah Wah Tah (White Eagle) as told in the *THE ILLUMINED ONES*. And this is how I have usually seen her since, and always felt her young and vital enthusiasm and inspiration of the work.

She is with me now as I conclude this writing. Her love and interest extends to everyone who is endeavoring to practise all these teachings in their family lives. Family life and family love is all important in our new age of Aquarius. I feel her saying so in White Eagle's words, "Keep on Keeping on!"

Wings of Protection

by Joan Hodgson

Along with meeting Jenny and Geoffrey Dent at the White Eagle Lodge, we were very privileged to spend time with Jenny's mother, Joan Hodgson, whose very being seems to breathe the essence of White Eagle's teachings. Shortly after sitting down with her, Jenny came into the room carrying two perfectly-formed golden-yellow roses branching out symmetrically from a shared stem. This she gently gave to Joyce and me and then said, "I'm sorry for interrupting, but I strongly felt that grandmother (Grace Cooke) wanted the two of you to have these roses. They are a gift from her." Then she quickly left the room.

Joan looked fondly at the roses and said they reminded her of the beautiful golden temples in the higher realms. She closed her eyes, continuing to talk about these lovely places of healing and learning, and soon, with her help, all three of us were lifted up in consciousness into a great golden temple, where we bathed in the radiant presence of angels and masters.

Here, she talks briefly about her childhood.

When we were children my mother, Mrs. Grace Cooke, made the world of spirit, the inner world of light, very real to us. Every night before we went to bed she would sing one of the old lullabys, songs that comforted her so much after she, as a child, had lost her mother. Night after night she would sing to us:

Hand in hand with angels,
through the world we go.
Bright our eyes are honest
then we blind ones know
Tender our voices cheer us
then meet death alone
Never walking heavenward
can we walk alone.

I can truly say that we had a most blessed childhood because my mother herself was so close to the world of spirit. Her life was spent helping those who were bereaved, especially those who had tragically lost loved ones in the first world war. She herself had been brought up to live hand in hand with angels and she was continually trying to help us to realize the closeness of the spirit world around us.

Back row (L to R): Ylana Hayward, Grace Cooke, Ivan Cooke.
Front: Joan Hodgson, Jenny (Dent), Rose (Elliot).
August, 1950.

I can remember as a tiny child walking with her through the park. I became aware of the little fairy beings in the flowers. I talked about them to her in a most natural way and she was very matter of fact about it; she didn't either encourage or discourage. She just accepted it as a fact that I was aware of these little beings.

As we'd grow older, she helped us whenever we had to face an ordeal. She encouraged us to attune ourselves to the great light of the spirit and to feel the help of the angels and of wise people who would draw close to help us.

I remember as a child being very frightened of the dark. And again she would help me to have courage by talking about the beautiful angel who was there, holding my hand, leading me through the darkness. She used to assure us nothing could hurt us, that angel wings were always around us protecting us. We found this sense of protection most helpful when, during the second world war, we found ourselves alone in the London branch of the White Eagle Lodge during one of the worst nights of the blitz. The air raid siren went off about nine in the evening and almost immediately the explosions started and continued throughout the night until about five in the morning. It was a continual barrage of noise and explosions and war airplanes. My sister and I were very frightened because, at that time, there was little air raid protection in The Lodge. We'd only just moved there. She got under the desk in the office and I was under the upturned armchair. We just didn't dare to move. Every moment we thought our end was coming. But suddenly, I had the most wonderful feeling of wings all around me. I thought of White Eagle and his beautiful strength and protection. It seemed as if he had great wings which he tenderly placed around us. Just at the same moment, Ylana said to me, "You know it's strange but I feel that White Eagle has got wings and that they are around us." The sensation was so real and strong that I can even remember smelling the feathers of those lovely protective wings. And although the barrage and the noise went on somehow we just felt secure under those lovely wings. This experience gave us both an even greater realization of the wonderful presence of White Eagle, and his great love, strength and wisdom which guided the work of The Lodge through the ensuing years. We were constantly reminded at difficult times in our childhood of the loving care of a guardian angel or our beautiful teacher who was there to help and inspire us in our work.

fifteen

The Child's Best Friend

God's love is all around
God's love is in everyone
God's love fills each space
God loves me through the trees and flowers
Through wind, sun and rain
Through so many people who I love
And through my little teddy bear.

RAMI, AGE 7

The child's best friend is within. Through becoming their own best friend, children will acquaint themselves with the real *Best Friend*—the God Presence inside them. We can help our children to find this "inner friend" by cultivating the love of solitude. Our children will treasure and draw strength from this gift their entire lives.

The trend these days is early socialization, making our children social as quickly as possible. Play groups are started as early as four months of age, pre-schools as early as one year old, and on it goes. These early experiences are excellent, if parents balance them with the child's need to be alone.

A woman I was counseling was determined to be a perfect mother. She thought that if her child grew up to have good relationships with others, he would always be happy. She herself was always seeking fulfillment in outside relationships and never succeeding. When her boy was six months old she started taking him to play groups. By the time he was two years old he was a member of seven different play groups. She would then proudly report that her boy could play with fifty different children. The child meanwhile was growing terrified of being alone and was needing to always be surrounded by others. There was discord between him and the mother, which she tried to remedy by exposing him to even more children. The mother was so burned out from taking him to play groups and having children over all day that she had no interest in spending quiet time with him or in being with him as he went to sleep. She felt she had done enough yet she was missing the greatest gift she could give: the cultivation of her son's inner relationship with himself.

As a parent of young children, I know of the pressure to begin early socialization. Parents proudly discuss their child's social abilities. "My son isn't shy of anyone." "My daughter is friendly to everyone." "My daughter never cries when I take her to the nursery—she loves to be with people." "My two-year-old answers the phone." But how many parents proudly report "My child loves to be alone." Shyness and quiet inner qualities are sometimes even looked down upon.

The first class I ever taught was for a small group of pregnant women. These women very patiently sat through my early fumblings and nervousness. I was particularly fond of one woman who had been a yoga teacher for many years. She was one of the leaders in her own yoga group which had grown to include hundreds of people. The way she carried her baby while pregnant was magnificent to behold. She truly looked liked a queen. She gave birth to a very beautiful baby boy, who radiated great wisdom and strength. We felt that this child was very special. Five months later the woman made an appointment to see me and came with her baby. She immediately burst into tears and sobbed, "The whole yoga group is laughing at my baby and calling him too serious." I looked at the baby, smiled at him, and offered him a little toy. His lips didn't part once into a smile—his look was very intense. I looked into his eyes and realized that he was seeing right into me. He seemed to be studying my very life. I realized that of course he wasn't smiling at people—he was too busy studying them. When I told this to the mother she laughed and said that this was her perception as well, but because so many people made jokes about his "seriousness" and seemed almost offended when he didn't smile, her vision had become clouded.

We are so attached to "normal" babies who gurgle and smile a lot. When a being comes along and looks intently at us, we don't know how to respond. We think there is something wrong with the child.

When parents are blessed with a child who has special inner qualities, it takes a tremendous strength to withstand the social pressure to make the child like everyone else. In the early years, these inner qualities may mark the child as different or even odd. Grandparents, well-meaning friends and relatives will offer all sorts of suggestions, hoping the child will ultimately become "normal". Behind these suggestions is the subtle idea that you are failing the child.

I know the sufferings of such a parent, for I was one. From the time Rami was a baby, she was different from those of her peer group. She was extremely shy and would turn her head away from people to avoid eye contact. Until the age of one and a half, she would only go into buildings where there was a pure and peaceful vibration. In all others she would scream and scream until we took her out. Until the age of three, she would strongly cling to me in large gatherings of people and beg to be taken home. She let very few people touch her and didn't want to play with other children.

I received many pitying stares and much advice all assuming that I was failing Rami. Barry was steady and reassuring, which saved me from succumbing to all the outside pressure and perhaps really letting her down.

Now I see clearly what I then intuitively felt inside but didn't always have the strength to hold to. Rami just wasn't ready for socialization until she was three. She needed to be sheltered. In her extremely sensitive state, she did not have the means of protecting herself. She was like a wide open door. She was also too busy cultivating her heavenly relationships and making them a part of her earth home. Nap time was her favorite time of the day. After a brief nap in her crib, she would wake up and start singing wonderfully sweet songs. As she gained vocabulary, the words of the songs were of angels and God. The singing usually lasted two hours, at which time she wanted to get out and play. She often spoke to me of her angel friends and the little gnomes and fairies that lived in our garden. Aside from Barry and I and a few others, these were her only friends for the first three years of her life.

When I learned to walk and could go to the garden by myself, I played with my fairy friends.

Once I picked a flower and looked down and saw a tiny fairy. She told me that she loved me and wanted to be my friend.

Once, when I was by a tree, I saw a tiny little man and he was chopping on a rock, trying to open it. I asked him why he was doing that and he answered, "Because I am a gnome and am looking for precious stones." He had a little house. He became my close little friend.

Once on my birthday, the little gnome gave me a special stone. I keep it in a special place.

The gnomes and fairies have brought me a lot of joy. That is why I love flowers so much.

RAMI, AGE 7

I was generally at peace with Rami's manner until another person would enter our home. Upon seeing another human being, she would run at top speed into her room and refuse to come out. If this person, who was usually a sweet, loving friend, persisted and went into her room, she would crouch in the corner and not look. This went on until she was two and a half. From two and a half to three years old she would stay in the same room either clinging to me or watching from behind a chair. Many people thought Rami was very strange. Looks of doubt, disapproval and sometimes pity pierced me like an arrow. Having devoted a large part of my life to the study of childhood behavior and having trained pediatric residents in how to detect early emotional difficulties, I couldn't help but worry about her in my mind. But the voice of my heart kept reminding me of Rami's unique beauty and that in time she would be ready for others.

Shortly before Rami was three and a half, she announced that she wasn't going to take a nap anymore and wanted to go to a little

school. In the school she developed lasting friendships and opened
to other adults. Adult friends are now amazed at how much love
they receive from Rami.

Socialization is a question of timing—the child's timing—not
ours. I believe that if I would have forced Rami into being social, in
the way everyone advised me to, I would have stifled an important
part of her inner growth.

The children being born now seem very special, with unique
gifts and power. In guiding and raising them, we need to give special
attention to their inner being. Allowing the child space, quiet,
aloneness and the right to be different, will usually assure the needed
soul growth.

Children seem to need a little place in the home that they can call
their own. In going to this little corner or area they can then feel
secure in being alone. When small, both of our girls were very fond
of their cribs and spent many long hours there singing and playing
quietly with their dolls and books. Mira at age two and three was so
fond of her alone time after she napped that she would become
disappointed if one of us had to go in to get her early.

Once a very special friend was visiting us for several days. He
was an older man who had spent time as a disciple of Paramahansa
Yogananda. Our friend possessed the gift of clearly seeing the
heavenly influences of angels, guides and masters. Rami was just
one-year-old at the time and loved this man dearly. While we were
taking Rami for a walk, he went in to meditate in Rami's room. After
his meditation, he opened his eyes and saw the great light of several
angels hovering around Rami's crib. He told us that the area of her
crib has become a great power spot recharging her continually
whenever she is there. Then I knew why she yearned to go there each
afternoon and evening. As Rami grew she wanted to have a small
altar where she could go and pray. Her idea of an altar and mine
were very different. I had to learn to let go of my idea to appreciate
hers. She filled her little table with rocks, dirt, dried leaves and
flowers, a snake skin, a piece of rabbit fur, a picture of our dogs and
a candle. She went there often, saying short prayers and rearranging
the leaves and flowers. Her alter now is actually an old foot stool
covered with a little white cloth. She has it crowded with porcelain
angels, dried flowers, candles, leaves, a statue of St. Francis, and an
odd assortment of other treasures. She made up a little ceremony in
which she rings a bell, lights the candle, sings a song, and then says a
short prayer. The entire ceremony lasts only five minutes each day,
but it is an important part of her day. When Rami is saddened by a

happening in school, or a scolding from me, I notice that she always goes to her altar table and repeats her little ceremony until she feels better.

The vibrations of a child's own special spot in the house helps the child to remember who she really is each time she returns to it. This is a place where she feels happy and secure in being alone. Since our home is so small, Rami has her altar set up in our bedroom. Children should have a tiny inside or outside space that they can call their own, if even for a short time each day.

Whenever I feel confused and am needing help in guiding Rami, I go to her altar and pray. The strength and sincerity of her time there always serves to help me to understand her better. I can almost hear her guardian angel whispering insights into my ears.

Cultivating the art of aloneness in our children really starts with pregnancy. It starts with the parents' attitude about being alone with themselves. The first step is to acquire a love of solitude, a love of being alone with God. Then it is naturally passed on to the child.

Many people feel an infant should be constantly surrounded by the love and warmth of humans. Through natural childbirth, both at home and in the hospital, mothers are more aware of their baby's arrival and hold them immediately. Fathers are also encouraged to hold their newborn as much as possible. Fortunately, fewer and fewer infants have to be isolated in the newborn nursery right after birth. The closeness and warmth shared between the parents and their new baby is beautiful to behold, but at some point, even shortly after their arrival, we need to start letting them go. We need to let them experience their unique soul beauty apart from mommy and daddy.

When Rami was born, I assumed that she needed to be held constantly while awake, to always feel the security of Barry's or my presence close to her. At night she slept right next to me. When she was ten days old she started waking four or five times during the night with cries of agitation. She wasn't wet or hungry. I sensed she was more upset in her inner being than because of her body. After one more week of this pattern, Barry and I were becoming exhausted physically and Rami was becoming more irritable.

The following night, when Rami woke after just two hours of sleep, I looked into her eyes and saw clearly that something was disturbing her. I asked God to show me how I could help her. I was shown that my wanting to protect and comfort Rami each night while she slept was actually inhibiting her. She was needing to soar from her body to her heavenhome for an extended period of time for recharging and further instruction. The nearness of our bodies, the sleep noises we made, and dreams we had, kept pulling her back to earth and to the consciousness of her body. It must have been frustrating for Rami to have the ability to rise to such a high level of consciousness as an ego-less infant, only to be brought right down again by our level of sleep consciousness.

Barry and I decided that we must move her into her own room. The decision was very hard to make. Rami seemed so helpless alone in a big room in her little basket. There was a part of us that felt almost heartless , that we were abandoning her.

As parents, we often forget that we are not the only protectors of our children. They have higher beings who watch over them. We need to give them the space to return in consciousness to these heavenly protectors.

Barry and I did not sleep well on Rami's first night alone. We kept awake listening for her cry. She woke only once that night and the next day she was much more peaceful and content. This went on until she was three months old, when she started sleeping a twelve-hour stretch in her own little room. She would awake each morning with a deep sense of joy, making sweet sounds rather than crying.

Other parents describe a similar experience after removing their infant from their presence at night. If a private room was not available, some used the living room, dining room or even kitchen. The important factor seemed to be the space away from the parents rather than which room it is.

I know many people who sleep with their babies from infancy through childhood. That seems right for them. All babies are different, as are their parents. Parents need to be very sensitive about whether their infant is needing the space from them or not. After several months, sleeping with parents becomes a habit which is hard to break, so it is important to listen carefully in the beginning.

One little boy became so used to sleeping with his mother that he insisted on it until he was a toddler. He woke frequently to nurse, which was hard on the mother. He couldn't sleep with the father present, so the daddy had to sleep in the nursery each night by himself. The father soon began to resent not being able to sleep with his wife and there was a strain on the relationship. The mother recalled that her baby did wake often in the middle of the night as an infant and did seem agitated. Perhaps he was asking for space. Listen inwardly and the little ones will tell you.

A close friend and her husband sleep with all four of their children. As each new baby came along, they made their bed a little bigger. Sleeping together is very special to this family and the children seem to receive much nourishment and love from the close time with their parents. Children are so different in their needs—as are the parents. What works wonderfully for one family may not work at all for the next. The important thing is to follow your heart and listen to the need of your child, rather than doing what people say or even following popular notions.

As mentioned before, the most important factor in bringing forth our child's innate love of solitude and stillness is the parents' attitude. Deep within every human being is a strong desire for stillness and aloneness. This is perhaps the deepest desire within us, for we cannot fully experience God, except in silence. In a state of perfect aloneness, we can experience the vastness of our own being and in turn realize our oneness with all other beings. Only those who can bear the sound of silence can hear God. "Be still and know that I Am God," is a basic foundation for all of the religions. We all yearn to return to the place of the "I Am", the place of God's Presence, our heaven home. This state of consciousness can only be reached when we are at peace within ourself. As long as we are endeavoring to seek fulfillment in outside relationships, material possessions, work or distracting activities, we will never fully experience the fulfillment of knowing God within our being.

Knowing deeply that God's love, wisdom and power reside within our hearts is perhaps the most ecstatic of all knowledge. If children can experience that inner joy from their parent they will naturally seek that same joy within themselves. Even if the parent struggles like crazy to find even one moment of inner peace and joy, the child will absorb and experience that one moment through the parent and will be inwardly inspired for his or her own inward journey. The commitment a parent makes to seek God's Presence within is indeed a major commitment and is perhaps the greatest gift we can give ourselves and our child.

When Pir Vilayat Khan, head of the Sufi Order in the West, was asked to share a special childhood memory of his father, Hazrat Inayat Khan, a great Sufi teacher, he lovingly related the following scene. He and his sister Noor-un-nisa were playing outside while waiting for their father to come out from his room where he had been meditating. Noor-un-nisa ran into the house to check on their father and saw him just as he had finished meditating and coming out of his room. She ran back to Pir Vilayat and excitedly called out,

Pir Vilayat with sisters Noor-un-nisa and Khair-un-nisa and brother Hidayat.

"Abha's (Father's) eyes are so bright! Wait until you see Abha's eyes!" The two young children ran back to their father and gazed into his eyes. They felt as if they were looking into the sun, for the light coming out of him was that intense. That experience had a profound effect upon Pir Vilayat, one that helped to inspire and enrich his entire life.

Any amount of effort on the parents part to still their own being and feel God's Presence will greatly benefit both themselves and their children. With family life, there needs to be a certain amount of flexibility, creativity and humor in trying to meditate and be alone. Success is only measured by our intention and sincerity, not by the outcome.

Before having children I was quite rigid about my meditation practice. I had a special spot to sit with pretty green plants and pictures of saints. That spot is still there, but the saints' pictures have

gradually been replaced by Rami's drawings and an entire doll collection (so I wouldn't be lonely). The candles and special incense have been replaced by toys and the smell of dinner cooking. The regular one to two hours of meditation has become limited to fifteen to twenty minutes depending on the children's schedule. Though the duration of meditation has decreased, the benefits have remained the same or even increased. Before, I was meditating for my own benefit. Now I meditate for myself and my children. God just seems to give special assistance to parents when the intention of their spiritual practice is to be more loving toward their children.

I used to enjoy ending my meditation with a spoken prayer. Now my quiet time is usually ended a bit earlier than I would wish by a warm little body on my lap asking if I can come and play. I say my prayer out loud anyway, and it always includes thanking God for the beautiful child on my lap. My reward is usually a loving hug.

The rewards of encouraging children to spend some time alone are very great. Often, we as parents cannot see the effects and benefits with our physical eyes. We need to know that God is always there for our children, loving, nurturing, and opening their souls to perfect beauty, much the way the warmth of the sun helps to open a flower in full glory. I vividly remember a spring morning when four-year-old Rami was sitting out under our apple tree. She did not appear to be doing anything but sitting. I hurried about in the kitchen, trying to finish my chores and checking on her periodically from the window. Every time I saw her sitting there so sweetly, my heart just melted with love. Then thoughts of doubt would flash across my mind, "Maybe she is lonely. I should go and play with her or have a little friend over. Maybe I should take her a toy to play with." Fortunately, the peace in my heart was stronger than my doubt and I left Rami alone under the apple tree.

Over an hour later she came into the house to find me. Her little face was shining brightly. "Oh Mama," her voice sang so dearly, "my angel came to visit me under the apple tree and told me how much she loved me. We had a wonderful time."

The tears of joy welling up in my eyes reminded me I need never doubt Rami's happiness in being alone.

sixteen

Television And Our Children

The absence of television watching in a home makes it much easier to cultivate the love of solitude in a child. Without the over-stimulation and distraction of TV filling their impressionable minds, they are free to remember the heavenly home they just left, free to slowly integrate their new experiences of earth, and free to develop their own imaginations.

When I was four years old our family was the first family on our city block to get a TV. It was a really big thrill and we watched it continually. Nine years later, the TV needed repair and our family was without finances to fix it. Then at age thirteen, I discovered that a large part of my life had been spent relating to a TV and I felt lost without it. I had two or three extra hours each day that had previously been spent watching TV. My mother started teaching me how to cook and bake. Soon I was making many of the family meals. I started sewing and exercising more. Since my brother was away at college and both parents had to work away from home, I was often alone. TV had been my companion before, and now I needed a new friend, so I turned to reading. I started with the Bible and a book about the life of Gandhi. Day by day I gradually became aware of a friend inside of me who was a great comfort, a far greater comfort than the TV had ever been.

When the money came to fix the TV, I begged my parents not to repair it. I had discovered a wonderful new life without TV and didn't want to return to the other. After much insisting, they relented and we lived without TV for the remaining several years that I lived in their home. I haven't had a TV since.

A friend of mine carried the TV out of her home when her two boys, ages seven and five, refused to go on a family outing because they preferred to watch the Saturday cartoons. It pained the mother to see how addicted they had already become to the TV.

Another family removed the TV from their home when they realized that the only songs their children liked to sing were those of the commercials. The children also seemed dominated by desires for the toys advertised on TV. Their Christmas list had hundreds of items on it which the children felt they had to have to be happy.

The argument I hear most from parents regarding the merits of TV for children is that by the age of two or three their children learn the alphabet, pre-reading skills, to count, and so on. We are moving into the Aquarian Age, the age of both spirit and of mind. The tendency of these times has been to magnify the power of the intellect more than that of the spirit. This creates imbalance. Early over-stimulation of the mind can set up a pattern in the growing child in which the mind will seek dominion over the intuitive, imaginative, spiritual aspect of their being. The tendency to glorify intellect is so strong in Western Civilization that it seems a shame to nurture that in a two-year-old.

Many parents proudly report, "My child can read at four years old." "My three-year-old can use a computer." But how many report with pride that their little child has an imaginary friend or sings to himself? If we strengthen the spiritual, intuitive, and imaginative part of the child in the early years, the mind will in turn grow to be strong while attaining a proper balance with the heart. The mind will be the child's friend and his willing servant, rather than his master. If we are earnestly endeavoring to set early patterns of spirituality in our children, why have an instrument around which can so easily and quickly draw a child into material thought?

I have noticed that children adjust very readily to the absence of TV, if given creative alternatives to fill their time. In the beginning it might be necessary for parents to spend extra time with the children doing interesting things. It gives parents an opportunity to be parents. In time the void of no TV will be filled with more enriching activities.

An eight-year-old boy whose parents removed their TV went to visit a new friend after school. The little boy was surprised that his friend watched TV. His comment to the boy was, "Come on outside and I'll teach you an exciting new game. TV is old- fashioned now." The mother of the friend happily reported that the two boys went outside and played a very imaginative game with their bikes. A child's deepest desire is to play and learn about life in an active, participating way, as opposed to sitting back and watching. TV teaches children to watch things happen rather than make things happen.

Children can easily live without TV. But how about the parents? For most parents, television watching is a life-long habit. An interesting experiment would be to put the television set completely away for six months and watch for changes within yourself. Parents who have tried this experiment have reported that communication among family members improved. They enjoyed each other's company more, sleep came more naturally, they awoke more rested, meditation came easier, and life seemed fuller as more nourishing ways were found to spend the time.

Other parents have found that careful monitoring of the child's and their television watching has proved a good solution. These parents found that if they were strong within themselves and consciously watched only wholesome programs, it set an example for the children. Many people, however, find that television watching is like any habit. Try telling a smoker to cut down, or a heavy drinker to limit himself to one drink at a party. Television, too, is extremely seductive. It is often much easier to sell the TV than to try to cut down. As one small boy said to his mother, "I don't want to watch so much TV, but it makes me."

We need to also know that we have other options available to us. One ingenious father attached a generator to a stationary bicycle, and he adapted the TV to be powered only by the generator. Whoever wanted to watch TV had to pedal the bicycle to power the TV. It required deliberate motivation and real desire before his children, or anyone else, watched television. You can imagine how well the programs were selected!

For parents who would like to read more about the negative effects of television, I would strongly recommend the book *FOUR ARGUMENTS FOR THE ELIMINATION OF TELEVISION* by Jerry Mander. Here are some typical complaints he found from parents whose children watched television:

"My kids look like zombies when they are watching TV."
"My kids walk around like they're in a dream."
"How can I get my kids off of it and back into life?"

He discusses inherent biases of television. One which stands out for me is:

> War is better television than peace. It is filled with highlighted moments, contains action and resolution, and delivers a powerful emotion: fear. Peace is amorphous and broad. The emotions connected with it are subtle, personal and internal. These are far more difficult to televise.

In conclusion he states:

> What is lost because we can no longer flip a switch for instant "entertainment" will be more than offset by human contact, enlivened minds and resurgence of personal investigation and activation.

> What is lost because we can no longer see fuzzy and reduced versions of drama or forests will be more than offset by the actual experience of life and environment directly lived, and the resurgence of the human feeling that will accompany this.

> Overall chances are excellent that human beings, once outside the cloud of television images, would be happier than they have been of late, once again living in a reality which is less artificial, less imposed, and more responsive to personal action.

The Effects Of TV
by Karen Karima Rivers

It is "aliveness" that must be the guiding principle...

RUDOLF STEINER

A mother and Waldorf school teacher, Karen Karima Rivers has done extensive research on the effects of television in childhood. Karen lives in Nicasio, California with her husband and daughter Cheri. She was in charge of the children's section of a camp we attended one summer. Both of our girls had a very positive experience. Karen is devoted to bringing out the best in children.

A child requires careful guidance by parents and teachers if he is to blossom into the radiant flower whose seed lives within his soul. The cultivation and care of a child is a challenging task, for his needs are complex. The development of the will, the heart, the intellect, and spirit of a child must be tended with insight and care.

A serious question facing parents and educators is: "How does the experience of watching television effect a child in these areas of development?"

> *...we now have evidence that habitual viewing can affect a young person's basic outlook and sensibilities, predisposition to violence and hyperactivity, IQ, reading ability, imagination, play, language patterns, critical thinking, self-image, perception of others, and values in general. Further, habitual TV viewing can effect the physical self as it can alter brain waves, reduce critical eye movements, immobilize the hands and body, and undermine nutrition and eating habits.*
>
> KATE MOODY
> *GROWING UP ON TELEVISION*

These findings are frightening, almost paralyzing. Yet we must understand their import if we are to make intelligent decisions for our children. Let us look closely at the specific effects television has on particular aspects of human life.

Physical Effects

A child's behavior reflects his mental state and his emotional and physical well-being. It is an indication of his inner equilibrium. Children's behavior deteriorate just after watching television. They become victims of hyperactivity. This is the consequence of images projected into the brain of a child who is sitting still. The images stimulate the impulse to move, but the stimulation is repressed. The physical energy which is created by the images, but not used, is physically stored. Then, when the TV set is off, it comes bursting forth in aimless, random, speedy activity. This is an exhibition of "sensory overload," a condition which is damaging to all human beings, but especially to the young. A child needs physical activity which strengthens his body so that it may work harmoniously with his heart, mind and spirit.

Effect on a Child's Self-Image

As a child watches television, he internalizes what he sees. It affects his ideas of his own abilities and potential. He becomes willing to let the television image answer the question: "Who am I?" The answer to this question evolves from the unconscious frustration of sitting in front of a wall of indifference. A child cannot communicate with the television. The people on the screen do not even know he exists. As a result, a child learns that his existence is inconsequential; it has no effect. In response to this feeling, some children resort to hostility, extreme aggressiveness, physical violence, constant screaming and yelling. This is their attempt to convince themselves and the world that they can affect their environment, and their existence does have some consequence. Other children withdraw, feel apathetic, and "tune out" the world around them. They internalize this sense of impotence, which erodes the will of these children. The strong primal impulse of the will lies in the depths of every human being. This impulse must be protected and nurtured if a child is to grow into adulthood with the confidence and capability to meet the demands of our society. A primary gift one can offer a child is to preserve and nurture his will for life on this earth.

Effects on Human Values and Relationships

Television has profoundly affected the way in which members of the human race learn to become human beings.

GEORGE GERBNER
DEAN U. OF PENN. ANNENBERG SCHOOL OF COMMUNICATION

The hours that a child spends in a one-way relationship with television characters, an involvement that allows for no communication or interaction, affects his relationships with real people. In many families the television has replaced the parents' role in the socialization of the child, the development of human values, family rituals and special events. "Like the sorcerer of old," writes Urie Brofenbrenner, "the television set casts its magic spell, freezing speech and action, turning the living into silent statues so long as the enchantment lasts. The primary danger of the television screen lies not so much in the behavior it produces—although there is danger there—as in the behavior it prevents: the talks, the games, the family festivals, and the arguments through which much of the child's learning takes place and through which his character is formed. Turning on the television set can turn off the process that transforms children into people." Television images teach values and behavior patterns to a child. He accepts television characters as models for his own attitudes and actions. At some level, a child begins to judge his own meaning, dignity, and worth in comparison with the television characters. What are these portrayals teaching children about family relationships, sexuality, violence, racial groups? *A child becomes conditioned to see problems resolved in 30 or 60 minutes;* this creates a low tolerance for the frustration of learning and problem-solving of any real stature. The traditional opportunities for expressing love within the family have been usurped by the television. It has become difficult for many families to find the time to express love for one another in truly meaningful ways. A child needs to learn through love expressed in everyday participation in family life. Then he will grow to understand what the gift of human life truly is.

Effects on Reading

It is required of a child who grows up in a literate society that he develop skills in concentration, reading, writing, and verbal communication. This includes the capacity for analytical thinking. Concentration is a skill that requires practice to develop, and it is necessary in order to learn to read and write. The capacity to speak, write, read, count, compute, and reason, are functions of the left side of the brain, the hemisphere that orders data. This is necessary when the brain perceives printed letters, scans them, and joins them to make meaning. The right side of the brain works in a different way; it perceives the world holistically rather than through analytical structures. It works through pattern recognition, which is the antithesis of the coding and decoding process of the left side of the brain. Television viewing is a process of the right hemisphere of the brain. It is primarily the language of pictures, perceived through right-brain pattern recognition. Habitual television viewing has proven to be counter-productive to analytical thinking and the mental process needed for reading. Reading requires perceptual continuity to persevere line after line. Television habituates the mind to short sequences, not to the continuity of thought required in reading. The pace and speed of television cause children to be easily distracted. They become inundated with so many messages that they cannot stop to make sense of them. This deteriorates their ability to focus and concentrate on the printed word.

The written word provides humanity with a looking glass into the wisdom of humankind. It is a wonderful resource for understanding our evolution on the earth. If we are to send our children forth into adulthood with freedom, they must not only develop the skills necessary to read, write and think analytically, they must develop a love for learning by these means.

Effects on Imagination

The imagination can and must be trained just as scrupulously as the intellect is schooled, to perceive and adhere to truth and reality. The imagination is one of the eyes through which we can see into the lawfulness, wholeness and transformations in the universe.

RISA LEVENSON

Daydreaming and imaginative play promote a child's perceptual maturity, emotional growth and creative development. Imagination is the capacity of the mind to project itself beyond its own perceptions and sensations. Imaginative play allows a child to become an active user rather than a passive recipient of experience. He finds ways to work out difficulties and adjust the realities of his life to his inner requirements. In make-believe play a child can take on the roles of his parents and redress grievances that have caused him suffering; he can reenact painful scenes from everyday life and transform them into more satisfactory experiences. In the course of his play a child structures a world for himself in which he has the power to act and to affect his position in the real world.

Television projects adult-created images into the child's brain, which he in turn imitates. He can become dependent on outside sources to create his ideas and visual pictures for him. This stifles a child's opportunity and ability to create from his innate source of imagery, which cripples his maturing process toward healthy adulthood. Margaret Meyerkort stated that it is the imagination which provides the capacity to love. It is our imagination which sees the perfection in our beloved, the intention behind the imperfect human act. Without this capacity we would not have the vision to love. It is the imagination which is the threshhold to the spirit of man.

Cheri.

Effects on a Child's Spiritual Development

Know thyself!

SOCRATES

Through his imagination a child finds expression for his innermost reality. He discovers his innate resources, his feelings and his thoughts. These are an expression of his sense of self. To nurture a child's inner growth he must spend some quiet time each day when he has the opportunity for reflection, processing the events of the day, and resolving conflicts that are burdening him. Parents usually recognize that children need some quiet time each day, but many parents use the television to facilitate this. Rather than providing a child with the opportunity to work through his experiences of the day, the television fills him with more stimuli, overloading his faculties rather than relieving them. Television fills a child's mind with other people's ideas and images, denying him the freedom to discover his own. Without this opportunity a child will feel frustrated, over-loaded, and most crucially, lack self-knowledge. A child must have the opportunity to know himself, a process that evolves from within. Given this opportunity a child will develop the capacity to explore his inner world and begin to grapple with the question, "Who am I?". The responsibility lies with us, as parents and teachers, to cultivate imagination, a sense of truth, and a feeling of responsibility. It takes courage and conviction to lovingly tend the seeds that live within our children. But it is the most worthy work we can undertake, for our children are our gift to the world.

Reclaiming Our Children
by T. Mike Walker

Our friend and single father, T. Mike Walker, shares some very strong feelings and describes his experiment with eliminating television from his home. Mike has fathered four children. Two daughters are now grown and on their own. It warms our hearts to see this man's closeness to his children.

Following a recent jazz-dance concert in Santa Cruz, several small children skipped down from the audience and began to dance at the foot of the stage, playfully copying steps and routines they had just witnessed. Quick mimics of everything we see, it struck me suddenly how impressionable we are.

Like living patchworks of behaviors, we are each stitched together from images we absorb and then reflect through our actions. During our early years members of our immediate family mold us and establish our personal images and values. But the greatest image-shapers in America today are no longer Mom and Dad. Uncle Telly and Aunty Media have moved in to stay, and their amoral messages may well be a

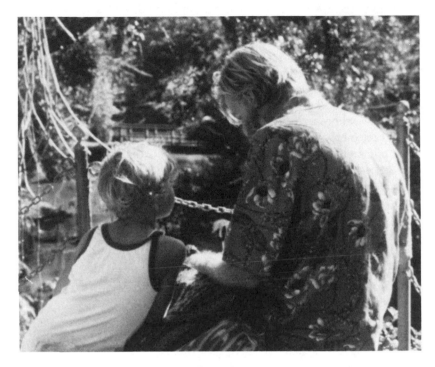

Mike and son.

cause of increasing public violence, especially in small children who fantasize and role-play, bringing this violence into their games.

Images of rude, abusive, macho men smashing into our lives to murder us are big box office; Conan and Terminator are worshiped by millions. Our collective unconsciousness is saying something to us about our values, but the volume's too loud during the commercial to hear. Television and its multi-billion dollar advertising industry bombard us with images and messages which tell us how to dress, what and where to eat, dictating a full spectrum of consumer-oriented values which are devoid of substance and perhaps even dangerous to our personal health, as well as to our survival as a species.

A recent Reader's Digest poll indicated that the average American father spends less than ten minutes a week of quality time with his children. Yet that same man spends between ten and twenty hours watching TV! Watching Monday night football preempts prime time with our kids. Television has become a parallel educational system, urging instant sense gratification and encouraging personal greed.

Can the Soaps really teach us to love? How often has a TV cop or cowboy ever expressed real sorrow or regret over the killing of another human being? Other than rage and revenge, where do we find tenderness or compassion?

If we permit our children to be bombarded with these images, won't they dance it out?

Several months ago, in a fit of despair over my thirteen-year-old son's poor school marks and aggressive attitude, I unplugged his TV set, canceled his cable connection and forced him to move back into my life. I plucked him out of his room to take walks on the beach with me and trips to local parks. We started talking about nutrition and planning wholesome meals together. We took turns reading books to each other, went camping and swimming, but most important, we began to talk and listen to each other's real needs, dreams and desires.

It took nearly half a year, but his grades have raised from "D's" to "B's", his attitude has become more thoughtful and considerate. Most important, we have become friends again!

We must be willing to set an example by being the change we wish to see in the world.

seventeen

The Courage To Discipline

Train up a child in the way he should go, and when he is old he will not depart from it.

PROVERBS 22:6

Discipline, in the sense of setting limits, is one of the greatest gifts a parent can give their child. Many parents sense their child's greatness. Some even feel that their child is their spiritual teacher. Therefore it seems to those parents quite absurd to discipline their child, for on some level he/she is wiser than the parent. However, even the most advanced soul still needs discipline as a child. Discipline is a basic need. A child who lacks defined limits will scream and kick, begging for this need to be fulfilled.

Several years ago a single mother and child visited me for counseling. The girl, who was nine years old at the time, had been asked to leave two schools because of her behavior. She was unhappy at home, and didn't get along with her younger brother and sister. Her mother told me about the profound experience she had when this child was born. She had recognized her baby as her teacher of love. Thereafter, she had honored and respected the child as one would a teacher, yet at the same time had given her complete freedom to grow as she desired. She loved her daughter and gave her plenty of attention, and wondered what she had done to encourage her child's present behavior.

It became clear to me that the child had not received enough discipline. The mother felt that it was wrong to set limits with so high a soul. I studied the mother and saw her deep sincerity to be a pure instrument of mother love. I studied the girl and saw that indeed she seemed wise beyond her years, yet her eyes also revealed a great unhappiness. She was lost in her own desires and lacked direction in her life.

I explained to the mother the girl's basic need for discipline. I gave several examples from my work with disturbed children, and how they readily responded to consistent discipline given with love. The mother listened politely, but she was not convinced. She was needing a deeper explanation of why her "teacher" should be subject to discipline. Several months later the answer came to me in the form of one man's story:

It was snowing heavily January 13, 1982, in Washington, D.C. By mid-day many of the office workers in the city were informed that they should leave work early due to blizzard conditions. One man, Lenny Skutnik, was slowly making his way out of the city along with thousands of motorists. As they passed over the 14th Street Bridge they noticed a crowd looking down at the icy river. Stopping to investigate, he saw that a large aircraft had crashed into the river. Luggage and debris were scattered everywhere, while the distinct odor of jet fuel hung in the air. Someone shouted that the plane had just gone down after take off. There were people clinging desperately to the wreckage with chunks of ice floating all around them. The bystanders gathered ropes and tied them together and one man tried to swim out to the people with the rope. Bt the frigid water overcame him and he had to be pulled back. The small crowd felt helpless. Lenny Skutnik was among many standing there who started to pray for the people.

Soon a small helicopter came and a cheer went up from the growing crowd on the shore. First one man was saved by the helicopter's rope and immediately the pilot went back for more. The second time two people clung to the rope. As the pilot was bringing them to shore, one of them, a young woman, lost her grip and fell back into the water. The pilot brought the one person to safety and immediately went back for the woman who had fallen. The woman seemed to be in shock, for even with the rope and ring dangling right in front of her she seemed unable to grasp it. Finally she held onto it weakly while the helicopter slowly flew to shore. On the way, one of her arms slipped out of the ring and then the other one. It was obvious she wasn't going to be able to grasp the ring again. If she wasn't saved in a few moments she was going to die.

It was at this point that Lenny Skutnik received the strong inner prompting to swim in after her. He immediately pulled off his boots and coat and jumped into the icy water. He remembered that he didn't even feel the coldness of the water, nor did he have a plan of how to save her when he got there. All he knew was that he was acting out of an inner guidance, a strong urgency to get her to safety. He pushed her back to shore where waiting hands pulled her up. As soon as he was on land he felt so grateful he started to cry and give thanks. He looked down at his clothes and saw they had immediately crystallized into ice. Then an ambulance carried him off to the hospital to be treated for hypothermia.

Sitting in a hot tub of water he began to think about the incident. He wondered what had given him the courage to jump into the water. Fear of people had always been the biggest obstacle in his life, especially being singled out in front of people. Here he had done something which TV would carry throughout the nation.

He remembered his childhood and the loving but strict discipline of his father. When his father spoke, he learned to listen and obey. Then he realized that a higher power had taken command out there in the icy Potomac River. The power that moved Lenny to save the woman's life had spoken to him as a loving father would his son. Lenny had been trained as a child to listen and obey, so he didn't question when the inner command came to jump into the water.

In the highest sense, disciplining our children is actually attuning them to listen to their own inner voice. The lower self often rebels at the promptings from the higher self. We are so used to being led by our human thoughts and desires. In order to be "master of our ship," (our body, mind and emotions), we need to listen to the true captain—the still small voice within. It is through this voice that God can speak to us and help direct our lives. We cannot easily listen to this inner voice and obey its commands unless we have received some kind of assistance in childhood to listen to and obey a parent or guardian.

"No, you can't have another cookie. I told you, you could only have two." "But I *want* another one," your two year old defiantly

GURRU GHOSH
Mother of Paramahansa Yogananda

BHAGABATI CHARAN GHOSH
Father of Paramahansa Yogananda

YOGANANDA AT THE AGE OF SIX

As a child, Yogananda was disciplined with love and consistency by his parents.

responds. "You can have an apple or a banana if you are still hungry, but not another cookie. "I want another cookie!!" "No," you definitely conclude. What then begins is what all parents of two-year-olds dread—the tantrum. How silly to be fighting over one more cookie! It is so tempting at this point to just give the cookie and avoid the tantrum, especially if Grandma is standing there and she was the one who baked the cookies. However, to give in would be to fail your child. If we as parents can understand that a dispute over another cookie can really be a major life training, teaching the child to obey a command that is difficult rather than always getting what he wants.

The commands of the Higher Self, or God-Self, are sometimes very difficult to obey; jumping into an icy river, forgiving a friend who has hurt you very deeply, or sitting down to pray with your partner when you would rather shout angry words. Special friends of ours, an elderly couple, are living examples of true attunement to the inner voice. In the midst of a busy day, the husband received an inner prompting to travel to a favorite camping place some hours away as soon as possible. The couple immediately started packing up their camper and hitched up their small boat behind it. When they got to their camping spot they unpacked their equipment, put the boat in the water and got out the lawn chairs, happy for a moment to finally rest. The very minute they sat down, they both received an inner prompting to return home immediately. Without hesitating, they packed up all of their things, pulled the boat out of the water, hitched it to the camper and set off for home. They had driven ten minutes when they saw a big gas truck in trouble. The woman felt strongly to help clear away the crowd that had gathered. Just as she did that, the truck exploded into flames and would have killed all those who were standing around. As it was, no one was hurt. By listening to their inner guidance rather than to their own desires to stay at home, or to relax even a few more minutes at their camp spot, many lives were saved.

A parent's wise discipline can help their child to begin a pattern of listening and obeying a higher guidance. Through the years, the parent can then increasingly guide their child to look within for their own inner discipline. When Rami turned seven we started a "game" of asking her angel to help in certain small decisions in her life. Once, a friend was begging Rami to come to her house and spend the night. I knew Rami didn't want to go and also saw her being persuaded by the constant nagging of her friend. I took Rami aside and asked her to go into her room, sit quietly, and ask her guardian angel what she should do. She skipped out five minutes later and happily told her friend that she wanted to stay home. Her friend seemed satisfied and left. Rami played happily the rest of the afternoon, knowing her angel had helped her make the right decision. A very special family evening confirmed this.

It takes great courage to discipline a child. Children will test a parent over and over to see who is boss. They will persistently try to win and get their own way. If they do win and feel as if they are running the show, they will feel very insecure and unhappy. This will probably lead to further testing as if to say, "Do you love me enough to discipline me?"

Once I counseled an eleven-year-old boy and his single mother. Through prolonged use of drugs, the mother became very weak-willed and seemed unable to set limits for the boy. He always got his own way. Consequently, he did even worse things at home, unconsciously hoping for discipline. When this didn't bring the desired result he would run out and deliberately break something—like a large store-front window. Then he would just stand there waiting for the police to take him to the juvenile authorities where he would receive the discipline he so desperately needed. The boy had to be transferred from his mother's house to a situation where he could receive discipline in a consistent way.

Children need to know that the adult watching them is in charge, and that their behavior is subject to correction. When Rami was four years old, Barry and I needed to go away for an afternoon. We asked a special friend if he could watch Rami. He was delighted and arrived at our home loaded down with games, puzzles and puppets. Rami was also very excited. We returned four hours later. The man shuffled out of our house looking completely downcast. Rami came out next looking very unhappy. She said she never wanted to see our friend again. They had had a wonderful time until Rami wanted to do something against our friend's wishes. Not wanting to scold her, he had gently explained his reasons for saying no. She tested him so much that he finally just gave in to her and walked out of the room. By hesitating to take command of the situation, they had both become very unhappy.

Once a parent is forced to limit a child's behavior, all measures should be taken to follow through. This sometimes takes the greatest courage of all. Children will often test their parent in front of others, just to see if the parent loves them enough to follow through when others are around. If the parent backs down, the child loses some respect and subsequent discipline will be all the more difficult.

Another time, when Rami was also four years old, she and I went shopping in a downtown mall. We had a lovely day buying her new clothes, a new doll, and going out to lunch. As we were walking back to our car, Rami spotted a teddy bear that she liked in a store window. "I want that teddy bear!" It sounded somewhere between and request and a demand. "No," I gently responded. "I want that teddy bear right now!" Her response was now a demand. "We'll go say hello to the teddy bear," I reassured her as we walked into the store. Once in the store we both hugged the teddy bear and talked to it. I noticed that it was one of those $100.00 bears so I knew I could never justify buying it for her. "Now say good-by to the teddy bear. We need to go, Rami." "No, I want the teddy bear!"

Once outside, the kicking, jumping, and screaming began. More than simply desiring a teddy bear, I felt she was wanting limits to be set on her behavior. Much of the day had been spent in pleasing her. Now she seemed to be asking where the limits were. In her own way, she needed to know if she was in fact a princess whom everyone could wait upon, or a child growing up in a family with discipline and limits. Holding her new doll she started jumping up and down screaming, "I want that Teddy Bear!" "I held her face firmly, looked straight into her eyes and said, "If you don't stop screaming I'm going to take your new birthday doll away until tomorrow."

Just then I spotted a woman coming towards me who had recently been in one of our workshops. Because of a healing that had taken place within her at that time, she had placed me on quite a high pedestal. She had that sparkley far-away look in her eyes and I knew intuitively that she expected me to be a certain way. Just as she approached saying, "Oh how wonderful to see you and your darling daughter!", Rami started screaming louder than ever. I excused myself from the woman and began the difficult process of taking the doll from Rami's clutched hands. Screams filled the downtown mall. The woman watched a moment, a look of horror appeared upon her face, and then she quickly departed. Perhaps she was simply surprised, or perhaps she was convinced that I was a horrible mother. It really didn't matter.

By the time we returned to the car, Rami had settled down and her sweetness returned. The teddy bear was never mentioned again. "Can I play with my new doll tomorrow, mama? Can I just let daddy have a peek tonight?" "Yes," I said, giving her a kiss.

I thought about that scene for quite some time. If I had ignored Rami to receive the woman's appreciation, I would have failed

Rami, for I would have given her the message that an image someone held of me was more important to me than taking the risk to discipline my child.

The pain children may cause us is nothing compared to the revelation they offer at every moment.

STEPHEN GASKIN
SPIRITUAL MIDWIFERY

Through disciplining our children, we sometimes become subject to all kinds of disapproval from friends and relatives. As parents, we need to see that our child's need for discipline is more important than people's judgments and criticism. I have been strongly criticized twice while disciplining Rami. One woman felt I was too strict with Rami. Another felt that I was too lenient. Both of these experiences were very hard and forced me to ask deeply inside, "Am I too strict?"—and then "Am I too lenient and pampering?" Finally, in each case, as the hurt healed within me, I realized that the force behind their words revealed their own inner hurt—not mine!

The first woman later revealed that seeing me punish Rami reminded her of her mother punishing her in a similar way. Later that day the mother had been killed in a car accident. Her last contact with her mother had been the punishment. She never knew if her mother had really loved her at the moment of death. While talking, she understood how much love it takes for a parent to discipline a child. This helped her to open her heart to her mother, perhaps for the first time.

Concerning the second woman's criticism of me, I realized on my own that jealousy was the bottom line. I had previously spent time with this woman alone, away from the children. When we came together next, the children were there too and she was hurt to discover that my connection to the children was deeper than my connection to her. Her unconscious way of communicating this was to blame me for being lenient and pampering with Rami. We have often seen this happen with persons entering a relationship with a parent. Their jealousy over the parent's intimate relationship with their children can manifest as criticism.

I learned and grew through these experiences as well as by listening to others with similar experiences. I realized that sensitive, valid criticism from another, however hard it is to hear, will cause a stirring of inspiration within the heart. When you receive constructive feedback given compassionately, your heart will sense something true and you won't feel defensive. If the criticism comes in anger and you feel hurt and defensive from the words, then chances are that criticism comes from unclear feelings on the part of the sender. This is especially a problem in the relationship between parents, where one parent will criticize the other when it is they themselves who feels inadequate or frustrated. It is very easy to project these feelings onto a spouse.

Mothers and fathers need to continuously support each other in discipline. Parents need to support other parents. Whenever I observe a parent appropriately disciplining their child, I try to give a little twinkle with my eye, or a nod of approval, to let them both know they are beautiful—even as discipliner and disciplinee. We need to continuously remind ourselves and others that conscious discipline is a form of love and early spiritual training.

Barry and I try to support each other as much as possible. However, when Rami was two we struggled against each other. Though we had been together thirteen years, the discipline experience was new and we had to learn to work together. The more we struggled against one another the worse each situation became and the more unhappy we all became. Just like a newly married couple sometimes struggle in learning to live together, so do new parents often struggle in learning to discipline together. Like all new parents, we needed to learn how to work together—uniting our energies in disciplining our children. We learned a little more about trusting one another. Now we have frequent planning talks on how we should handle various types of behavior.

Discipline is such a creative process. Sometimes we discover the perfect solution, sometimes we fail. We need to always allow room for mistakes. Sometimes, when we are trying a new approach, Rami looks at us as if to say, "Mom and Dad, you are way off this time." Barry and I have to laugh at ourselves.

It is important for a single mom or dad to have a special friend with whom they can talk over and laugh over certain discipline problems. A single father I know meets regularly with a single mother with similar aged children. They discuss discipline and try to support each other. They find it helpful to receive the male/female balance on certain issues.

I have found it helpful to have the support of another mother. Barry finds it helpful to share with other men on fathering. I have a friend who has two girls almost the same ages as Rami and Mira. From time to time I might call her with something like, "I'm not letting Rami go to the party because of her behavior. What do you think?" My loving friend knows that I'm not really calling for advice, but to hear her tell me that I'm a good mother and to remind me of how much I love my children. Having been reminded, strength returns and I can be more loving to the children.

Parents cannot support each other too much. Don't miss an opportunity to tell your friend, husband or wife that they are a good parent. We are all a bit unsure of what we are doing and honest appreciation helps us to become the parent we are seeking to be.

Remember that outside help is always available. It may take the form of a book or a person. Nutritional counseling or medical advice have proven helpful for some parents. We have found it helpful to ask an outsider. The teachers at Rami's school have been very helpful, as well as older persons who have raised many children. On occasion the grandparents suggestions have been excellent.

When Rami was six, she had a habit of throwing tantrums before each dinner. Try as we may, we couldn't break her of the pattern. We consulted her kindergarten teacher who was shocked—Rami was the ideal child in class. "Princess Rami, misbehaving!" She could hardly believe it. When she recovered from the shock, she asked us to examine our expectations. Were we each evening actually expecting Rami to misbehave before dinner, and thus perpetuating her tantrums? She suggested that we change the scene entirely, perhaps sitting in front of the fireplace for dinner or eating in Rami's little play house or sitting in a circle of candles. We tried her ideas with the expectation that Rami would love the new arrangements. Rami responded beautifully, and eventually we were able to go back to eating at the dinner table in peace.

Parents are usually the ones to see the worst behavior in their children. When children feel secure and confident in their parents' love, they then feel free to experiment with all different behaviors and to allow their worst selves to emerge. In a way this is a complement to a parent. A parent would need to worry if their child was a total angel at home and misbehaved away from them. This might be a symptom of fear in the child, and the need for a more nurturing atmosphere at home.

The most important quality for a parent to develop when disciplining children is self-love and self-forgiveness. Sometimes Rami's and Mira's behavior can really make me angry and perhaps I yell a little louder than necessary. There have also been times when I just didn't think I could last another minute alone with them and days when everything seems to go wrong. These are the times when I can so easily be upset with myself and feel as if I am a bad mother. These are the times when it is so important to forgive ourselves. Negative thoughts about ourselves take so much precious energy. By practice, a parent can learn to live in the consciousness of self-forgiveness, for we all make so many mistakes.

Once, when Rami was five, I had a particularly trying day with her. Barry was working at the hospital. While Rami was in the bathtub playing with some toys, I tried to sort out the day and understand my mistakes. I picked up a little book written by a well known spiritual teacher. This man wrote a section in his book on things not to do when disciplining children. I grew very sad as I read it over, for I had done all of these things in just one day. Negative thoughts raced through my mind: "I'm ruining Rami." "Why did she pick such a lousy mother." Finally I caught myself and realized that developing self-forgiveness is far more important than concentrating on my mistakes. As I started forgiving myself I started seeing all the positive parts of the day. With each thought of love for myself, I could also love and forgive Rami. I felt so uplifted. Rami sensed this and we had such a happy story time together.

Conscious people are attracting very powerful souls as their children. These children are sometimes very difficult to discipline and require our inner strength to match theirs. Rather than grumbling about a "difficult" child to raise, see it as a marvelous God-given opportunity to grow and be strengthened yourself.

About ten years ago we were visiting a dear woman teacher in Mt. Shasta. This woman is very intuitive and had sensed the birth of a very advanced soul. She told us of the boy's birth, who his parents were, and that he had been a great ruler in a past life. Two years later we visited the boy and his parents. As Rami was also almost two, we decided to take the children to the park to play. As soon as we got to the park the little boy ran over to one of the bigger boys and hit him, then ran over to a group of younger boys and knocked them down. The parents sharply disciplined he boy. Soon after, a new boy appeared on the play ground and was promptly knocked down by "the little ruler." The parents explained that wherever they went their son immediately pushed or hit any unfamiliar child in the area. The children, big or small, usually backed off from the boy. It seemed as if the boy was sensing something of the power he had known. Being in a two year old body with a two year old personality, he was unable to know what to do with the power within his being, so he turned to knocking other children around. The boy required tremendous strength and courage from the parents to guide and discipline him in the proper use of his inner power. With joy, I watched the great change in his parents. Before he was born they were rather shy, withdrawn people. After several years of living with their son they became strong, confident people who began assuming leadership themselves.

I recently had a lengthy talk with a friend who has two young boys. The oldest, who was five years old, had several problem behaviors. The parents had tried many different forms of discipline and could not seem to curb the boy's behavior. Nutritional counseling and a holistic doctor had helped considerably, but the misbehavior still persisted. My friend reported that her embarrassment over her son's behavior was the most difficult part of the situation. She felt everyone was judging her and her husband. Occasionally, people even told her negative things about her mothering. Her husband had received similar comments about his fathering. And yet both of these people are tremendous parents with so much love for their children. Their test in this period is to repeatedly remember their own beauty as parents. Even in the midst of a struggle with the boy, they need to affirm their strength and love.

Rather than seeing a child's behavior as the fault of a parent and therefore blaming the parents, if we could just see that children have definite behavior tendencies from past lives and are drawn to a particular parent or parents who have unique strength, understanding and ability to guide them. The parents' inner attitude can then change from one of embarrassment and failure to feeling that they have been blessed by God in receiving a "challenging" child. This type of child demands that the true greatness be brought forth from the parents. And, in truth, every child is a unique challenge.

I still have people blame me from time to time for Rami's shyness. They see her behavior as wrong and my fault. Sometimes I feel hurt, for even close friends have misunderstood. I then need to go within and see how Rami was drawn to us because we understand her shyness. Even at age nine, she is too busy cultivating her inner spiritual life to give much attention to the social world. People's judgments about me have forced me to discover an inner strength.

A parent needs to be very mindful to watch for and praise their child's thoughtful and kind actions. A parent's appreciation needs to be much more abundant than criticism. If a child hears more criticism of his behavior than appreciation the effect will be harmful.

In disciplining, always remember that we are disciplining a child's behavior, not the child. Words such as "You are not going to be allowed to throw your toys at your sister anymore, are more effective than saying, "You bad boy, stop throwing your toys at your sister." In the first, the child understands that it is his behavior that is wrong. In the second the child receives the message that *he* is bad. If told often enough that he is bad, the child will begin to believe it and form an image of himself which could last a lifetime.

Take every opportunity to appreciate your children. If your family has a problem with siblings bickering and you catch them in a rare moment being loving to each other, seize that opportunity to really let them know how happy it makes you.

If the day has been particularly hard and you have had to discipline a certain child often, try to have a warm and cozy time with that child before he or she goes to sleep. May they feel your love and forgiveness as they drift off to sleep. If they have done one hundred things to upset you and one beautiful, talk about the beautiful. These are the days that children need our love and approval the most and will carry that with them to sleep.

If it is not possible to spend this time, then go into their room while they sleep and "talk" to them. Let them know how deeply you love them and how really beautiful they are.

The highest form of discipline that we can give our child is to first discipline ourselves, since we can only give our child what we ourselves possess. Many of us possess an outer discipline in our lives. We get up at the same time and go to work. We watch our diet. We jog every day. We study hard at night school. We practice the guitar. All of these disciplines are valuable and help in the momentum of disciplining our child, but an equally important discipline is to make peace with ourselves. We then become the captain of our "ship," and gain control of our thoughts, speech, feelings, body and desires. At times we feel so far away from this mastry, and yet each small step that we make towards this ideal is a valuable gift given to our child as well as ourselves.

When parents become master of their own being, they become a model of discipline and their vibration alone guides the child.

Barry and I had the privilege of spending a summer in France

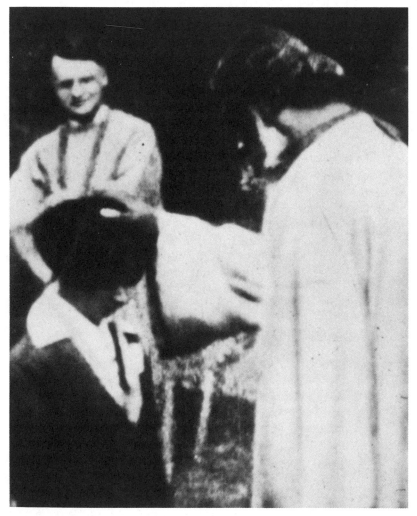

The initiation of Pir Vilayat Inayat Khan by his father Hazrat Inayat Khan.

with Pir Vilayat Khan, head of the Sufi order in the West. In a moment of intimacy he told our little group a touching story of his father, Hazrat Inayat Khan, a Sufi Master. Once, as a small child, Pir Vilayat was misbehaving. His father came out of the house some distance away and simply glanced at him. No words were spoken.

He then returned to the house. In that one glance Pir Vilayat deeply understood the message. There was no need to repeat that behavior.

Each day may we strive to become more like the Master, and be a model of discipline rather than preaching it to our children. We will then be giving them a gift to last a life time.

I love Thee in the temple of discipline.
I love Thee in the temple of devotion.
I worship Thee in the temple of my love.
I touch Thy feet in the temple of stillness.
I behold Thine eyes in the temple of delight.
I feel Thee in the temple of emotion.
I fight for Thee in the temple of activity.
I enjoy Thee in the temple of peace.

PARAMAHANSA YOGANANDA
METAPHYSICAL MEDITATIONS

eighteen

Laughing at Ourselves

Humor is the great thing, the saving thing after all, the minute it crops up, all our hardnesses yield, all our irritations and resentments slip away and a sunny spirit takes their place.

MARK TWAIN

A merry heart doeth good like a medicine, but a broken spirit drieth the bones.

PROVERBS 17:22

Love may make the world go round, but laughter keeps us from getting dizzy.

DON ZOCHERT

A person without a sense of humor is like a wagon without springs—jolted by every pebble in the road.

HENRY WARD BEECHER

As parents we can be jolted along our course, knocked about by the many irritations and difficulties of parenting and life in general. Or we can roll along smoothly with springs of laughter gently bouncing us over the hard aspects of our life and responsibility as parents. We constantly choose to either laugh or be uptight, to bring relief to a situation or make it worse. We can either model to our children that life is a constant struggle or that life can be lived with light and joy, which is what our children are modeling to us.

When I was a teenager my father had to work away from home for several months during the winter. My brother was away at college, leaving my mother and me to tend to the house. While my father was away everything seemed to go wrong with the house. It had been a particularly severe winter and the heating and plumbing difficulties had been quite an inconvenience. Then there was a rise in temperature, snow was rapidly melting and heavy rains were causing flooding conditions. My mother arrived home late from her job as church secretary, fatigue written all over her face. As the oven had also broken we decided to go out to dinner to cheer ourselves up. Over dinner we laughed over what a hard time we had been having keeping the house in running order with my dad and brother away. Laughingly my mother stated, "Well we should be thankful that the worst thing of all didn't happen—the flooding of our basement." We both laughed remembering the one time the basement flooded and the week of work involved to dry it out again.

When we arrived home after our dinner, my mother picked up the newspaper that had been delivered to our house. "Oh, I'll just throw this down in the basement for now and put it away tomorrow," she said flinging the rolled up paper down the basement steps. We both heard an unmistakable "Splash!". We looked at each other for an instant as the truth slowly hit. The basement was flooded! Suddenly my mother started laughing and laughing. Then I started laughing and laughing and soon we could hardly contain ourselves as our laughter grew and grew. We held each other as we made our way to the living room couch where we sat down and laughed some more. Our laughter healed the agony of the moment, giving us the strength and right spirit to then begin the week's worth of work drying and cleaning out the basement.

I have forgotten many things from my teenage years, but the night my mother and I laughed so wonderfully and deeply together is a permanent part of my memory. By her laughter she showed that we can moment by moment choose either uptightness and irritability or peace and joy.

Barry Sultanoff MD, editor of the American Holistic Medical Association Journal, writes that:

> By joining in humor and acknowledging our oneness, we can have a profound experience of unity and cooperation. When we laugh with another, we enfold that person in our loving, reach out with caring, understanding and support. That in itself may be one of the most profound expressions of healing energy of which we are capable...laughing together can be a time of intimacy and communion, a time when we come forward, fully present and touch into each other's human-ness and vulnerability.

A mother of a teenager discovered that when her child attacked her verbally it was in a sense best to step out of the way and let the angry words ride by. She further discovered that a touch of humor, if done in the spirit of compassion, helped to eliminate the attacks all together. Here are some examples:

TEENAGER:	MOTHER:
"I hate you!"	*"You're just saying that to make me feel better."*
"I'm going to run away from home!"	*"Can I come with you?"*
"It's not my turn!"	*"You have been so wonderful this week, I'm letting you have an extra turn."*
"You're the meanest mother in the whole world!"	*"Actually not, but I did make the semi-finals this year."*

When a parent can laugh at themselves, it shows a strong sense of self-confidence. By laughing at ourselves and our own mistakes and weaknesses, we are helping our children laugh at themselves and their own mistakes.

I remember so well a little play the girls performed for Barry and I one rainy Sunday afternoon. Rami played the mama and Mira was daddy. It was wonderful to see them act out in such a cute way how Barry and I parent them. We were enjoying the play immensely until the girls started to act out a rather uptight scene that occurred perhaps once a week. I held my breath and wondered how Barry would respond. In the scene Mama comes to the kitchen to begin making breakfast, joined by Rami and Mira (who are unseen due to the lack of actresses). The three scurry around the kitchen and in their hurry one of them spills a small amount of water or juice on the kitchen floor. When finished the three leave the kitchen to get dressed for the day.

Daddy then hurries into the kitchen to make a thermos of herb tea for his day at the medical clinic. He is dressed in good clothes and stocking feet (we don't wear shoes in our house since they are usually muddy from living in the country). "Who spilled water on the floor?!," yells the daddy. "Now my only pair of clean matching socks is all wet!" Mama, Rami and Mira slowly enter, guilty once again. Scene ends.

Mira had done such a good job portraying Barry in that scene that I waited to see his response. Barry is quite sensitive about his feet. Suddenly I heard a slight giggle which built and built until it became deep, rolling laughter. Barry fell to the floor laughing hysterically. The girls were thrilled and jumped on top of him and soon we were all laughing together about something that previously was very serious. Mira then announced, "Daddy I'm going to call you "Mr. Feety." The name has stuck and now whenever that same uptight scene is repeated, (which it infrequently is now. Barry purchased a pair of slippers.) Rami or Mira will lovingly call out, "There goes Mr. Feety again!" Laughter than replaces the uptightness.

If you are too busy to laugh, you are too busy.

ANONYMOUS

nineteen

A Father's Tenderness

by Bill Knight-Weiler

My son can dish out a solid punch—for a 20 month old—yet is extremely gentle and cuddly, content to hug and be hugged. Our child-rearing goal as peace-conscious fathers is to turn sluggers into huggers. Children, as was depicted in "Pinochio", are challenged by good and bad influences on their path of growing up. On which side of the fence they end up may be determined by the guidance of fathers. Dad can train his children to be peacemakers by (1) modeling gentleness (2) treating sons and daughters equally (3) practicing non-violent discipline at home and (4) demonstrating a respectful attitude towards work.

Traditionally, instilling peaceful ways has been the mother's job. Far too often, in raising her sons, she could not compete against a father who desired to raise warriors, and against a society in which courage and esteem were crowned only in battle, and in which mental and physical preparation for war was a cornerstone of "proper" education. Although civilization has progressed to a degree, today's father faces a stiff challenge from present-day American society, as it prods boys into macho men complete with the latest camouflage uniforms and even G.I. Joe cereal. Instead, we need to create a new American way which sees gentleness as strength and non-violent actions as manly. We men can learn from the Chinese who say, "Water conquers by yielding; it never attacks, but always wins the last battle. The sage who makes himself as water is distinguished for his humility; he embraces passivity...and conquers the world."

One way to pass the peace pipe is for fathers to hug their children, especially their sons, frequently and not just when they're tiny. Today, such overt expressions of love and caring must replace yesterday's angry switch and withheld affection.

Practicing non-violent discipline is essential. The use of force is a far too easy way of administering punishment. It generally replaces forethought and counseling. When force is threatened, the child views the father as someone to be feared. A child's tender loving feelings will have difficulty surviving that fear. Children are easily frightened, and Dad, being physically large, is already imposing. The other day my four-year old burst into tears when she thought I would "break her muscles" by swinging her.

Another way of waging peace is through raising children as human beings rather than stereotyping son and daughter roles. We don't differentiate their basic needs by feeding one lasagna and the other lima beans, so why do we differentiate when it comes to their higher needs? Both need unconditional love, spiritual guidance, and careful discipline.

Fathers invariably steer their sons toward sports, which is fine, but daughters should also be included. Sports can be used as an opportunity for learning a sense of sportsmanship, fair play, and losing gracefully.

Lastly, through a father's approach to his daily work, he has an excellent opportunity to influence his child's attitude toward service and constructive achievement. He should make frequent positive mention of his job, and be careful of subtle innuendos such as "Today's my day off—I'm sure glad I don't have to work!" One's work life should not be viewed as an existence separate from life at home, but as a continuum. Coming home each day, Dad has the

Barry and Mira.

potential of bringing with him an olive branch or bringing home
thorns. Fathers don't need to bury every hatchet before opening the
front door, as good and bad experiences from the day should be
shared with family members; nevertheless, creating a generally
positive work attitude will spill over into a better home life and
vice-versa.

Fathers must now take their place alongside mothers in bringing
peace to the home. It is a responsibility which can be joyfully
undertaken. When there is peace at home, there is peace in one part
of the world. Our dear children are in our homes for only a moment
in time. When they fling the door open, it should not be as a
dandelion seed which is being freed to go wherever the wind blows,
but rather as a dove, whose flight is his own and whose mission is
magnificently clear.

Children are even as a branch that is fresh and green; they will grow up in whatever way ye train them. Take the utmost care to give them high ideals and goals, so that once they come of age, they will cast their beams like brilliant candles on the world.

'ABDU'L-BAHA

twenty

Awakening the Goddess

by Emily Sanford

Emily Sanford is the minister of the Unity Temple of Santa Cruz. She is a mother of five grown children and grandmother of seven.

I first arrived at the Unity Temple and into Emily's acquaintance in a rather embarrassing way. Day-light savings time occurred and, as usual, I was unaware of it. Several friends had urged me to come to this church on this particular Sunday. Since Barry was working in the hospital, I went by myself with the children. I was totally unaware that I was an hour late as I struggled toward a seat in the front of the large church, carrying baby Mira with six-year-old Rami holding tight to my skirt. Finally, I plopped down making more noise than I would have wished. Emily looked at me with a mixture of humor and love and then said to the congregation, "Close your eyes for the final prayer." My face reddened as I realized my mistake.

I thought of all the effort it had taken me to get there. I was starting to get upset at myself for my mistake, but the feeling of Emily's prayer soothed me like a forgiving mother would her child. She has continued to nourish my soul ever since and is a beautiful example of all that she speaks.

The following is a brief excerpt of a talk she gave to a group of thirty mothers in our home. The feeling of her words still lives in my heart.

The Goddess is the spirit of the mother within each one of us, men *and* women. An aspect of her presence is referred to in almost every religion in the world. Her history goes back even farther than that of a patriarchal God. All people are drawn to her. Even the strongest male societies have been drawn to the Mother-Goddess. She is the flow of life. Our intuitive nurturing and giving nature comes from her. She is the reason for the undying connection between children and parents.

There are so many details in caring for a child, so much that has to be done. Parents easily get caught up in the doing of it, rather than being aware of the nurturing part of it. Parents don't have to be constantly concerned about their child. The energy that flows between parent and child is what is most important. That energy truly nurtures a child. It unveils the knowledge latent within the parent of how to care for the child. There is a big difference between being a nourishing parent and being a martyr. The martyr sees all the work to be done. The nourishing parent is more concerned with the energy flow of love.

Once you open up to this energy flow, you can have it for all children. All children can become your children. When this really begins to work for humanity, the whole world will change. We do this by totally accepting our womanhood, our Goddess-nature.

When the nurturing, receptive, and intuitive part of us is developed and we allow that depth of connection to go forth to another human being in the way we do to our children, then we are doing what we came here to do. The Goddess has tremendous power. We are afraid of so much power. We don't know how to let it move forth. Fully loving our children and being aware of the inner connection—this will show us the way.

There is a tremendous need for us as women in this twentieth century to open ourselves and allow our power of love to flow forth to bless the world. May the Goddess within each one of us bless the whole of humanity.

I choose you now dear child
As you have chosen me.
You flutter softly
             'neath my heart
Our mingled blood
             flows as the sea...

Deep-rooted is my love for thee
Strong, supple as a Spirit-tree...
             Blessed be!

The secret song we share
Resounds beyond this sphere
Our auras blend in
             rainbow hues
Our love, our paths
             co-mingle here...

We meet, again, dear child of Light
As we have met before in Life...
             Blessed be!

EMILY SANFORD

twenty-one

Single Parenting

Single parenting is a reality of our time. The problem we tend to have is one of judgement. It is often easy to look upon single parents as failures in the same way that we look upon divorces as failures. This is often far from the truth. The path of life does not require us to always remain in a relationship. Relationships are powerful tools for our spiritual growth, yet many times we will be called upon to learn lessons by ourselves.

As Joyce and I delve deeper into the truths of parenting, we feel the beauty of single parenting as well. We believe that the souls of unborn children know exactly what they're getting themselves into. Who are we to deny that perhaps certain children are best raised by one parent. We certainly have seen single parents do an extraordinary job of loving and raising their children. We've also seen couples all but ignore their children.

If a single parent is committed to walking the path of consciousness, if he or she is committed to drawing out the highest soul-gifts of their chidren, then what better situation could a child be in?

Single Mothering

With the increase of divorce in this country, more and more women are finding themselves raising their children without the help of the father. Many of my friends and at least one third of all the women who attend my mothers' workshops and come to me for counseling are single mothers. I have grown to respect and admire these women, as well as understand several common threads that weave among them.

I feel that these women have in some way chosen a particular path of mastery in their lives. Single mothering demands not only the softness and compassion of the mother, but also the power and strength of the father. Many women tend to be either too feminine or too masculine in their approach to life. Children of single mothers need their parent to be balanced, allowing both their female and male qualities to be expressed. When women accept this great challenge in their lives with gratitude, they are walking the path of self-mastery and love. Truly then they shine with both the light of the mother and the father as a beacon for all.

I have seen two common pitfalls that single mothers must overcome to achieve this quality of mastery in their life. This first is the feeling of self-pity. I have seen women wallow in negative thoughts about how hard their job is, feeling that they are much less fortunate than their friends who have husbands to help; feeling they are not good enough to be married; even feeling punished by a difficult task because of their unworthiness. Negative thoughts and an attitude such as this surrounds a person in a cloud of self-pity. It is hard then to see the light and goodness of the situation through this cloud. If we could see all our difficulties as gifts which bring strength and mastery into our being, we could then be grateful. Gratitude then gives us clearer vision of the higher purpose for our lives.

Another stumbling block for a single mom is the unwillingness to forgive the father of her children. Carrying a grudge or negative feelings about the father, directly blocks a woman from allowing the purity of her own father energy to flow forth to her children.

A good friend of mine, Karen Backinoff, who is pictured here with her two boys, shared her story of ten years of single parenting:

When she was sixteen her mother died, which was a great shock to her. At age eighteen she met a man who was not much older. They became married but the relationship was difficult. After three years she became pregnant. It was while pregnant with her first child that she started to feel close to God and to acknowledge the strengthening presence of a Divine Mother.

Karen, Ian and Tim.

During her eighth month of pregnancy her husband announced that he had fallen in love with another woman. At first she felt devastated, but later the birth of her son allowed her to feel joy again. Then she felt how deeply she loved her son and this gave her the courage to ask her husband to leave so she could fully devote herself to caring for young Ian.

One month later, her husband came back and after a year she became pregnant again. A week after the birth of her second son, her husband announced that he wanted to meditate in the desert for several months. He said he couldn't handle being a father. When he left this second time, Karen knew that they were never to be together again. She described a beautiful walk she took in the moonlight with two-week-old Tim and two-year-old Ian. She experienced a profound surrender to single mothering as her path to God. A beautiful peace setted upon her as she accepted this path with gratefulness. Just at that moment little Ian reached up to take her hand and Karen knew that she did not walk alone—she would receive much help and strength from God and her two boys.

In that moment Karen had overcome the stumbling block of self-pity and had turned her face towards acceptance and gratefulness.

Three years later she became very sick. Another obstacle had to be overcome along her road of single mothering. She lay in bed for two weeks. Even though medical doctors were treating her for pneumonia, she felt strongly it was something else. She was not getting better.

Finally, she went to a counselor who helped her through the use of guided imagery. She realized she was still carrying deep resentment towards her husband, who never showed the slightest interest in the boys. By holding on to resentment and anger toward him, she found herself resenting the male part of herself as well. She felt her male side asking to be acknowledged, and to be married to her female side; asking not only for forgiveness of her husband but for all men. When she was able to forgive her husband and divorce him, her health returned.

Now she was able to let the Father-God flow through her. For the first time she began consistently disciplining her boys. She started jogging and getting her body in shape, and started her own career. For the first time in her life she felt whole and fulfilled. She shared with me:

> Much of that time I was very lonely and always longed for a true mate. As there wasn't one I had to learn to find another kind of strength to help me. I learned to call upon my Heavenly Father to be the head of our household and also to allow myself to be comforted and nourished by my Heavenly Mother. This learning process began with accepting the feminine *and* masculine aspects within me and then integrating them into an internal marriage in my psyche.

Several years later Karen and I sat talking. Things were going well for her and the boys were developing beautifully. She wanted to be in a relationship and held the happy dream of a loving marriage, yet whenever she came close to fulfilling this dream, something would happen and the man would leave. She felt there was something within her that was still unclear and was pushing men away. We started talking about the father of the boys. Though she had done much work on forgiving him, she still did not feel love for him and so the forgiveness was not complete. I asked her to recall her earliest memories of when they were falling in love. Tears came to her eyes and her face softened. I then asked her to look upon his abandonment of her not as a rejection but as a part of his immaturity. Suddenly she was seeing her first husband through the compassionate eyes of a mother who understands when a boy is afraid to become a man. Her face lit up with understanding and love. Her forgiveness was now complete. I asked her to hold that feeling of understanding and love in her heart for all men.

Soon after, she met Steve and eventually they were married. True forgiveness of her first husband had opened the door for a deep and lasting relationship with her second husband. The self-mastery she learned in the ten years of single mothering brought rich gifts of love, compassion, and wisdom to her second marriage. In her own words:

> I feel it is very important for parents to respect the inner being of the Child. Encourage them and tell them often how good they are and how much you love them.

> Try to give your children a positive feeling about their father— they must feel good about both sides of the family. Arrange for the children to be cared for and nurtured by uncles or male friends, as this will help balance the needs of the child for a father figure.

> May we mothers have inner reliance on God's love and Guidance. May we take time alone to uncover and integrate the qualities of the opposite sex within ourselves. May we develop an open devotional heart and forgiveness, for we are all children and make mistakes which our Cosmic Parents can heal, if we let them.

> A verse which helped me in my single parenting is: "As one whom his mother comforted. So will I comfort you." Isaiah 66:13.

I have known women who remained single mothers throughout the growing-up years of their children. These children felt the dedication, love and self-mastery of their mothers and grew into well-adjusted men and women. Single mothering is not an easy path, but with the right attitude it can transform a woman into a powerful, wise and compassionate channel of God's love.

Single Fathering
by Brian Graham

Although single mothers far outnumber single fathers, we know men who are dedicating their lives to fathering. A dear friend, Brian Graham, is an example. The editor of "The Science of Thought Review" in England and author of CLARE CAMERON: A HUMAN AND SPIRITUAL JOURNEY (London: Werner Shaw Ltd, 1984), he is a father first and foremost. He knows this to be his most important job in life. His busy life is scheduled around the needs of his now sixteen-year-old son, Kaladin. While visiting him, we were deeply moved whenever he spoke about his son, so much caring was expressed in his words.

Perhaps Brian's greatest strength as a father is to see the humorous side of every situation. We were first introduced to Brian in a rather fumbling way. He originally wrote to us because of THE SHARED HEART. We had felt such a strong connection with him through our letters and traveled to his small English town of Bosham to meet him and do a workshop at his home. The last part of the journey was by train. As it was late at night and we seemed to be just abut the only ones on the train, we decided to treat ourselves to a short ride in the first class section. We prepared ourselves for our first meeting with Brian who would be waiting at the next stop for us. Secretly we hoped we'd make a good first impression.

Suddenly, the train stopped. Being new to the British railways we couldn't figure out how to open the door. Frantically, Barry flung our suitcase out the window. Brian, who had been the only one waiting at the station, was amazed to see the train stop and a large blue suitcase tumble out of the window while the train started up once again. His first incredulous thought was, "Barry and Joyce, I really had no idea you looked like that!" Fortunately the train finally stopped for us and we fell into his arms laughing. It is with the same sense of joy that he fathers his son and all who come to him for counsel.

Being a father has taught me most of all about loving and remaining in touch with the spontaneous flow of my inner child.

I have two daughters, Lalena (12 years old) and Sasha (9 years old) and one son, Kaladin (16 years old).

My marriage broke-up in 1980 and my daughters at present live with their Mother and her new husband in Australia; my son lives here in England with me. All of the children have coped very well with the difficulties resulting from divorce and both their mother and I remain close friends. Although their mother and I live separate lives, the children know that the love from each of us remains the same. It is the unbroken strength of that love which has helped them to integrate all that has arisen out of the divorce. Though the girls now live 12,000 miles apart from Kaladin and myself, we all know that the love we share contains no distance and transcends any passage of time.

Being a Father has given me so much joy. I am certainly not a perfect parent (I have never met one!) though I have felt it important to give as much as I can to the children. I feel the greatest thing we can give our children is our time. I have taken time to play with them, swim with them, climb trees, dress up, laugh, sing, read bedtime stories, walk in nature, picnic, bathe together, hold their hand at the dentist. I take them on picnics, to the pantomime, fun-fairs, playground and have many other adventures. I myself have become a child again to fully participate in so many different activities with them. I have comforted them in their sorrows and rejoiced with them in their happiness.

I have always found it so important to be honest with them. I have taught them to pray to the God within and established a belief in the continuity of life after death.

Children are so often old souls in young bodies and I have tried to acknowledge that reality in my relationship with them. I have found the need to teach them truth and the difference between right and wrong, and to have compassion for all living things.

They too have been my teachers in so many ways. So often I have found them to be much more wise and intuitive than I thought. Their joyful spontaneity has so often broken asunder my own rigid patterns of thought and behaviour, and their sensitivity has so often touched me deeply. Just before their mother and I separated and I was going through a lot of inner turmoil, my eldest daughter, Lalena (then about 6 years old) gently placed the palm of her hand on my face and looked deeply and with such compassion into my eyes. It was a look of, "I understand how you are feeling, Daddy." Such empathy from one so young—I felt so comforted.

Children love so completely and they so much need to know that we truly love them. I have found it very important to express my Love to them, not just in the giving of gifts or my time, but to actually hold them and say, "I love you."

I have also found that it is the continuity of fair discipline which has helped my children find a measure of security. There have been many times when I have found it necessary to discipline them because of naughty behaviour. As I let them know that I will not accept unruly behaviour, I also emphasise that I do love them. I have learned that it is so important that a child does not feel rejected for themselves, but they need to learn that certain kinds of behaviour will not be accepted. There is a big difference between rejecting wrong behaviour and rejecting the child himself (or herself).

I have learned that touching, hugging and snuggling each other is also so important. Such vital expressions of our care and love for each other make us all feel so good. Sometimes a heart-felt hug can say so much more than hundreds of words.

My son, Kaladin, has been living here with me for well over a year now. He is a strong-willed adolescent with a fiery temper at times who

Brian and Kaladin.

needs discipline but also a lot of love. I hope that I give him both. Whenever possible, his needs come before my own. I don't go out much as I like him to know that I am around should he need me. I take an interest in his school work and other activities and I encourage him to achieve set goals and to put the best he can into all that he does. When he does well at school or in other activities I tell him how proud I am of what he has accomplished. Even at 16, I tell him that I love him. I sometimes get mad and shout at him when he doesn't do something he should have. In many ways I try to draw the best out of him and help him to become more aware of all the potential he has within himself. Though I do quite a lot for him as both a mother as well as a father, I also do my best to encourage him to develop his own independence. I wrestle with him and have water fights. I teach him to care about people and all forms of life. I have realised that he learns more by what I am, the way I live my life, the way I react and deal with things, than he does by what I may "preach" to him. He is rebellious at times and he reminds me so often of what a pain I must have been to my parents at his age!

Amongst other things, I clean and polish his shoes for him every morning. How much he appreciates this I do not know, but to me it is important. To me it is an acknowledgement of my giving in humility to him, serving the Being that he is. It is also part of a tradition. My father always cleaned my shoes for me every day. It means a lot to me that my father did such a thing for me though I didn't express my gratitude at the time. Whether or not this small act says anything to Kal does not matter—it is important to me to do it.

We also watch movies together, go for walks with Arwen our dog and tell each other jokes. If I feel I have wrongly reacted to him about something, I apologise and tell him that I do not always get things right. Recently when a friend joined us for dinner, our guest asked Kaladin what it was like bringing up his father? He smiled wryly and said, "difficult". We all had a good laugh about that. Sometimes when I have my rather zany periods he tells me that I'll be all right if I keep taking the "tablets"!

His sense of humour amuses me. Sometimes, when I get stuck in certain patterns of thought, I tell him that he has to be patient with me.

I like to think that we have a caring and healthy relationship. Though he may not be aware of it, he continues to teach me many things. I am firm with him when I feel it is appropriate. I feel he needs a firm discipline at times to establish his own boundaries. He is slightly taller than me now and, when I look up at him I sometimes think, who is teaching who? I learn a lot from his enthusiasm and from his consuming, creative interests.

I love being a father. It is not easy at times. Being a parent is an on-going learning process which I hope will make us both more integrated and whole. It is a big responsibility to be very honest about myself and to be willing to make changes in the way I handle things at times...to give more of myself and to love more.

twenty-two

Growing with Teenagers

by Qahira Qalbi

Qahira is a poet with a marvelous sense of humor. Her life is now devoted to traveling and teaching the Sufi message. Her father was the personal secretary to Hazrat Inayat Khan. Both parents helped to spread Sufism in the United States. Qahira was their only child and was raised in a deeply spiritual environment.

She and her husband Tansen have six children; their youngest daughter is now sixteen. Recently she has been leading camps and programs for teenagers.

Our favorite memory of Qahira is from a summer we spent together at a meditation camp in the French Alps. For three weeks we endured hard driving rains and snow. Most of the sixty campers had continually wet feet, and many were developing runny noses and coughs. Qahira's smile and inner sense of joy were like a ray of sunshine warming all of our hearts.

The teachings of Love may not always be gentle,
but the one with a gentle heart
will always be a teacher of Love.

One beautiful spring Southern California morning on awakening years ago, the wind seemed to fill my room and it was saying over and over again, faster and faster,

"Say 'Yes' to the Universe!"

"Say 'Yess' to the Universe!"

"Say 'Yesss' to the Universe!"

Faster and still faster came the sounds—like a freight train and I heard myself saying aloud, "all right! all right! I will, I will!!!"

Now, before this awakening, I wasn't at all a negative person; in fact, pretty positive, considering we had six children, assorted chickens, roosters, cats, dogs, rats, birds, and 100 avocado trees! But I must say, after the wind incident, I found myself saying "Yes!" to so many more things that my teenagers were asking:

"Mom, can I have watermelon instead of supper tonight?" "Sure, that sounds like a great idea; sometimes I'm not that hungry either."

"Mom, is it O.K. if I go to a slumber party at Lorraine's Friday night?" "That sounds like a lot of fun. Do you want to bring something for supper?"

"Can I borrow the keys to the car?" "No problem; fill it with gas and be home at a reasonable hour; or give me a quick call if there's a problem. Oh, can you use some extra money?" (That'll blow 'em away every time!)

Why not?...Why not!! Saying "Yes" is such a relief, instead of a string of constant "No's" because as guardians we are supposed to play some role as "The Great Controller." That role so often leads to rebellion and leaving home as soon as possible.

Now, you must know I don't advocate *never* saying "No". I

remember a real "No" arose inside me when my 15-year old son asked to go to a friend's party. I really wanted to say "yes", but it wouldn't come out.

"Is his mother and father going to be at home? "Yes". "Do you know if there'll be drugs or alcohol at the party?" "No, I don't think so." "Well, something doesn't feel right; do you mind if I call his folks?" "It's O.K. with me."

I found out that the boy's parents were going out of town for the weekend, and didn't know anything about the party.

So, "no" has a proper place in our vocabulary; but not as much as we tend to use it. And when "No" is few and far between, it is heard loud and clear and often not argued with, because, "Yes" has been such a healing bond and vote of confidence to the budding, young psyche.

The word discipline is born of the word disciple, and when a human being is born, discipleship begins, or maybe, continues. To the wise, the state of discipleship is an attunement throughout life.

When the age of adolescence arrives, the state of discipleship intensifies. The spirit is that in us which is *very* living, and in no other age group does this "livingness" come forth with as much energy, combined with high idealism, as in the Tremendous Terrific Teens...hereafter called the TTT's!

Far from any thought of bringing spirituality to these treasured, young-adult children, the adult companion of this age group can best harmonize with them by listening. Do we really know how to listen? If we think that waiting patiently for our turn to speak is listening; if we think that composing our thoughts, our arguments for the next opening of our mouth is listening; if we think stony silence with no caring acknowledgment is listening; then, we are ignorant of the Art of Listening.

As adults, we have accumulated many years of treasured ideas and concepts about ourselves and about life. In the questioning, searching adolescent, we find "ready ground" for transplanting our seedlings of thoughts, many of which, unfortunately, suffer from root-rot or get so condensed and entangled that they choke.

What does this "ready ground" *really* need when we think about cultivation? Certainly it needs nourishment; the nourishment of: the grounded security of acceptance, the water of compassion, the fire

Qahira, Tansen and family.

of enthusiasm, and the fresh air of freedom. Earth, water, fire, air; just the elements all growth needs.

And *what* is being nourished? Not transplanted seedlings from our own soil, but the new and vital seeds within each TTT. These seeds came with the package. They have all the potential of magnificent brilliance and beauty which our own seeds have. They have, of course, been sprouting forever, but now the Age of Adolescence calls for special care and wisdom on the part of the gardener—or guardian.

Sunshine, rain, wind, fire, birds and bees, all play important roles in deciding how these seeds will grow—or if they will ever sprout at all.

The right amount of all these in the form of encouragement, listening, and applause, coax the sprouting process. Too much of these factors, in the form of criticism, ridicule, and indifference, cause each seed to shrivel up and die, until finally the ground becomes barren.

We are not talking about someone else in this process, but rather about another aspect of ourselves. What does that mean? Could it be that we are indeed so inter-related that these precious TTT's are the continuation of our own being? Is it possible that what we ourselves could not bring forward as vital, living action in our own lives, is now given a chance to come forth again?

Of course, it's true. We are a continuum of all our ancestors who have passed on, and the link to all beings yet to come. Personally, I never believed that "opportunity only knocks once"; to me it knocks again and again and again—only in different guises!

How do we teach spirituality to our TTT's? Not only do we *not* have to drag them to our churches, our meditation classes and our yoga lessons, but *if we listen to them,* they will help *us* evolve fresh, new forms and ways to put spirituality back into *our* own lives. They, in fact, can recharge us with ideas for really living! For instance, has a TTT ever told you:

"The feeling of coming down that ski slope was so fantastic! I felt like an eagle flying and like I was one with everything!" (could this be the peak experience for which we meditate for years?)

"Mom, the dune-buggy rolled over and over after hitting the embankment, and I didn't even have time to think; but when it stopped and we turned it over again, it was great to keep on going. Boy, am I exhausted!" (Perhaps here, a lesson in daring and courage and persistence which we hope will be inspired in us through studying the lives of great saints and masters.)

"The itching from this poison oak is driving me crazy!" And Dad says, "Are you going back there to hike again?" "Oh, sure, it's so beautiful in those mountains, and diving into that waterhole without clothes on is a terrific (actually the word these days is 'rad') feeling! (Can this experience of freedom...despite the poison oak...be what we long to recapture from our youth and reawaken in our adulthood?)

Nature (and what is natural) is the finest environment we can give young people. Classrooms as well as holy places all play their part in spiritual training and must not be neglected but if we can nurture their spiritual seeds in a setting of natural beauty, in a climate of listening love, we, the parents, will find that *we* are the disciples of these Tremendous, Terrific Teens, and in truth they have come onto the planet to remind us of the Living Deity by their beauty, freshness, vitality and faith.

Our best guideline may come from the thought of the Sufi master, Hazrat Inayat Khan:

There is One Holy Book, the sacred manuscript of Nature, which alone can enlighten the reader.

If as a guardian we have gone with our young child to explore in Nature, to be awed by the simple beauty of the worm and butterfly; if we have *listened* well, rather than teaching and preaching; if we have poured many "Yes's" on their hearts as well as a few well-placed "No's", honoring their intelligence and natural wish to please and yet explore; we can then safely and with confidence free our adolescent eaglettes to the mountains, deserts and oceans of this planet without us tagging along. And they will return with spirituality such as we have seldom seen.

The key is trust....trust in the inherent goodness of TTT's, their occasional mistakes in judgement soothed by the love of our understanding, their doubts and fears evaporated by the light of our insight; and their sometimes-lack-of confidence bolstered by our faith in the human process of growth through achievement.

Let us hail these beautiful people; let us humbly teach them and learn from them, and then go forward as their respected companions on the path of human life, which gratitude alone will enrich for all of us.

twenty-three

Schooling

Our highest endeavor must be to develop free human beings, who are able of themselves to impart purpose and direction to their lives.

RUDOLF STEINER

Real education consists in drawing the best out of yourself. What better book can there be than the book of humanity.

GANDHI

The real purpose of education is to nurture and guide the soul to blossom in its own time and space as it pursues its destiny.

MURSHIDA VERA J. CORDA

The preschool years are not the time to teach reading or math. We should use life's most impressionable years to teach life's most important lesson—how to be happy!

LINDA AND RICHARD EYRE
TEACHING CHILDREN JOY

In the early years of children's lives, our highest responsibility is to expand their sense of wonder and joy about life, to bring forth their innate creativity and imagination.

Academic excellence may come, but in the child's time—not ours. David Elkin, in his book, *THE HURRIED CHILD*, describes the dangers of forcing a child to grow up too soon. Pushing academics before a child is ready can retard the child's emotional development.

I once saw in counseling a twenty-five year old woman who might be described as a genius. Her parents had taught her to read and write by age four. She went to a private school on the east coast which excelled in academics. Her developed intellect allowed her to skip several elementary grades so she graduated from high school at age fifteen. She was admitted to one of the finest women's colleges in the east and graduated in three years. By age twenty-one she had a doctorate in mathematics and found a prestigious job. Her parents were very proud of her. She had excelled in academics, but never-the-less she was suffering. Her emotional development had been severely retarded. She felt lost and empty inside, knowing only her intellect as God. Her body had aged considerably from years of tension and stress. She sought out almost daily massages for relaxation. It might take this woman a lifetime to catch up on the emotional and spiritual lessons that she missed as a child.

Nothing is so disillusioning today as talking to numerous college graduates who have spent five years or more in higher education and still do not know who they are or where they are going.

MURSHIDA VERA J. CORDA

Rami went to a Waldorf School for kindergarten. She entered into a magical world and had a delightful time learning of gnomes and color fairies, acting out Snow White, and playing house. The summer before first grade, I investigated a few local schools in Santa Cruz. I found one private school I liked which was close to our home. The principal who interviewed me was in disbelief that Rami didn't know the alphabet, pre-reading skills, and early math. She suggested that Rami repeat kindergarten and be tutored so that she would be at kindergarten level. I was really shocked at how early academics was pushed. I remembered my own carefree kindergarten years at a country school. Though a long distance from home, Rami returned to the Waldorf School for three more years. There she was allowed to develop academically at her own pace. Her teacher always praised her abilities, rather than criticizing her weaknesses. In many ways, Waldorf and other similar forms of education are ideal because they allow the integration of academic, emotional and spiritual development.

If children learn slowly, with plenty of time to reflect upon what they have experienced, they seem on the surface to be behind other children who are learning facts, facts, and more facts. However, when the teenage years are over, the children who have integrated their experiences as they went along keep learning and growing because they have never tired of learning, while their companions, dizzy with facts, begin to avoid learning, and only want to slip into a welcomed unconsciousness as a relief from all those years of being forced to be too awake too soon. The one child builds a high tower, impressive to look at, but too quickly constructed and unstable because of its narrow foundation. The other builds a pyramid, which seems for years to be going nowhere, but long after the tower has been destroyed by the fierce winds of life, the pyramid is still rising, finally ascending high above all other structures, a monument of lasting strength and beauty.

LAWRENCE WILLIAMS
HOW TO RELEASE YOUR CHILD'S
NATURAL GENIUS

In choosing a school for your child be certain that the teacher cares more for your child as a whole person than for his academic development. There are beautiful, dedicated holistic teachers in both private and public schools. With a little diligence the right one will be found. Barry strongly disliked his first grade experience in the public school. His teacher only cared that the students all conform to standards and learn the academic subjects. He withdrew and did very poorly in school. He was hardly noticed and received poor grades. His second grade teacher cared for each student as a human being first, and secondly their academic performance. Barry blossomed and began to enjoy school and learning.

When children are attending public schools, parents need to be careful to balance their child's left and right brain development. They need to balance the school's push for academics with creative and imaginative outlets and spiritual inspiration at home.

If a child's learning pace is slower than what is expected, he or she can be made to feel inferior in school, and needs the support and encouragement from the parents. Some children are just not ready to read until they are older. Rudolf Steiner, whose inspiration started Waldorf Education, and Albert Einstein are beautiful examples, as they did not learn to read until after the age of ten. It is now thought that up until that time they were too busy formulating their own creative thinking process to be concerned about reading other people's ideas. A friend's nine-year-old son had been passionately interested in science since the age of four. He can read words such as hydrogen and oxygen, but is unable to read other simple elementary words and is tested on a first grade level. Fortunately his Montessori teacher understands his process of learning and helps him to fill his day with meaningful activities.

Parents need to be careful to not readily accept labels placed upon their child such as "slow learner", "border-line mentally retarded," or "learning disabled". A man I know was labeled as border-line mentally retarded in first grade. His mother would not accept the label. She felt that he was really very intelligent, with a keen interest in motors and machines. She never let him know that the school thought he was slightly retarded. This man did not learn to read or do mathematics until he was thirteen. At this age he suddenly became ready for academics and went on to become a genius in the field of engineering.

In the first three grades of school I did very poorly in academics. My teachers were very concerned about me. I once overheard my third grade teacher whisper to another teacher that I would probably fail third grade and perhaps never be able to learn very well. I know now that she had also told my parents the same thing. However, they believed in me and knew in their hearts that I was intelligent. My teacher's remark, when filtered through my parents strong belief in me, lost its power to affect me. By this time, I was poor in spelling, reading and math. My parents tried to encourage my strengths rather than dwell on my weaknesses. I used my vivid imagination to put on puppet shows and plays for neighborhood children. By fifth grade I was one of the top students in the class. The skill in puppetry that my parents encouraged me to develop served as such a valuable tool in my later work with disturbed children. I feel that if my parents had become affected by my teacher's negative comments, I also might have been affected. I might have been afraid to really try later on. By encouraging me to develop a talent, I developed not only a valuable skill for my profession, but also the self-confidence needed to blossom academically.

A parent's belief in their child's inherent greatness can carry children through many difficult situations in school—as well as life in general. Perhaps their belief, as well as a genuine interest and enthusiasm for all they are learning, is a parent's central responsibility in the education of their child.

Remember always that what you believe you will teach.

COURSE IN MIRACLES

An Experiment in Schooling

Rami, Barry, and I were happy with her Waldorf schooling, yet it was clear to us that she wanted to be home more. We saw so little of her because she was gone from eight in the morning until four in the afternoon, five days a week. On Saturdays she was usually tired and wanted to play quietly in her room. Our only real family day was Sunday. Thoughts would pass through my mind like, "I am missing a large part of her childhood," or "I wish I could be with her more."

One morning as we brought her to the carpool pickup point and watched her go off, Barry announced, "Next year I want us both to teach Rami. We hardly ever see her now." The idea of homeschool began to fill our minds. Rami, too, was very enthusiastic about the idea.

Fourth grade is now in our home. Barry squeezes out two mornings a week from his crowded schedule to teach Rami. He shifts the morning work to the evenings. Never having taught before, he is proving to be an excellent teacher. Usually I hear Rami giggling and laughing as Barry makes up little games to teach spelling words and math. They meditate together, hold each other, and for three hours twice a week are alone and growing very close because of this.

I have the two mornings that Barry takes Mira to playschool on his way to work. These two mornings a week with Rami are proving to be a precious and valuable time in my mothering. She really wants to learn, which makes teaching her a joy. Each morning before we begin our lessons, we close our eyes and visualize Rami's angel of learning. Her colors, according to Rami, are violet and yellow. Later during our lesson, if a problem seems too hard for Rami she closes her eyes and pictures her angel of learning or even just the colors. This opens up the non-linear, intuitive aspect of her intelligence, which then helps her to think in a more balanced way, to solve problems with less strain.

I was sitting on a chair reading a book. I stopped at a word. I didn't know it. I closed my eyes and prayed to my learning Angel. She told me what the word was, and she blessed me.

Rami and I end each home-school session with a meditation and then art. First we talk about God; then I share a thought or feeling and listen in awe as she adds her own ideas. Our meditation time is very short, sometimes just five minutes. Children receive pictures and inspirations so quickly. Rami draws what she has seen, and then writes her experience, combining creative writing, spelling, and cursive writing practice. This is our favorite time of the day. I learn so much from Rami about the nature of life and God.

Usually I have a lesson planned each morning. Many times my plans need to change and adjust to where Rami is in that moment. One morning she jumped out of bed, dressed quickly, made her bed and ran out of the house yelling to me, "Mama, a bird is calling to me." I watched as she ran out into the orchard below our house calling, "Birdie, birdie I hear you." Then she stood silently for a long time in front of a tree, laboriously building a nest for the bird. She returned to the house very radiant. That day's lesson, needless to say, centered on her whole experience that morning.

In addition to our work, talented friends are teaching her special subjects like ceramics, poetry, swimming, and violin. She enjoys the interest of other adults. We invite children over to our home and she also takes a few creative classes with other children. Rami's days are fulfilled and happy—and so are ours.

When I got up in the morning
I heard the birds singing. One
bird seemed to be colling to me. I
ran out to greet it. I stood very still
as it sang. I could hear him telling
me to always love birds and animals
and they will always love me too.

*What is most important and valuable about the home as a base for
children's growth into the world is not that it is a better school than
the schools but that it isn't a school at all. It is not an artificial
place, set up to make "learning" happen. It is a natural, organic,
central, fundamental human institution, one might easily and
rightly say the foundation of all other institutions.*

JOHN HOLT
TEACH YOUR OWN

Homeschool is proving to be a wonderful experience for our
entire family. Though there are difficult moments, as with anything,
the closeness we all feel as a family more than compensates. Never
having taught children before, I worried that I wouldn't do a good
job. I'm finding, however, that Rami is showing me exactly how she
is needing to learn. Our job as home teachers is simply to open the
doors to what is already latent in our child. A helpful home school
curriculum based on this concept comes from The Oak Meadow
School*.

Homeschool isn't for all families, nor is it for all children. There
are valuable lessons to be learned in a classroom working with other
children that can't be learned at home. My favorite memory is when
Rami was Eve in the class play, "Adam and Eve", and spoke before
the entire group of parents. What a victory that was for her. Mira
can't wait for her two school days each week. Being away from
home with four other children is serving as an important part of her
life right now. She is growing tremendously through the experience.

*Oak Meadow Publications, P.O. Box G, Ojai, CA 93023.

Rami may or may not want to return to her class next year, although she loves her school and class teacher very much. We parents need to listen to each child's desires as well as needs. Even if she returns to school for the rest of her education, this one year at home will have proved to be a strengthening experience for her whole life. It certainly has been for Barry and me.

As you teach so will you learn
If that is true, and it is true indeed,
do not forget that what you teach
is teaching you.

COURSE IN MIRACLES

Parents may want to try homeschool for a year or more. The bonding and closeness experienced with your child will be a gift to last a life time. Perhaps parents could homeschool one child at a time. Maybe you have a middle child who never received the individual attention that the others did. A year at home alone with mom or dad might prove so valuable to his or her awakening process.

Another idea for schooling is for several families to join together and share the responsibility of teaching their children. A group of five families in Northern California actually built their own little school for their combined twelve children. All of the parents participate in the education of the children. I also know of a very successful program where several families joined together and hired a teacher for the main subjects, while the parents brought in extra subjects.

We have learned that education is a continual process of listening to your own heart, believing in the inherent greatness of each child and allowing them situations where this greatness can come forth. We need to be willing to work hard and be flexible. If we stay in tune with our child's unfoldment process, we will find ourselves unfolding as well.

There was a time when pioneering teachers sought supporting parents. Today as often as not, it is pioneering parents who are calling out for the right teachers... We need more and more pioneering parents as well as pioneering teachers, parents who are not only sympathetic but who make themselves articulate for an education not only for their own children but for the generation to which their children belong.

FRANCIS EDMUNDS,
FOUNDER, EMERSON COLLEGE, ENGLAND

*Could I but kindle every man
With the Spirit of the Cosmos
That he might be a flame
And unfold his being's essence
As a flame!
Others would take water from the Cosmos
To quench that flame
And make all being
Watery and dull within.
Oh joy, to see the human flame
Burning brightly, even when at rest!
Oh bitterness, to see man like a thing,
Bound when he would be free.*

RUDOLF STEINER

twenty-four

Affirmations

With God's help I can do anything.

ABRAHAM LINCOLN

God is us.

KIRPAL, AGE 9

God is in our hearts.

CHERI, AGE 7

God is everywhere.

SOLOMON, AGE 8

*I think that God is everything and
can be whatever he wants.*

AMINA, AGE 9

God is always looking and we can't hide from Him.
He is even in plastic.

TACHINA, AGE 11

Through the use of affirmations, children can be taught at an early age to think positively. With each affirmation we can send a message or instruction deep within our unconscious mind. If a child is lovingly told often enough that he or she is a beautiful child of God, they will know the truth of it and will eventually begin to use the affirmation themselves. Parents can begin affirming positive thoughts for the child, which teaches them to affirm these same thoughts for themselves.

Each heartfelt affirmation we give our child is like planting deep in fertile soil a seed which will later take root and bear flowers and fruit. If we affirm the negative for our children by telling them "You are bad" or "You are mean and stupid", we are also planting seeds deep within their unconscious. These seeds will also root and grow and cause difficulties as they grow. An affirmation such as "You are so loving and giving", will bring forth such beauty within a child.

Giving a child an affirmation may be most effective while also touching them. Children receive so much through touch. The combination of gentle touching and a spoken affirmation can have a very valuable effect upon a child. When I was in nursing school, one of my friends did a careful study of pediatric nurses who worked with dying children. My friend noticed that a particular child would cry when attended by some nurses and not with others. She discovered that when a nurse took time before each procedure to gently talk to the child while gently stroking his body with her hands, then the child did not cry. When another nurse would also gently reassure the child but without the physical contact, the child usually cried. The physical touch was a powerful reinforcing factor which enabled children to more deeply receive the affirmation. Bedtime is often a wonderful opportunity to affirm the highest qualities of your children, all the while stroking and caressing their bodies.

A negative affirmation can likewise be reinforced when combined with physical contact. I once heard a story about a teenage boy who was unable to read. He was a very bright boy, who had an unexplainable reading block. Tutoring and extra help were in vain. Finally, his parents took him to a well known child psychiatrist. The doctor hypnotized the boy and guided him back to the point where he received the message that he could not read. The boy suddenly described sitting in his first grade class, struggling with a reading assignment. The teacher, who was in a very impatient mood, called upon him to read before the class. The boy was so scared to read out loud to everyone that he couldn't speak. The teacher walked over to him, put both of her hands upon his shoulders, and said in an exasperated tone, "You will never learn to read!" The combination of the affirmation with the physical contact had made such a deep impression upon his subconscious, that he had since been unable to read. Fortunately, the doctor was able to replace the negative affirmation with a positive one and to everyone's delight, the boy rapidly learned to read.

We hear so much nowadays about the use of affirmations for outer things—money, intellectual development, jobs, relationships, etc. Of far more importance is the affirming of inner qualities, such as the development of the child's heart. Telling the child "There is so much love pouring from your heart," will begin a momentum of opening their hearts to express unconditional love.

We can also begin from infancy to affirm the beauty of our child's body while touching and hugging them. Our bodies are all uniquely beautiful. We should all be proud of them. A child should not be taught to compare their body with others or to see their body as more or less beautiful. The beauty of each body is that there are no two totally alike. By saying, "Your body is so beautiful in every way," as you tenderly hug your little one, will create such a lovely thought-form for your child to carry throughout life. It will help if your son is the shortest in his class; your teenage girl develops facial skin problems; or if your child is handicapped in some way.

A parent can also affirm their child's inner power to overcome all worries, sickness and weakness. This affirmation can be phrased in a variety of ways according to the age of the child. One could say to a little child, "Your guardian angel is always protecting and guiding you." Affirmations of this nature allow the child to discover his or her higher consciousness. Through constant affirmation they learn to trust that they have a wonderful inner power which is always available to them.

Creative visualization can also be introduced at an early age. Simply have the child visualize a positive affirmation. Repeat this each evening and, if possible, several other times in the day. A child who is lonely could affirm, "I am a good friend," as she visualizes love pouring out from her heart to her classmates.

Each night before sleep, parents can visualize that their child will remember God's Presence throughout their life. We can use our inner eyes to "see" a radiant angel above our child's head with our child responding to that Presence. We can affirm and visualize ourselves becoming the fullness of parental love.

Ilse Klipper has a marvelous little book for children, entitled *MAGIC JOURNEY*. In it she tells seven short stories about people, fish, animals and birds. In each story the person or creature was helped in some way by repeating magic phrases. These phrases are: I am loved, I am good, I am happy, I am content, I am great, I am brave, and I am a friend. After reading this book together, Rami and I started to practice the magic words in everyday situations.

Once, while on a camping trip, a woman camped a quarter mile away from us had three lovely kittens with her. Mira was napping while Barry and I were writing nearby. Rami came and begged me to go with her to ask the woman if she could borrow a kitty for the afternoon. I explained that I couldn't, but that I would watch while she went by herself. Rami felt scared to go alone. Then we remembered the magic words "I am brave." She hesitatingly started off down the road repeating the words "I am brave, I am brave." A short while later she triumphantly returned with a kitty in her coat. She told me that every time she felt like running back she just repeated her magic words and they helped her to keep going. In these simple ways children teach themselves the valuable skill of positive affirmation.

Parents need to continually affirm for themselves and for their child that our planet is becoming ever more peaceful. In a recent workshop entitled *The Healing of Mothers*, one woman explained that she was afraid of having children for fear of the entire world blowing up. A woman who was newly pregnant with her first child burst out crying, saying that she feared the same thing. The rest of us, forty-eight women, all had at least one child under five. Ironically, none of us were worried about the world coming to an end. Those of us who live with a young child (who seems to carry the latest news of heaven in its aura!) are constantly reassured that the light and wisdom coming with these little ones will make this planet a much brighter place. God would not be sending so many pure and beautiful souls to earth, if there were not a pure and beautiful plan for them to help fulfill.

In a recent study of high school seniors, over half felt that they would not be able to live a full life due to nuclear war and the destruction of the planet. So much in the media seems to be pointing in this direction. If parents affirm to their children that peace is coming to the planet, the child will grow to trust this and will be reassured of the opportunity to live a full life. One of the most powerful ways to help make our planet a peaceful place is first to be peaceful ourselves and second to affirm the positive. Whatever it is we affirm, we are in that moment sending out a powerful energy which works toward the fulfilling of that affirmation.

Today is the International Day of Peace, the third Tuesday of every September. People all over the world are asked to respond by concentrating their thoughts towards peace. This morning we sat with the children, asked them to imagine a bright shining star, and see the entire planet bathed in the light of the star. Then we all affirmed that greater light and peace would be continually coming to our world.

God is the world.

ABRAHAM, AGE 7

Many people despair about conditions in the world and say they will never get any better. We can ourselves speak of what we have seen for the future of mankind—of a coming life which can only be described in earth language as celestial, when the light of the Sun of God is shining through men's faces, so that they live without sickness, pain or distress, a life which is harmonious and beautiful in every detail but still warm and human—where the fullest expression of the spirit can be given. Believe us if you can: nothing is too good to be true!

How can such a life ever dawn while humanity is as it is at present? My children, you do not know how rapidly the human family is now progressing. Wars shall cease. Untruth will fade away. There will be no more deception or illusion. Life will be lived from the centre of the Sun, from the heart of the Christ. The whole purpose of life on earth is the continued etherealisation of the planet. Do you know that there are planets in existence in your solar system which have become so spiritualised that they are invisible? These are planets of light; and this earth planet, very dark at present, is slowly quickening in vibration until it too will be a planet of light. This is where all of you have a great work waiting. Don't just listen to our words and forget them. Try to put into practice the truth of the Christ-thought, the Christ-life. Then you will be aiding in the creation of a brighter world. This dense matter, this darkness will gradually be dissolved.

So, my children, good thought, positive thought, loving thought—that is the way; for if you think positively, kindly and lovingly you must act so; because this is the spontaneous reaction to good thought. In the same way that thought affects action so it affects physical matter, quickening its vibration, so that eventually the whole earth will not only be beautiful to look at and live upon but it will be made of a finer, more delicate, more ethereal form of matter.

WHITE EAGLE

twenty-five

The Family Retreat

Kinship with all creatures of the earth sky and water was a real and active principle. For in the animal and the bird world there existed a brotherly feeling that kept the Lakota safe among them and so close did some of the Lakotas come to their feathered and furred friends that in true brotherhood they spoke a common tongue.

The old Lakota was wise. He knew that man's heart away from nature becomes hard, he knew that lack of respect for growing living things soon led to lack of respect for humans too. So he kept his youth close to its softening influence.

CHIEF LUTHER STANDING BEAR

Unlike the wise Lakota Indians, many of us "civilized" folk have gotten too far away from the "softening influence" of nature. This may be especially true for those of us who live in urban areas, but it is equally true for many country-dwellers. We all have a need for retreat—not running away, but a change in environment and simplification of life-style for a period of time. Many of us work

275

ourselves into ruts, becoming preoccupied with our daily work and lives. Time away in a natural setting can renew us, giving us a new vantage point from which to view our lives, to remember who we are—separate from our work and the roles we play.

Joyce and I regularly pack up our old camper and take off for the mountains with the children and dogs. We have found something magical about camping—not in sardine-can-like camp-grounds —but in far-from-everything secret wild places which we have discovered over the years. We have learned the beauty of the family retreat, living simply and very intimately with nature.

We feel a deep attunement with our brothers and sisters, the American Indians. These people knew and loved simplicity. They loved the fire. They saw it as releasing the sunlight locked into the dead wood for the purpose of warming themselves and cooking their food. They sat on the ground rather than chairs, for they felt best when in close contact with their Earth-Mother. They loved and spent as much time as they could in the sun, for they knew the sun was an instrument of the Great White Spirit, their Sky-Father. They ate simply and only as much as they needed. All of nature was treated with reverence and kindness; the soil and rocks as much as the plants and animals.

While camping, nature's simplicity works its magic on our whole family. Joyce and I touch back upon the roots of our love, letting ourselves be nourished by our Mother Earth and our Father Spirit. We find so much more time to be truly *with* Rami and Mira, without the seemingly endless distractions we busy ourselves with at home. It reminds me of Donovan's song inspired by St. Francis,

Brother Sun and Sister Moon,
I seldom see you
Seldom hear your tune,
Preoccupied with selfish misery.

Rami and Mira come into a deeper harmony with one another. If we come to a new place, one of the first things they do is seek out their own "power spot", a special boulder on which to climb and play games far beyond limited adult imagination; or a tiny ring of trees which instantly becomes a house, while branches are magically transformed into everything from kitchen stove to beds. They play for hours; their five year difference, which at home can loom significant, dissolves in the presence of earth, rocks and trees. Finally, just when Joyce and I have forgotten that we have children,

Mira goes camping.

we hear their joyful voices calling us. Then we go to them and are privileged to enter their world and witness their creation.

Once, while younger Mira was napping in the afternoon, Rami was walking past a pile of rocks. They seemed to call out to her. She sat down next to them and instantly each rock became a living being, and a whole drama unfolded in her imagination that lasted all afternoon. The "lead" rock had to learn about good and evil, and then conquer evil through the power of love alone, while the other rocks took their appointed places in destiny. I remember walking by, noticing Rami moving some rocks around, totally unaware of the fantastic drama of creation and life going on in front of my nose.

The famous American Indian mystic, Ohiyesa, says, "As a child I understood how to give; I have forgotten this grace since I became civilized. I lived the natural life, whereas I now live the artificial. Any pretty pebble was valuable to me then; every growing tree an object of reverence. Now I worship with the white man before a painted landscape, whose value is estimated in dollars!"

I am writing this at one of our favorite spots, close to the five thousand foot elevation on the western side of California's Sierra

Nevada Mountains. It is early September. We've been here two weeks, enduring everything *but* sunny, warm weather. Yesterday morning it even snowed on us. I am still hopeful for some warm late summer sunshine, as I look up into the sky and see yet another massive ominously gray cloud-system moving rapidly toward us, almost as if to say, "So you want warm sunny weather, do you. How 'bout some hail?"

Even the harsh weather has had a favorable effect upon our family, drawing us all closer to one another. The wind, the cold, the rain and snow all teach reverence and humility to us. Starting a campfire with wet wood presents a challenge, but all four of us team together. Even little Mira comes running down from the woods, a jubilant smile on her face as she shows me the dry pine needles she was able to find.

Similar to an individual retreat, the first few days are a time of adjustment. The simpler, quieter life-style brings up the stored tensions to the surface. We find we need more sleep initially. Sometimes we find ourselves a little more irritable, and our minds seem to be racing with every kind of thought. We might even wonder to ourselves, "What kind of retreat is this? I was better off at home!" But we need to weather this initial adjustment period. It is so much like an individual retreat. I remember so many of my own retreats. I used to do many more of them than I do now, but I still find them very useful at times in my life when my mind seems to be overly cluttered and "preoccupied with selfish misery." I would arrive at some special or sacred spot and initially seem to go crazy with almost totally uncontrolled thoughts and images. I remember once sitting on a mountain top viewing the whole world spread out below me, and being unable to stop thinking about details of my income tax preparation. It's at times like these that meditation techniques can be useful. I find conscious breathing techniques help me the most. I know so many of them that sometimes I have to be clever and make up a new one. Regardless, they help. They brought me through the craziness, the sleepiness, the irritability, and the judging and condemning of myself because of how crazy I was. Then I would break through my darkness into the light, which might start as a moment of forgiveness, or perhaps I would burst out laughing at the ridiculousness of my situation, and the feeling of a compassionate mother or father would fill my being.

The same with the family retreat. When we allow ourselves to go through the adjustment period, knowing it will pass, we will break through the occasional chaos into the harmonious flow of nature. This reminds me of a rocket blasting off from the earth's surface. The acceleration is not easy, nor is the breaking away from earth's dense atmosphere. Yet, all this is required before entering the serenity of space.

Once we inspired another family about the joys of the family retreat. They were so stuck in their mundane affairs and unhappy with the lack of harmony between them that they agreed to go camping together. However, we made a mistake. We neglected to inform them about the possible initial difficulties. So off they went, happily anticipating a miracle. Everything went wrong! They forgot to bring "important" camping gear. (Every trip we forget something "important" too.) They had car trouble. (We do too—every time!) The weather was inhospitable. (Guess what!) Their disharmony grew so bad that they were almost fighting non-stop with each other. And their thoughts about us were anything but pleasant—we who inspired them about the "joys of the family retreat."

Well, somehow, they stuck it out. Some form of superhuman help prevented them from (1) totally blowing it, and (2) going home miserable failures. Closeness to nature did finally work its magic with its "softening influence". The earth and trees seemed to willingly absorb the inharmonious vibrations. The whole family settled down into the rhythm of nature. The wind in the treetops during the day, the campfire in the evening, the symphony of crickets while they slept, the physical exercise, the simple meals all had a soothing influence on their troubled souls. By the time they returned home they were unrecognizable, so much had they been transformed. They had received the necessary help to make the changes they needed at home and were grateful.

Much of the writing of THE SHARED HEART and this book took place on our family retreats, and over ninety percent was written in nature. (When at home we write in the woods and grasslands surrounding our house.) This gives our camping trips the added bonus of creative expression. Even if you don't think you can write, I encourage you to keep some kind of journal. Camping trips are such ideal times for reflection, for writing down all your thoughts, feelings, inspirations and problems you're working on. Write for yourself. It'll help you later on. It'll help you right then and there. Don't worry about grammar or sentence structure. It's the feeling that matters. You'll be surprised at how being away from home and all the daily routines gives you a higher perspective and the added clarity for deeper understanding.

Now a little about going home—ending the family retreat. It's always surprising to us how much we've gained in these times away. We're partly aware of our gain in the form of creative expression, inspiring decisions we make about our lives or, to some degree, the peace and harmony in our family and ourselves. However, it takes the return to the home environment to really make clear the full extent of the inner growth. It's like our home and possessions and the very atmosphere around it all have stood still in time, reflecting an image of who we were before we left. Upon setting foot into this atmosphere, we instantly see or feel by comparison how much we've changed.

As a spacecraft returns to earth, there is a re-entry process which must be respected. If it decides to ignore natural laws and plunge straight down through the atmosphere, it will burn up and disintegrate just like a meteor. A safe re-entry needs to be a gradual, orbiting process. We may not be coming from outer space (most of us, anyway), but we still need to respect certain laws. If we expect ourselves to dive back into our everyday lives without a proper transition period, we may not become burned up like the meteors, but we probably will become "burned-out" in a hurry. A gradual re-entry would be wise. After burning ourselves out a number of times arriving home at the last minute, late at night before some big work day, we now allow ourselves a day or two at home to relax and integrate the changes. The atmosphere at home that we left behind when we went away has a certain amount of momentum. It can easily pull us back into our "old" selves, especially if we immediately busy ourselves with all the duties of being at home. Moving slowly helps us to keep our awareness focused so we're not caught up in this momentum.

Another tendency is for the family to split up in all directions, running here and there checking everything out. Our house with two bedrooms is small by comparison to many, but compared to our eight foot camper and tent it is a huge castle with a labyrinth of rooms to get lost in. It makes us very aware of how close we've all gotten to one another and how our auras have blended into such a harmonious whole. So now when we arrive home we enter our house, join hands in our living room and have a little welcoming ritual. We take turns blessing the house as well as blessing our new lives there. We ask for the divine strength to make full use of the gifts we've been given—in service to one another and the world. We thank each other and God for the gift of family, a group of persons learning to love one another totally and unconditionally, as the first step in creating peace on this planet.

Walk away quietly in any direction and taste the freedom of the mountain air. Camp out among the grasses and gentians of glacial meadows, in craggy garden nooks full of nature's darlings. Climb the mountains and get their good tidings. Nature's peace will flow into you as sunshine flows into trees. The winds will blow their own freshness into you, and the storms their energies, while cares drop off like autumn leaves.

JOHN MUIR

twenty-six

Birthdays: An Inner Celebration

Tomorrow is my 39th birthday and I'm choosing to spend most of the day by myself. I gave hugs and kisses to my sweet family and felt deeply appreciative of Barry as I drove off for two days at a monastery retreat center in Big Sur. A kindly monk greeted me and showed me to my small room. Then he led me to where a rather plain, uninviting pot of soup was waiting.

The first night I felt homesick for the warmth and joy of my family in comparison to this simple cell which will be my home for two days. I am the only woman on retreat here, along with eight elderly gentlemen. There are twenty-eight monks who live here full time. "What an absurd way to be spending your birthday!", my mind nags. "Hush, crazy thoughts! The guidance was very clear that I come here," as I remember the inspiration I received several months ago. I had read from *THE REVELATION OF RAMALA:*

*For those of you who have begun to advance your
consciousnesses, who are aware of the link of humanity with life
eternal and of the planes of existence beyond the physical, the true
awareness of a birthday brings great reward; for at the moment of
the anniversary of your births you can assess the true spirituality
of your being.*

As a child, my parents gave me two big parties to celebrate each
birthday. One party was for all my school and neighborhood
friends; the other included dozens of relatives. By the time my
birthday was over, I always had a huge pile of birthday presents. I so
totally enjoyed the two parties and all the attention I received.

My first birthday away from home at age 18 was almost
unbearable, even though I received a big box of surprises from
parents and relatives. I missed all of the special attention I had gotten
for eighteen years at home. I had been conditioned to feel that
birthdays meant a tremendous amount of human love and
attention. To not receive this as an adult was painful. Barry always
tried to be very sensitive to my feelings around my birthday. Still,
something always felt missing and I would feel a strange ache in my
heart through out the day. I always felt glad when the day had
passed.

Some years I tried ignoring the fact that it was my birthday.
Other years I tried distracting myself by having big parties. One
year we traveled three thousand miles so I could again be with all my
relatives on my birthday. No matter how I tried to spend a birthday,
there was always a strange emptiness that pervaded the day.

Then several years ago I realized that in all of my outward
seekings for the perfect people with whom to spend a birthday, I had
been ignoring the very ones with whom I *needed* to celebrate my
birthday. Again, from *THE REVELATION OF RAMALA:*

*At the moment of birth many forces herald the arrival of that
spark of Infinite Spirit into matter. At the time of a soul's birth into
physical matter there are literally hundreds of influences present,
ranging from the angelic and devic realms to the spirit guides, the
guardian angels, the masters and teachers and those who are to
walk with that soul throughout its life. They are all present to
witness this act of creation, and their power, their influence, their
presence, are strongest at the time of birth.*

It is important that you discover that moment in time when you were born, and as your birthday comes around each year you should sit in deep meditation and attune yourself to those influences which bear down upon you, for they will be present fulfilling their duties to help you as you walk your path in life.

Each year as I began to take more inward time to experience these higher influences, my birthdays have become richer and more rewarding. The empty, lonely feeling is replaced by an inward joy and companionship with those who watch over and direct my life.

I believe it is possible to help our children from the time they are very young to realize that each birthday is a very inner and sacred event in their lives. As they grow and leave home they will naturally seek inner fulfillment on their birthdays, rather than looking for it in a material way or feeling the inner emptiness that I experienced.

On Rami's eighth birthday, Barry and I made elaborate plans as loving parents often do. We invited all the girls from Rami's class and gave a very special party. We had six extra adults over, each sharing their favorite party game. There were hats and balloons, carrot cake and ice cream, giggles and fun. All the girls agreed that it was the best party of the year.

After everyone had left, Rami sat looking at her big pile of presents. She had received very special gifts from everyone, but as I looked at her more closely I observed a sadness in her eyes. "Did you like your party?", I ventured hopefully. "Oh yes, very much. It was perfect. And I love all of my presents, too," she sweetly replied. She then looked out the window. Her gaze was very far away. I knew Rami didn't realize it consciously, for her birthday party had been just the way she had dreamed, but she was missing her *real* birthday celebration.

On her ninth birthday we planned the same great party for all of her girl-friends, except that on the morning of her birthday I rose very early and gently woke her up with "Let's have a birthday party first with the angels!" We woke up her teddy bear and doll and told them to get ready for the most special birthday party of all. Armed with blankets, stuffed toys and oranges, we crept out of the house very quietly. The sky was just beginning to lighten as we sat in the tall grasses of the apple orchard. After we set up bear and doll, we sang a little song to the gnomes and flower fairies inviting them to come to our party. (Rami made up the song.) Then we closed our eyes and asked that Rami's guardian angel and all the great beings who are helping and watching over her, come close to join us for her

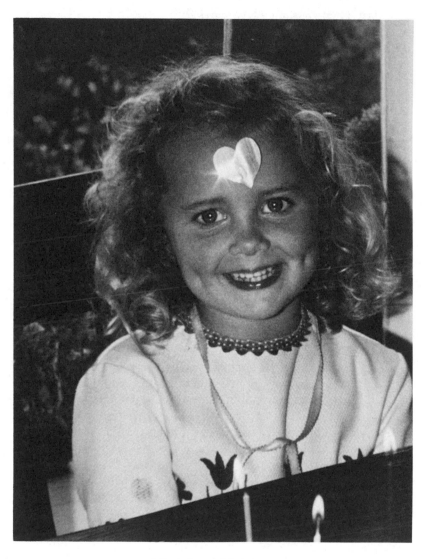

Mira's fourth birthday.

birthday. Then we sang a few songs that we both knew. I affirmed our feeling that her angel was very close to her and was blessing us both. Rami's eyes were sparkling with joy. Then we again closed our eyes and I prayed outloud that God reveal why Rami was sent to earth. Momentarily she opened her bright eyes and joyfully exclaimed, "I'm here to love everyone!"

We sang some more songs in celebration and giggled as we ate our oranges and fed part to bear and doll. We skipped home after just 30 minutes. I could tell that Rami was really happy, and something had been fulfilled within her being by our little "party with the angels."

Later that day we had the big party with all of Rami's friends. Everyone had great fun. After her friends left, there was the usual pile of presents, popped balloons, and cake crumbs on the floor. When I looked over at Rami I could sense an inner peace within her. She came to hug me and said, "I loved my party so much, but best of all I loved our party with the angels." I also felt happy for I so enjoyed the quiet time with Rami. It gave me a chance to experience her inner being and feel why she was brought to us. Barry, who unknowingly slept through our little party in the early morning, definitely wants to be included next year after seeing how happy it had made Rami and me.

The party out in the orchard in the early morning probably wouldn't have been enough of a celebration for Rami by itself. But the combination with an outer celebration seemed perfect. I wish I would have started the "angel party" at a much earlier age. As Rami grows, we will emphasize the inner more and the outer less. We all look forward to Mira's fourth birthday and a family party with the angels.

I awakened in the morning to the early bells of the monastery. The monks rise at 5:30am to pray and meditate. I eagerly jumped out of bed. This was my birthday and, as the time of my birth was soon approaching, I hastily gathered my note book to record the images and visualizations that might come to me at the exact moment of my birth. I had picked a special spot where I could meditate over looking the vast panorama of the Big Sur coastline.

My feet fairly flew as I walked the half mile to my special spot. As I sat I couldn't help wondering what God would reveal to me. I held my notebook and pen, ready to record all the images I received at my birth moment. I began to think of all the many things I hoped to accomplish in the year; finishing this book, making instructional tapes for families, various workshops, new books; the list when on and on. This then led to thinking of what I wanted to accomplish in the next several years. Soon my mind was off and running. My birth moment came, and my mind was too busy with outer accomplishments to feel the inspiration of my birth. I slowly walked back to the monastery, feeling a sense of failure.

As I drew near to the monastery chapel, I saw the monks leaving from their two hour period of prayer and meditation. I felt myself drawn to the chapel. They have a room which is used only for meditation. Not one word has been spoken within that room since the monastery was built many years ago. Walking into the room, I noticed ten of the older monks still deeply involved in prayer. I sat among them.

The absolute stillness in that room brought my feelings of failure very clearly to my awareness. I realized that I had been so much in my head thinking about accomplishments that I had failed to receive the true inspiration of my birth and life. With that realization, a flood of feeling broke loose from within me and I began to cry. Soon I was sobbing uncontrollably as I inwardly asked for help to feel the inspiration of my birth.

The room was filled with the sound of my crying. I was acutely aware of the presence of all ten monks as they sat praying—*for me*. With their help and the grace of God, my true path and the inspiration for my life on earth was revealed in all of its simplicity: to love and desire God as fully and deeply as possible. The accomplishments are important only so far as they increase and strengthen our desire for God. I saw that my role as a parent is bringing the greatest understanding and desire for God right now. I believe this is true for all parents who are sincerely serving their children. I saw Rami and Mira as Goddesses and Barry and I as their devoted disciples as well as teachers, guiding them as they guide us. I felt renewed, strengthened, and prepared for the challenges of parenting and life.

So I ask all of you to begin to use your birthdays, and when your next birthday comes along to look at it with a fresh vision, to see it not as you have probably seen all your other birthdays but to look upon it as an opportunity given to you by your Creator for a moment of rebirth. At that time you can change, for all the power, all the love, of your Creator is bearing down upon you. At that moment the whole of the Heavens are pouring down their powers onto you to revitalize and strengthen you for your next cycle. You are surrounded by the angelic realms and what you ask for will be granted, but it will not be given to you unless you ask. Will you begin to do so?

REVELATION OF RAMALA

twenty-seven

Mother's and Father's Day

Mother's Day 1985

My gift from my family on this sunny, lovely Mother's Day is time alone to write my feelings. I feel so at one with mothers throughout the world. The gift of motherhood is truly sacred. My eyes fill with tears as I feel how blessed I am to be allowed to mother and nurture two of God's precious children. Through motherhood, darkened areas of my being are becoming opened up and filled with light. My children are healing me, and their tiny hands are guiding me ever onward into the light. I love my two girls so much. I pray to be worthy of their love and devotion to me.

This morning, small hands opened our bedroom door and there by my side of the bed stood nine-year-old Rami. "Happy Mother's Day", she sang, and gave me a card she had been working on all week. Tears filled my eyes. As I looked at Rami she was beaming such love. With her whole heart she really believed, as does each little child, that her mother is the best mother in the world. Her devotion to me in that moment was pure and uninhibited, for she

Dear Mama,
I love you so so much.
I love you when you love me.
I Love you when you say a prayer with
me in the morning.
I love you when you have a special
time with me,
I love you when you are happy and
when you are sad
I love you dear sweet mama
because you are the very best
mother. Love Rami

truly sees me as one with the Mother-God. Even a few moments of this complete devotion is enough to transform a woman, to make her want to become all that her child so adoringly sees in her. In that moment Rami was my spiritual teacher, revealing God in my heart.

Bang! The door crashes open and in marches Mira. (Why do three- year-olds make so much noise?) She gives me a wet kiss and warm hug around my neck. Mira's love makes me feel good all over. "Happy Mama's Day my sweet gorgeous mama, I luv you!" Then she hands me a present all wrapped up in her old baby blanket. Inside is Gray Bunny, fur mostly rubbed off, ears sticky from spilled jelly, and torn red ribbon. Bunny is Mira's favorite toy so I'm surprised she is giving it to me. "You can give bunny a special hug today." Her voice is joyful as her arms reach out to reclaim her special toy.

Now I understand. Mira is letting me share in her joy and love of life. Then her reclaiming bunny tells me that I can share her joy but it's not mine to keep. We can join in the happiness of our children, but from even the early age of three and younger they demand that we as easily let go.

My children have grounded my feet to the earth, yet have shown me the way to rise to the heavens. Thank you Rami and Mira. Through your love and devotion to me you are bringing me home to my beloved Heavenly Parents.

*And a woman who held a babe against
    her bosom said, Speak to us of Children
And he said:
Your children are not your children.
They are the sons and daughters of Life's
    longing for itself.
They come through you but not from you,
And though they are with you yet they
    belong not to you.*

*You may give them your love but not
    your thoughts
For they have their own thoughts.
You may house their bodies but not
    their souls,
For their souls dwell in the house of
    tomorrow, which you cannot visit,
    not even in your dreams.
You may strive to be like them, but seek
    not to make them like you.
For life goes not backward nor tarries
    with yesterday.*

*You are the bows from which your
    children as living arrows are sent forth
The archer sees the mark upon the path
    of the infinite, and He bends you with His
    might that His arrows may go swift and far.
Let your bending in the archer's hand
    be for gladness;
For even as He loves the arrow that flies,
    so He loves also the bow that is stable.*

KAHLIL GIBRAN
THE PROPHET

Father's Day 1985

Today is Father's Day and neither Joyce nor I remembered until this morning. We woke up in our tent at our favorite camping/retreat spot in California's Sierra Mountains. We've been here almost a week, and each morning on arising we get dressed, wash in the lake, and then sit together for a time of morning stillness before the girls beckon.

This morning, however, was different. Joyce had a dream

about the unique blessing of parenting. While she was sharing this with me, she remembered a little piece she wrote on Mother's Day. She had read it to me on that day, and then it disappeared somewhere in the depths of her clipboard. Now she found it in an instant and we read it once again to each other. When we were done I suddenly said, "I think today is Father's Day." And it was!

Sitting on the lake shore in the shade of pine and fir trees, I now have a chance to reflect on my fatherhood and the universal fatherhood. I am realizing now that it has taken me almost this whole week in nature to settle down, to clear my head of all the clutter of worldly responsibilities. The first three or four days here I kept thinking I heard the phone ringing. We fathers can get so caught up in the outer duties of providing for our families and for everyone else. As a medical doctor, I always smile at how we are referred to as "providers"—and how easily I get caught in this role.

Now I'm reflecting on how God, the inner source of my being (and all being), is the real provider. We as fathers could be so much better providers if we remembered that we are the instruments of the Father-Spirit. Then we wouldn't have to get so tense and preoccupied.

That's what Rami and Mira have been teaching me, and once again it's taken simplicity and these humble surroundings to remind me of what is truly important. I hear squeals of laughter coming from our camp and I know that Joyce, Rami and little Mira are busily writing and coloring Father's Day cards for me. I feel so blessed to have these three beings so one-pointed in their devotion to me—so open to their need for who I really am. Thank you, Father-God, for deepening this message and lesson this Father's Day. Help me to always remember I can do nothing more important in the world than to play with my children, to learn from them how to be in my heart rather than in my head, to give them an example of what a father really is.

Now the air rings with calls of "Daddy, Daddy!" I go now to receive their gifts of love with renewed gratitude and a deeper listening. May I return them in kind.

I love my daddy because

He takes me for walks in the woods,
And reads me special stories,
Fixes my old wagon
And plays with me alot.
He makes me just so happy
when he plays those rough-house
                                games.
I can't believe how much I
                love my daddy.

twenty-eight

When Children Die

Birth is not the beginning, death is not an end.

CHUNG-TZU

As the children of the concentration camps at Majdanek scratched little butterflies with their fingernails on the walls before entering the gas chambers, so did your children know at the moment of death that they would emerge free into a land of peace and unconditional love, into a land where there is not time and where they can reach you at the speed of their thoughts. KNOW THAT and enjoy the spring with new flowers coming out after the deadly winter frosts, and enjoy the new leaves and life bursting forth all around you.

ELIZABETH KUBLER-ROSS
ON CHILDREN AND DEATH

Three days before our beloved eleven-year-old golden retriever Kriya, died, I lay with her on the floor petting and loving her. We had been told four days earlier that she had inoperable cancer and would die shortly. The news came as such a shock to us, for Kriya had been so healthy all of her life. She was the children's dog and we lovingly referred to her as our "nanny". Her mission in life was to protect and watch over Rami and Mira, a job she did with great skill. I could totally trust Kriya.

Now she lay on her favorite rug in our living room, unable to eat and barely able to stand. Each day her condition deteriorated rapidly. It caused me great sorrow to see our lively dog, who one week ago was swimming in the ocean and chasing balls, now almost too weak to lift her head. She was very conscious of my presence, however, and occasionally wagged her tail in appreciation of my love for her.

At one point tears streamed from my face and I felt as if my heart would break from the sadness I felt. I wanted to leave the room and distract myself to ease the pain. As I was getting up, a strong feeling rose within me, "Stay here and continue to look until you can see death as beautiful. This is Kriya's final gift to you."

I stayed and felt the beauty of Kriya's life. She had lived her life perfectly, with pure dedication to serving us with love and devotion and caring for the children. Now she was ready for a greater life, dwelling in her body of light to play with and protect the children of the heaven world. Her compassionate brown eyes told me that she was ready to leave her old body. Barry compared her dying process to a woman in labor about to give birth. Kriya was giving birth to a new life. Suddenly, death became as beautiful as birth. As soon as I felt this, Kriya's tail wagged and she bravely lifted her head. She wanted me to experience the beauty of her death.

Just at this moment of communion between dog and mistress, Barry solemnly walked into the room. He told me that our friends, Don and Margaret Ware had just called. Their baby boy, Nicholas, who was fourteen months old, had died suddenly two days ago. He had been operated upon for a congenital heart problem in San Francisco and seemed to be healing beautifully. The doctors and nurses were all very pleased with his progress. While Don was holding and playing with him, Nicholas gave his father a sweet smile, turned his head, and quietly died.

I knew in that moment that God was calling upon us to feel the beauty of this death also—only it was much harder.

The following evening we had a memorial service for Nicholas. As a small group, we lent strength to one another as well as to Don and Margaret. All gathered were parents and this death touched a fear deep within us all. The death of one's child is perhaps the hardest of all of life's pain to bear.

We asked each person to delve into their feelings until they could see the beauty and love of God in this death. People shared songs and poems. We all took turns around the circle speaking a prayer. All of us came to sense the radiant presence of Nicholas as he watched over us and gave us his love. We all came to trust that he was secure and happy in the heaven world. Still, however, all shared the pain of separation that the parents were feeling, especially the mother whose breasts were still full of milk for her nursing baby.

Towards the end of the service we were all feeling in God's will. There was a holy feeling of acceptance. Kriya had been watching the entire service from her lying down position on her favorite rug. As soon as the feeling of peace and acceptance came into the room she started wagging her tail and once again bravely lifted her head. This was 30 hours before her own death. She seemed to be wanting to tell all of us that death can be beautiful too. Nicholas smiled right before he died. So did Kriya!

That day which you fear as being the end of all things is the birthday of your eternity.

SENECA

Three days after Kriya peacefully died and one week after Nicholas' death, Margaret came over to visit with her four-year-old daughter Amethyst. Amethyst and Mira played happily. Neither one felt sadness over the deaths in their lives. Since they are so fresh and newly here from the heaven world themselves, the trip back to the spirit world seemed very natural to both of them. Both had watched their family's grief almost from a state of detachment. We knew they were probably feeling, "What could be sad about someone going to such a wonderful place?"

I sat with Margaret and asked her to share her grief, sorrow, and despair with me. Feeling so vulnerable myself from the recent death of Kriya, I felt Margaret's feelings throughout my body. I knew that these feelings must come out before the higher inspirations could come. Suddenly we both felt Nicholas' presence in the room and there was a definite assurance that he would not leave his parents alone. He still had work to do with them. Then we felt the promise of Easter, the promise of the resurrection. The powerful Christ-like presence of Nicholas would always be there for his family. They would be radiating his love as a blessing for the world. He came to

Nicholas Micah Ware
11/30/84 — 1/30/86

acquaint them with the beauty of his being, and strengthen and instruct them. He left because he had a great work to do.

These parents will never be the same again. Their son's death is transforming them, bringing to them greater love, understanding of God and a depth of compassion to serve others. Nicholas' birth, fourteen-month life, and death has been one of their greatest blessings in life.

Should you shield the canyons from the windstorms,
You would never see the beauty of their carvings.

OLD PROVERB

Mama, God sent me to be with you to bring you love.

AMETHYST, AGE 3

Messenger of Love
by Wendy Chapler

In the autumn of 1984, Wendy Chapler visited my mother's class and shared the story of her son's illness and death. We were all held spellbound for over an hour as she spoke. That night, each one of us felt we had been changed. Through Wendy's strength and courage to see the beauty of God's plan, she helped us get beyond our worst fear—the death of one of our children. Here follows Wendy's story:

Dan was our first born son who came to us as a gift from God. We enjoyed his infancy and his toddler days and amazed at each development along the way. He had twinkle in his eye and intrigue for life that inspired us to be the same. So, at two years old, when he was diagnosed as having leukemia, we were beyond upset. When the truth set in, we knew that if his life was to be so brief then he was going to have a lot of work to do in a short period of time and he was going to need us to help him.

Within hours of finding out the reason he had been so ill, we were at Children's Hospital at Stanford beginning the process of trying to overcome the disease. When things finally settled, there was our son hooked up to IV's and machines. And as hard as it was, we were already surrounded by love and support and the feeling of so much hope. We carried that hope with us and for almost three years his disease was kept in remission. From the day he was diagnosed our lives changed dramatically. What seemed so important before, all of the sudden became trivial. From that time on, for his true happiness, life had to be as normal as possible. We kept Dan in the mainstream as much as possible. He went to school, had friends and did all the things that normal 2, 3 and 4 year olds do. And all the time we protected him as much as possible from some of the harshness of life. Undeniably, we had the feeling that if we made life wonderful for him then he would want to stay.

For those three years he was in remission, not only did we try to heal him through our love and quality of life we tried to provide, but we also used every medical and alternative approach to insure that the disease didn't come back. We regularly saw a chiropractor, drank herbal teas, used polarity therapy, color therapy, imagery; anything that was attainable and would not put further stress on Dan, make him think of himself as sickly, or put too much focus on his condition.

Despite all of our efforts, he had a relapse of his disease when he was five. We had been told that if he should relapse there would no longer be any chance for a cure and that his life could possibly be maintained for about one year. That year was the most meaningful of all and brought with it so much good and so much love.

I had always felt that if he relapsed I didn't want to do anymore chemotherapy. That we had given it its fair chance and if it didn't work, I wasn't going to put Dan through it anymore. But, when the decision actually had to be made, I knew that chemotherapy was one way we could have more time together and I wasn't yet ready to say goodbye.

We also continued using alternative forms of healing. We had two people working with Dan from a distance through their meditations, trying to heal him on a soul level. Both of them would tell us that Dan had definitely made up his mind to stay but his body was taking a little bit longer to go through the healing process. That always gave us a ray of hope and it was obvious from his behavior that he did want to stay. However, slowly his condition started getting worse.

We had never told Dan that he was supposed to die. Not only did we wonder how he could ever be healed if he believed he was dying, but we felt that he was a five year old boy and he needed to have the innocence and carefreeness of a five year old, and not be burdened with the responsibility that comes with such knowledge.

We began working with Safiya Williams. After the first healing she did with Dan she told us of the beautiful beings she saw surrounding Dan. She told us that Dan was extremely nostalgic for these beings and he really wanted to be with them. She suggested that I meditate with Dan while he was asleep and go to where he goes when he sleeps. When I got there, I should be with him and then at the appropriate time, tell him it's time to come home, just as I would if he was playing at his friend's house and he really didn't want to come home because he was having so much fun. I tried it and it was easy. Effortlessly, I was right there. I was off a little way from him and it was a beautiful place, grassy and green. He was with a circle of children, all holding hands and going around in the circle. They were all laughing and there was so much love among them that I had a hard time telling him that he had to come home. He was so happy and so carefree and it was so beautiful there, but finally I told him it was time to come home and he took my hand in is little hand and we walked away. I did that several times. Sometimes we would walk away and sit by a very beautiful stream that had light bouncing off it. Dan and I became very close through these experiences, even though he was asleep.

Something else we did which was extremely helpful in understanding Dan and his situation was to have an astrology reading with William Lonsdale. It gave us so much insight into his being and why he came here. It confirmed what we innately knew but had yet to realize. It also aided us in protecting and guiding him.

When I met William, and told him that Dan had leukemia, he said he wondered how a child with a chart such as his was surviving in the world of today. The underlying theme of his reading was that Dan was a very refined person and knew only love and light. I was told that if he was to make up his mind to stay then he could do it, but life would always be harsh for him and he would have to learn how to protect himself. We could help him by realizing his intent on being wide open, which made him so vulnerable to his environment. It would be important for us to have him in an environment where subtle forces were recognized, where there is inward tranquility, acceptance and peace.

We continued to work with Safiya, continued chemotherapy, and continued to do everything that we could. I truly believed that he was going to live. I believed it until the day he died.

Even as his condition began to deteriorate, there was never any "date" set that he would die or what would be the actual cause of death. It wasn't until about a week before he died that we were informed he had only a few days left. He was in quite a lot of pain and we were admitted to the hospital for pain control with the hopes of being able to take him home when that was accomplished. It became apparent that for Dan pain control would be impossible at home. We told him that we could go home but we might all be a lot more comfortable in the hospital and he said that he wanted to stay. We had a room to ourselves with a nice big window and plenty of privacy. All of our phone calls were screened and we were taken care of. We didn't have to worry about what was happening. The hospital staff did all of the worrying for us so we could be 100% with Dan. We were able to be very intimate, more so than we could have been at home having all that responsibility ourselves. We allowed very few visitors during those last few days. Safiya came to be with Dan a couple of times. She would say that there was something very special about being in that room; that it smelled like roses. Indeed, there was something very special about our room and we were so told by several people.

We spent our final week in that room. The doctors, nurses and staff of the hospital were very fond of Dan. They were not afraid to get involved with the children and Dan had a particular knack for capturing the hearts of those he chose to capture. We encouraged him to be fond of his doctors and nurses. Starting at age two, the staff of the hospital became some of his first friends. When he'd see his doctor he'd run up to him and give him a big hug. Their love for Dan made it so special for us. Somehow we always knew that whatever happened was alright. Sometimes it was really frightening. It seemed like there was always one more thing to hold on to. One more chemotherapy, one more healing, one more... Always, always there was one more thing that kept our faith. We believed in miracles and felt no reason why we couldn't have a miracle. So many times I thought of him, "You can do it, I know you can. You can be healed. But if you need to go I can understand that too. You must do what you need to do." We became so close that we didn't need words anymore.

It seemed as if Dan actually died twice. One time with Bob (his father) and one time with me. Early in the morning, about 2 or 3 am, of the day he died he sat up in bed and said "Hold me!" From stories we had heard about dying we thought, "This is it." Bob was right there, holding him and telling him of the angels in the room; that he could see them and feel them that they were here with us. I was too tired to do anything but feel remorse that my son was dying and I was too tired to even know what to say or what to do. It was Bob and Dan, which seemed appropriate since the real connection had always been between Bob and Dan. After Bob held him and talked to him for awhile, seemingly out of nowhere Dan said, "When are you guys going to sleep?" With a chuckle and a great sense of relief we crawled back into our bed and laid there—and didn't sleep.

As dawn broke, he became more restless and uneasy from the pain. No amount of morphine could make him comfortable. I started telling him of all we had learned during the last year. Telling him of our meditation adventures and what a beautiful place it was; how warm and breezy and grassy and light. And the love of the children. And I retold stories we had read about where we go when we sleep and when we die. And I told him of the beautiful angels that Safiya had always seen around him. Finally, we chose to give him some medication to help him sleep and be less aware of his discomfort.

His dying process seemed to go on forever and, even though our room seemed to be touched with a presence of peace and love, the struggle was becoming unbearable. It was so obvious that Dan didn't want to die. Regardless of the pain and the stress on his body, his heart kept going. We both wanted to hold Dan, but because of his pain he was more comfortable to be in his bed with Bob sitting on one side and me on the other. At one point the frustration became so great I went over to Bob and wept and expressed that I never imagined his dying would be this hard; that there would be this amount of suffering and would take so long. After a hug for comfort and a few tears shared I went back to Dan. I feel that exchange finally freed Dan to start into his final stage of dying. His breathing became more labored and Bob and I sat and watched his every breath until finally, he looked right at me, his eyes wide open, then he closed them, took a few more breaths, and stopped. During this time I held his hand and told him that I loved him and I was with him and I would take him as far as I could. We were in motionless awe for a moment, then Bob and I shared a glance and hug reaching over Dan. We then sat in peace for quite awhile, 15 or 30 minutes, until the doctor came in and with a quick check confirmed his death and left us to ourselves again.

We continue to sit by his side in timelessness. And then we began to wash him, put clean pajamas on him and put him in a clean bed. He looked so peaceful and it was as if he sat there watching us as we went about fixing ourselves and gathering our things. Both of us spent more time with him, talking with him. I sat by him again and held his hand and told him not to worry about me. I would be alright. He had given me so much love I couldn't help but be alright. And I thanked him.

After quite some time there was a knock at our door; a nurse asking us if we felt up to seeing visitors yet because there were several people waiting to see us. We were ready and the doctors and nurses and staff who had grown to love Dan came in to say goodbye to Dan and give us their love. And there sat Dan in his bed, so lifeless yet still seeming to be so much a part of it all. His friends would go to his bedside and maybe say a few words and be with him in his death as in his life.

We had not thought much about what it would be like when Dan died. As a matter of fact we purposely did nothing about it. We put all our energy into his healing. I was more inclined to talk about it than Bob and I might ask, "If Dan dies..." and Bob would respond that he wasn't ready to deal with Dan dying and if he dies we'll have a whole lifetime to deal with it. We kept our spirits up by reminding each other that while he's alive there's no time for tears. It wasn't until a few days before he died that we started talking about and making plans for a funeral. And it all fell into place with very little effort. One thing Bob knew was that he didn't want to leave Dan at the hospital. So when we were finally packed and ready to leave, we laid Dan on the bed in the back of our Volkswagon van and drove him "home". What a ride home. Everybody busy going here and there, totally unaware and unaffected by the grandeur of our day. And to us it seemed as if everybody should see the angel and the Presence we felt surrounding us.

He is buried under a tree that is just like a tree we have in our backyard. It was always his special place to be, complete with treehouse. Bob had gone to the cemetery the day before the service and hung Dan's swing fom the tree. His swing was made for him by a friend and had his name engraved on it. It was the most precious part of the service.

About two weeks after he died I went on a retreat with Stephen Levine who is known for his work with death and dying. For those two weeks after Dan's death I wasn't feeling anything from him, or so I thought. Regardless of what anybody said, I was still worried about Dan; I didn't know where he was and if he was alright. One evening I got a chance to talk to Stephen. We were standing out on a porch and it was a clear and starry night. I told Stephen that I was still worried about Dan. He asked me if I talked to him. I answered that I talked to him all the time but that I wasn't hearing anything back. He said, "Right now, just listen to him". So I closed my eyes and then I heard as clear as a bell, "Mommy, I love you". I opened my eyes and Stephen smiled at me as he said, "What did he say?" And as I said it, Stephen said it too: "Mommy, I love you". I don't know if he had heard it also or if he just knew there was nothing else Dan would have said to me. I started crying and walked over to the love, comfort and embraces of those whom I had become close to on the retreat. I knew Dan was safe.

Everyone thinks to lose a child is such a tragedy. But to have

Daniel Lewis Chapler
1/16/77 – 4/22/83

been blessed with a child like Dan was a gift. As William, the astrologer revealed:

> Dan's was the chart of someone who came to serve. His coming was a gift. He came to help people out and, if he should pass on, he would continue to provide inspiration. For him, life was to be a sequence of lessons, but whatever he would learn would not only be for himself but for everyone.

For us the lessons were the experience of the beauty of God's Grace and unconditional love; and a glimpse at what lies on the other side of the thin veil that separates life and death. His father expresses it best:

> For those four days while Dan was dying there was nothing else going on but caring for him and giving him all our love absolutely unconditionally. Nothing else existed in the world. We were completely in the present moment and that moment for us was holy. The lack of sleep, the emotional drain, the turmoil of dying all combined to put us in a space that was transcendent, in a place where we could somehow cope in a peaceful state with all that was going on. It was as if we were on an island somewhere in space and the rest of the universe dropped away; there was nothing else for us but what was going on. After he died, the terrible pain that he endured for so long, that we endured also, left us. There was no more pain because we had used it all up. There was a knowing from the experience itself that this was not the end of Dan; but that this was only the end of his body. That knowing extended to our immortal selves and we knew all was well. At that point our beliefs were established in experience so they didn't need explaining; they didn't need justifying. It was beyond logic. We were living the experience of the eternal life of the soul.

As his last parting gift to us, he gave us the experience of his death. He taught us that life is eternal, that dying is just the next step. To experience the giving of unconditional love gave us the opportunity to be in that consciousness. We saw the life leave his body and yet we still felt him in the room. His body was dead yet the existence of his spirit was still there with us. Dan taught us that death is just like being born. They are both holy occasions and then we have life in between the two of them. Once in a while something happens, such as what happened to us, to remind us that the place between being born and dying is holy also, but that most of our lives we forget. With our son we were reminded again; not through the intellect or through the emotions only, but through the absolute undeniable experience of it.

Dan was and continues to be a Messenger of Love from the Heavens.

Thank you Dan
For the Hope and the Fighting Me

Thank you Dan,
For the Courage and the Loving Me

BRIAN (DAN'S BROTHER), AGE 4

I'M LETTING GOD DECIDE

It's hard to understand
They say that I've got Ewings
It's spread in my bloodstream,
I don't know what will happen
Maybe I might die,
It's hard to predict the future.
I'd like to live as long as possible,
but, I'm letting God decide,
He helped me kick it last year,
I hope he helps me again

I'M LETTING GOD DECIDE

It's hard to understand
They say its hard to bear,
I'm gonna give it my best shot
And hope I can defeat
This deadly disease called cancer.
But whether I'm to win or lose,

I'M LETTING GOD DECIDE

It's hard to understand
My veins are pretty shot,
I've only a few more veins
Then I'll get a Broviac,
At least that's what my doctor says
If God lets me win the fight,

I'll help other kids survive
By becoming a doctor and
  giving kids a chance.
If God decides, it's better I die
I'll think he's giving me a choice
to be happier than before.
I'm leaving it up to him,

I'M LETTING GOD DECIDE

12-YEAR-OLD GIRL
WRITTEN SIX MONTHS BEFORE SHE DIED

Loving Life Enough
by Mary Manachi

We'd just cut the watermelons at a Sunday-school picnic and I was laughing at the kids' antics—pretending to play harmonicas as they munched on the sweet pink slices, using the rind to make big green grins, and seeing who could spit seeds the farthest, when I felt the woman's hand on my arm and saw her sympathetic, questioning eyes. I knew what she'd say before she even spoke.

"You seem so happy. Really happy. How do you do it after...after all that's happened to you?"

Again and again people ask me that same question—people who know that Louis and I had three children born with the blood disorder called Cooley's anemia. First Mary Lou, then Rosemary, then George. One after the other, they were born with it, lived with it and died of it.

How can I be happy after all that's happened? Well...

Mary Lou was born in 1955. She was our second child, born two years after our strong and healthy daughter Ann. At first I'd thought Mary Lou's pale skin meant she took after my side of the family. Louis and I are both of Mediterranean descent, but he's the one with the olive complexion. When I took her to the pediatrician for her three-month checkup, he asked me to set up an appointment at a hospital in New York City for testing. "She seems to be anemic," he told me.

Anemia? It didn't sound too bad; lots of people have anemia. But after Mary Lou was tested at New York Hospital's Cornell Medical Center, the doctor called Louis and me in for a consultation.

"I'm sorry to have to tell you this," the doctor said. "Your baby has *thalassemia major.*" He explained that this is commonly known as Cooley's anemia, after the doctor who discovered it. A rare genetic blood disorder, it prevents the body from manufacturing hemoglobin, the part of the red blood cells that carries oxygen from the lungs to body tissues and muscles.

"It mainly affects people of Mediterranean heritage," he told us. He also said that Cornell Medical Center was head-quarters for the Harold Weill Clinic, which specializes in treating children with blood diseases. Mary Lou would have to go there every two weeks for a blood transfusion.

From then on I drove my small daughter into New York City from New Jersey regularly. After a few months she seemed to get used to it. And she had company; there were 19 other children being treated for the same illness.

Louis and I wanted more children, but now we wondered.

"Don't worry," our doctor assured us, "it is very rare that this happens in a family twice."

Rosemary was born in 1959. She looked fine—bright blue eyes and fine brown hair like Mary Lou's. But just to be certain, I quickly took her to the clinic to be examined. The doctors were non-committal. Weeks went by. One day she'd seem perfectly normal, the next her head would be sweating. The pattern had been the same with Mary Lou. Then, when she was six months old, the doctor gently told me that Rosemary would also need regular blood transfusions.

"Why didn't you tell me before?" I whispered. "Why did you let me hope?"

He shook his head sadly. "We knew how difficult it would be for you to hear this outright. We hoped you would recognize it gradually on your own."

So now I was driving two little girls into the city. It was easy to see how much Mary Lou and Rosemary depended on the transfusions. As the time for the treatments neared, they would tire easily and become irritable. But after their hospital visit—grueling as it was—they seemed fine. In the meantime, Louis and I tried to give our three daughters a normal life with music lessons, Monopoly games and plenty of family outings.

In 1961, our son George was born. We had yearned for a boy and we'd been assured that the chances of our having another child with the same affliction were absolutely nil.

But from the first moment I held my little boy in my arms, I knew. Deep down, I knew. Soon I was taking George into New York along with two-year-old Rosemary and six-year-old Mary Lou.

Even so, Louis and I were grateful for four lovely children. The blood transfusions simply became a regular part of our lives and we went on hoping that a medical breakthrough would make them unnecessary. Meanwhile we were busy with the usual family things—school activities, music lessons, outings and vacations; and the years passed.

Then came our shocking discovery.

One morning while I was waiting at the hospital, a mother of one of the other children quietly handed me a clipping from *The New York Times* headlined FATAL BLOOD DISORDER. It was about children coming to that very clinic. One sentence blazed out at me. *"They usually die before they are 20 years old."*

I couldn't believe it. I took the clipping to our doctor. "Is it true?" I asked.

"Yes," he sighed. "I'm afraid it is."

There were no drugs, no treatments, no known medical help to prevent my children's death at a young age.

For weeks, Louis and I lived in a daze. His reaction was to say little and concentrate on his work as a garment designer. Mine was to cry whenever I was alone.

The children? We couldn't bring ourselves to discuss it with them, though they were aware of the seriousness of their condition from talking with the other patients during their hospital visits. And then came one of those small moments, small but significant, that changes the way you see things.

I'd walked into 11-year-old Rosemary's room one evening and found her making a jeweled butterfly pin. She was already selling her work at craft shows.

"How beautiful," I said as I watched her carefully set a rhinestone.

"Thanks, Mom," she murmured. "I'm going to earn all I can toward college."

College? She was planning on *college?*

I cleared my throat. "Uh...what are you planning to study, hon?"

She looked up, eyes shining. "Nursing, Mom. I want to be like those nice women at the hospital who help me."

She turned back to her work and I walked slowly out of the

room, trying to take it all in. Rosemary was *not* thinking about death; she was focusing on life.

At Thanksgiving one of her teachers phoned me. The class had been asked to write about what they were most thankful for. The answers were the usual ones about home, parents and food. "I thought you'd like to hear Rosemary's answer: 'I thank God for my good health.'"

Good health? How could she write that? And then I remembered the other children Rosemary saw on her hospital visits, the ones with amputations or suffering from cancer. But Rosemary could walk...go to school...skip rope.

Rosemary had filled our house with Scripture plaques that she made herself. In her own room she'd hung the one that said: *This is the day which the Lord has made; let us rejoice and be glad in it.* (Psalm 118:24 RSV)

That Thanksgiving I looked around me. I saw that our house was not a house of shadows and sorrow: our children filled it with cheerfulness and bustling activity. Mary Lou's piano music rang through the rooms as she practiced for a recital. Rosemary busily crafted jewelry and wall plaques. Little George had an extensive rock collection; he was already talking about becoming a geologist. Slowly I began to see that my children, all of them, were rejoicing in life.

On July 4, 1969, Rosemary, now 12, was in the hospital with a minor cardiac problem, a side effect of Cooley's. "You seem better, honey," I said to her that night as I leaned down to kiss her good-bye. "I'll be back early in the morning."

Just after I got home, the telephone rang. Rosemary was gone. "Peacefully," the hospital said.

We mourned. Mary Lou and George had known their lives would be short, but now, with Rosemary gone, they were forced to face the fact head-on. Mary Lou, four years older than Rosemary, began carefully tending her sister's grave. I knew that she must be contemplating her own death. And yet, I watched carefully as she took up the business of her life with a new vitality. She began making the honor roll in high school and was very popular. And she made a suggestion that gave new direction to our lives.

Louis and I had been taking our children on more and more excursions, including a week's vacation in the Pennsylvania mountains. Soon after that trip, Mary Lou returned from her hospital visit in a thoughtful frame of mind.

"Mom," she said, "when I told the kids at the clinic about our visit to the Poconos, most of them said they'd never been to a place like that. Could we find a way to take them with us next time?"

"Of course we can," I said hugging her. Suddenly we had a project. Right away I started organizing a volunteer group to take the other children on trips. We held bake sales and raised enough money for an excursion to Mount Airy Lodge in the Poconos. Most of the children had never been together outside the hospital. How wonderful it was to see them laughing and having a good time away from the sting of needles, transfusions and spinal taps. We found ways to raise funds to see a Broadway play and even to visit Disney World.

In 1973, Mary Lou graduated from high school as a member of the National Honor Society. She had undergone surgery for removal of her spleen, so she had worked extra hard for these honors. In the fall, she entered William Paterson College as a fine-arts major. Soon she made the dean's list. She worked part time in a TV repair shop and her civic activities—everything from collecting for charity to volunteer work—put her in touch with almost everyone in town.

The following year she volunteered to participate in an experimental drug program for the treatment of Cooley's anemia. It took a lot out of her and she had to be hospitalized for three weeks. "But if it helps other kids, it's worth it," she said.

Mary Lou was 19 that Christmas of 1974. In January, our Christmas tree was still standing in the living room. For some reason I just couldn't take it down.

On January 20th it snowed heavily, keeping all of us at home. Mary Lou practiced her piano in the morning, but she was very tired. "I think I'll rest for a while," she said as she went up to bed. Later I brought her some lunch.

"Oh, this soup is so *good!*" she exclaimed. Then the light went out of her eyes and she fell back on her pillow.

Mary Lou's funeral was one of the largest ever seen in West Paterson. Louis and I had no idea that she had had so many friends. The mayor and the entire city council were there. In the words of the Cooley's volunteer group who honored her, she had been "A very special girl who lived and understood life better in her 19 years than most of us could possibly hope to if we lived to be 100."

Later, as a cold February rain battered our living-room window, I sat alone thinking about this radiant daughter. Sighing, I leaned back, staring at the wall. In my line of sight were three of the

Scripture plaques her sister Rosemary had made for us. *I will never leave thee, nor forsake thee.* (Hebrews 13:5) *Casting all your care upon him; for he careth for you.* (1 Peter 5:7) *Do not be anxious about tomorrow.* (Matthew 6:34 RSV)

The words wavered in my vision, then cleared. I got up immediately and began preparing dinner for my family.

Our oldest daughter Ann was involved in her career, and George, a typically noisy teenager, kept our house lively. His friends came and went and the telephone rang constantly. He dated and had an after- school job at a local restaurant. We continued to take the Cooley's children on trips and have get-togethers.

George graduated from high school and went on to Paterson College, where he threw himself into a full schedule of activities. He went on working part time at the restaurant, and the summer he was 19 he bought a Chevrolet Monza sports car—shiny black with fire-engine-red trim. It was a young man's dream—and always full of his friends. He kept it in showroom shape.

That's why, on the night of September 20, I knew something was wrong. George came home from a date and after he went to bed I happened to notice that his Monza was pulled into the garage at a careless angle. Always before he'd aligned it so neat and straight.

The next morning he stayed home from school. "Mom," he said, "I just can't make it anymore. I'm so tired."

Louis and I took him for a long ride that night, knowing the moving car's hum and rhythm would help him doze off. When we got back to the house, he sank down on the couch. "I know I'm going, Mom," he said wearily. He looked up at me with concern. "Promise me you won't cry? You know where I'll be."

"No, Georgie, I won't cry."

My son smiled, shook his head and lay back, eyes closed. Then he took a deep breath and was gone.

Mary Lou.

Rosemary.

George.

...And so, again and again, people ask that question, "How can you be happy after all that's happened?"

I'll tell you how.

My children understood that life is a holy gift from our Creator. They loved each day they were given, and their enjoyment and gratitude were like sunlight, warming and brightening our time together. In the face of early death, they embraced life. If they loved life as much as they did, honoring it, reaching out to soothe their stricken friends, using their days creatively, am *I* to love life less?

No! I will not dishonor God—or my children—with gloom and self-pity. I embrace life as they embraced it and I shall rejoice and be glad in it!

twenty-nine

Kriya Goes to the Heaven World

by Rami Vissell

I'm nine years old. Today our eleven year old dog Kriya is very sick. We don't know how much longer she will live. At first I cried as I was petting her and loving her. I felt like she was my sister because she has always been with me. I have played with Kriya every day of my life. She always follows me on my adventures and when we are swimming in the lake she likes to pull me on the float while I hold her tail. Once I remember I even dressed her up in necklaces and beads. She even sat in the wagon and let me pull her. I feel that Kriya is the best dog in the world. I love her so so much. I was crying because Kriya means so much to me and I wished she could always be with us.

Then I realized that it was up to God to either let Kriya go to the

Rami and Kriya in wagon.

Heaven World or to stay longer with us. I knew that even if she goes to the Heaven World she will still be with us in her body of light.

When I was four years old our nine-year-old dog Bokie died. We buried his body in the back yard and had a special service for him. We each told special memories and sang songs. Even though my parents told me Bokie was in the Heaven World I still felt as if he were buried in the dirt and I felt sad. That night I went to sleep and I could feel Bokie lying right beside me. He told me that he was very happy in the Heaven World and that he would always watch over me. I felt so happy and I came and told my parents. For several years after he died I felt him close to me every day. I still feel him now every once in a while. I know that Kriya will always stay with me too.

The Heaven World is a place where you go when you leave your earth body and take your light body up to where all the angels are. You walk up the golden pathway into a beautiful world where there is no sadness. You can talk to the animals and see the magical flowers. We can also go to the heaven world when we sleep or meditate. When Kriya dies Bokie will greet her at the magical arch of flowers.

When we die we stay in the heaven world for a nice rest. Whenever we are ready we can come back to earth for a new life in a new body.

(7 days later)

Kriya died yesterday before the sun even came up. Before we went to sleep we each prayed that she could go peacefully and soon to the heaven world. We wanted her to be able to leave her old sick body. Kriya's fur on the top of her head was as soft as a newborn puppy. I was sleeping in my mom and dad's room next to Kriya. In the middle of the night she woke us all up when she walked over to my mom's side of the bed. Then she walked back to me. We all knew that she was getting ready to go. We lit two candles and gathered around her. We sang a special song to her and told her we wanted her to go to her new home. She looked up at us once, stretched her legs, and breathed deep breaths. Then she stopped breathing and left very peacefully. We felt so happy for Kriya and filled with love for her. We said a few more prayers. Then we went back to sleep so we could be with her in her new home.

I woke up feeling filled with love. Kriya's old body still lay right beside me. It was sunny outside for the first time in two weeks. We all gathered around Kriya's body and had a little good-by service. We told each other the gifts that Kriya gave us in her life. I said, "Kriya always protected me in the woods and always loved me." Mira said, "Kriya took away my sickness and sadness." Daddy said, "Kriya kept me from thinking too much." My mom said "Kriya

Rami and Kriya shortly before Kriya's death.

taught me patience and devotion." We than closed our eyes and felt Kriya in our hearts. She was right with us smiling and happy in her body of light.

Then we went outside to dig her grave. We all helped, even Mira. We picked daisy flowers and put some on the bottom of the grave. Then we went into the house and Mira and I drew pictures to put in Kriya's grave. Then we went in to where Kriya's old body was to wrap her up in a sheet. Mama and I started to cry as we petted her body for the last time. The fur on the top of her head was still as soft as a puppy. Mira didn't know what to do so she started to pretend to cry. We cut some long hair off of her tail and put it into an envelope. Then we covered her up. We wrapped up the pictures with her and on the back of mine there was a love note to Kriya. Then we put her into the grave. We each took a hand-full of daisy flowers and said a prayer and sprinkled them on top of her body. My prayer was, "To fill the daisys with love and that the angels would surround Kriya with light." Mira prayed that Kriya would always be happy. All four of us put the dirt over her body using our hands and blessing the soil. We planted pretty flowers on the top.

Then we went on Kriya's favorite walk and we all felt her running along beside us. I know for sure that Kriya will always be with me in her body of light. She will always protect me when I'm down at my play-house. I will always love Kriya.

(Parent's note)

At the exact moment of death, Rami's eyes shone with wonder and joy as she sweetly said, "I never knew death was so beautiful."

thirty

Completing the Cycle

The great man is he who does not lose his child's heart.

MENCIUS

To be seventy years young is sometimes far more cheerful and hopeful than to be forty years old.

OLIVER WENDELL HOLMES

We had just turned 50 and 56 years of age when our first grandchild was born. We remember that day so well. We felt new life swelling through our entire being and a connection with the future here in our country and in our world. We were so uplifted that we felt young and full of energy. Each birth has made us feel that way and now there are six grandchildren.

GRANDMA AND GRANDPA WOLLENBERG

Reading and telling stories, kissing away hurts, singing, playing games, baking cookies, are part of the joys of being a grandparent. But there's more.

As the saying goes, your own children are like money in the bank, but your grandchildren are the interest on that money. They are also the promises of our dreams, the hopes of the future — they are our immortality.

GRANDMA AND GRANDPA VISSELL

Navajo grandfather and grandchildren.

Once, while at a retreat center near Big Sur, California, I sat on a lone bench overlooking the vast panorama of ocean, beach and rock. I was working on this book and feeling very peaceful inside when, from behind me walked an elderly gentleman, puffing from the strenuous climb. "Young lady," he asked, "may I share your bench for awhile? I fear I can't go on much longer." I made room for him and we sat looking at the beauty of nature. He told me he was a priest who worked with delinquent children. I told him about this book. I liked him immediately. We sat in silence for a long time, then he turned to me with bright shining eyes and asked, "Do you know why today's youth have so much trouble adjusting?" I quickly listed the reasons I could think of: "too much television; being forced to grow up too soon; unstable families and ..." "No young lady," he interrupted. "Today's youth don't see enough of their elders. They are not taught to respect them. When the old people once again have the proper respect of the youth and a place of importance in the family, there will be far less trouble among young people."

As he finished speaking I felt the truth of his words. Children need and learn so much from elderly people, great grandparents and grandparents (though many grandparents are really very young these days). Their presence in the life of a child is very special. Older people often take the time to just be with a child, to be very present with each word that is said. They often have wisdom of the ways of earth that can be passed down to the child by their mere presence. Many people have told me that it was their grandparent who helped them to have faith and understanding in God. My father is convinced that his grandmother is like a guardian angel watching over him.

How we treat our parents now will be a model for how our children will treat us when we are elderly. If we love and respect them, our children will naturally learn to love and respect us as we grow old.

Each Christmas Eve we go caroling at a nursing home with a small group of friends and their children. I shall never forget one experience. We walked into the room of a man in his late eighties. By himself, he had put on his best old-fashioned suit and a red tie. We all fell in love with him instantly. He loved our singing and wanted to shake hands with each small child. The children loved him and gathered very close. He showed us pictures of his children, grandchildren and great grandchildren. "I love them all so much," he proudly told the children. Then he looked up into the faces of the parents and tears came into his eyes as he said, "They are too busy for me now. I'm too old. Now I'm all alone." He leaned over and kissed the children. None of them wanted to leave. "We love you," a little voice piped in." The old man smiled.

We watched as his dinner was brought to him and sadly realized that he was all alone for Christmas. The children of that man are teaching their children by example that old age is to be put away and forgotten...that, in fact, their own old age is something to hide and repress into unconsciousness.

Birth and death are part of a cycle. Our parents helped bring us into the world and loved and cherished us to the best of their ability. Our need for them was very great as we grew up. Then parents grow old and *their* need for us is very great. As they loved and nurtured us as children, so in turn can we complete the cycle by loving and nurturing them in old age. As they helped bring us into the world, so can we help them leave the world, nurturing them through the transition of death. As we are given to, so also must we give. No matter how poorly we may feel our parent cared for us, we can be real models of love for our children, by treating our parents with respect, by recognizing that they tried. The American Indians, who in many ways are the tradition and pulse of our nation, treated their elders with great respect, and it's true, there was little trouble among the Indian youth. If you feel your parent doesn't deserve respect, then that is something to heal within yourself, for each human being deserves respect and honor. As we treat the elderly with reverence we are teaching our children that it's OK to grow old, and thus it's OK to live fully. As we honor and respect the elderly who we can see with our physical eyes, we are teaching our children to have reverence for the real elders—the great Masters and Beings who, though unseen, humbly continue to guide and protect all of earth's children. To these Ancient Ones all honor and reverence is due.

Afterword

One morning, while this book was being typeset, we sat together and realized all the imperfections in our writing—how it didn't adequately convey what we feel about parenthood. Then we realized that if we rewrote the whole book it would still be imperfect. It is the best we can do because it is the best we can be right now—imperfect and yet holding to the vision of perfection.

It is the same with us as parents. We all have wonderful ideals of what we can be as parents, but we fall short in our day-to-day lives. If we could just remember that our intention—our desire—is what really matters the most, our failures will then be in the proper perspective. We only need to keep trying to do our best. As the saying goes, "a saint is a sinner who never gave up".

We ask, therefore, that you overlook the imperfections of this book, and accept the sincerity of our hearts as our gift to you.

With much love
Barry and Joyce

About the Authors

Joyce and Barry Vissell have counseled individuals and couples, and led groups, classes and workshops since 1972. Since writing their first book, THE SHARED HEART, they have conducted talks and workshops on relationship and parenting throughout the U.S.A., England, and Findhorn, Scotland. They live near Santa Cruz, California with their two daughters, Rami and Mira.

If you would like to be notified of a workshop or event with Barry and Joyce to be held in your area, if you would like to sponsor or organize such an event, or if you would like to share your reactions and feelings about this book (which they welcome), they may be contacted through:

RAMIRA PUBLISHING
P.O.BOX 1707
APTOS, CALIFORNIA 95001

List of Contributors

Jeannine Parvati Baker, MA is the wife of Frederick "Rico" Baker, mother of Loi Caitlin, Oceana Violet, Cheyenne Coral, Gannon Hamilton and Quinn Ambriel. She is the author of *PRENATAL YOGA & NATURAL BIRTH, HYGIEIA: A WOMAN'S HERBAL, and CONSCIOUS CONCEPTION: ELEMENTAL JOURNEY THROUGH THE LABYRINTH OF SEXUALITY* (with Frederick Baker and Tamara Slayton).

Leo Buscaglia is the beloved author of *LOVE; THE WAY OF THE BULL; LIVING, LOVING, LEARNING;* and *LOVING EACH OTHER.* He lectures throughout the world, writes for the New York Times Syndicate and has been on numerous radio and television shows.

Eileen Caddy is the co-founder, along with Peter Caddy, of the famous Findhorn Community in northern Scotland. Her "guidance", the messages from her Higher Self coming through her writing and speaking, have helped thousands. She is the author of *GOD SPOKE TO ME, THE SPIRIT OF FINDHORN,* and others.

Wendy and Bob Chapler live in Santa Cruz, California. Their son Dan was diagnosed with leukemia 4/22/79 and died 4/22/83 at age 6. With the birth of Robert Daniel in May, 1985, they again have 2 sons. They helped found and presently co-chair Circle of Hope, a support group for families of children with chronic or life-threatening illness.

Jenny Dent, granddaughter of Grace and Ivan Cooke, is the General Secretary of the White Eagle Lodge and the author of *SPIRITUAL TEACHING FOR CHILDREN* and other books for children.

Brian Graham is the editor of "The Science of Thought Review" in England and author of *CLARE CAMERON: A HUMAN AND SPIRITUAL JOURNEY* (1984 Werner Shaw Ltd., London) He is a devoted father to his three children.

Joan Hodgson is the eldest daughter of Grace and Ivan Cooke and the author of *WISDOM IN THE STARS, PLANETARY HARMONIES, THE WHITE EAGLE BOOK OF HEALTH AND HEALING,* and the popular book for children, *HULLO SUN.*

Gerald G Jampolsky is the author of the best-sellers *LOVE IS LETTING GO OF FEAR* and *TEACH ONLY LOVE.* He is a psychiatrist and founder of the Center for Attitudinal Healing in Tiburon, California. His TV appearances have drawn world-wide attention to his work and center.

Bill Knight-Weiler, father of two young children, administers a 1,000-acre regional park near Portland, Oregon. He has been published as editor of *THE EARTH SPEAKS*, an anthology of inspirational nature writing, and contributes a regular column, "On Fathering", for SpiritualMothering Journal.

Jack Kornfield is a meditation teacher who was trained as a Buddhist monk for some years in monasteries of Thailand, Burma, and India. He is a founder of the Insight Meditation Society, author of *LIVING BUDDHIST MASTERS* and *A STILL FOREST POOL*, and has a PhD in clinical psychology. He lives in San Anselmo, California with his wife, Lee and his daughter, Caroline.

William Lonsdale is an astrologer, counselor, visionary, and founder of "Move Your Mountains", a focus for transformational astrology. He is the co-author and editor of *STAR RHYTHMS: READINGS IN A LIVING ASTROLOGY.* He lives in Bonny Doon, California with his wife Sara and his two daughters, Corin, age ten, and Audette, age six.

Mary Manachi in 1982 was named New Jersey's American Mother of the Year. She continues her work with the other Cooley's anemia children. As a mother of a teenage daughter in the clinic said: "She's the person we all confide in when we can't talk to doctors. She's the one who gives us faith."

Qahira Qalbi is a Sufi teacher whose father was the personal secretary to Hazrat Inayat Khan, the Sufi master well-known for bringing Sufism to the West. A mother of six children, she and her husband, Tansen live in Southern California.

Karen Karima Rivers is a teacher at the Marin Waldorf School. She lives in Nicasio, California with her husband and her daughter Cheri.

Emily Sanford is the beloved minister of the Unity Temple of Santa Cruz. She is a gifted speaker, counselor, and artist, a mother of five grown children and grandmother of seven.

Rami Vissell is Joyce and Barry's ten year old daughter. She is a talented artist and budding young writer who fully intends to write and illustrate children's books in a few years. Her illustrations have been published in *THE SHARED HEART*.

T. Mike Walker, a writer, teacher, and editor, is the author of *VOICES FROM THE BOTTOM OF THE WORLD: A POLICEMAN'S JOURNAL* (Grove Press) and currently, *THE LAST AMERICAN* (a novel about the Iranian revolution). His son, Griffon Walker, has survived the first years of puberty and is preparing to enter high school this coming fall.

Safiya Williams has a master's degree in children's literature and teaches poetry to children. She lives in Santa Cruz, California with her husband, Isaiah and their four children.

Available books and tapes by Barry and Joyce Vissell:

THE SHARED HEART: RELATIONSHIP INITIATIONS AND CELEBRATIONS

"...a map of the relationship journey." —Ram Dass. "...full to overflowing with immeasurable guidelines on using our relationships as tools for our further awakening." —Science of Thought Review, England. "...celebrates, in all its aspects, LOVE."—Newport This Week.

186 pages   ISBN 0-9612720-0-7 $8.95

THE SHARED HEART CASSETTE TAPE: THE RELATIONSHIP OF LOVE

This is a tape of inspiration and guided practices for individuals and couples interested in relationships as a journey of the heart. It captures on tape the essence of THE SHARED HEART. Side one is by Barry, side two by Joyce. Soul-nourishing background music by Steven Bergman and Charlie Thweatt. Produced by Steven Bergman Studios.

Cassette Tape $8.95

MODELS OF LOVE: THE PARENT-CHILD JOURNEY

This book is to the family relationship what THE SHARED HEART is to the love relationship. With a foreword by Eileen Caddy of Findhorn and contributions by seventeen others, it is an exceptional manual for the journey of parenting.

322 pages   ISBN 0-9612720-1-5 $10.95

TRANSITIONS INTO FATHERHOOD: PERSONAL GROWTH FOR EXPECTANT FATHERS

A tape to inspire and help men move through the transition (and transformation) into fatherhood.

Cassette tape $8.95

MOTHER-CHILD BONDING DURING PREGNANCY

A tape for pregnant women who wish to deepen their relationship with their unborn child.

Cassette tape $8.95

A JOURNEY OF LOVE: COUPLES MOVING INTO PARENTHOOD

This tape will help pregnant couples to understand and prepare for the changes parenthood brings. It includes relationship practices especially for use during pregnancy.

Cassette tape $8.95

(These last three tapes are produced by Steven Bergman and are accompanied by his gentle background music.)

See following page for ordering information

We would like to make available to our readers a few items which have particularly helped us and our children.

SPIRITUAL TEACHING FOR CHILDREN by Jenny Dent, White Eagle Lodge, England.
This is a series of four play-as-you-learn books. Included are: GOD LOVES US ALL, WHERE IS HEAVEN?, THE GIANT JIGSAW, and GREAT TEACHERS. This is the best introduction to universal spiritual truths and meditation that we have found for children. Although written primarily for children, teenagers and parents have enjoyed and learned from them also.

Set of four $9.95

ANGELS BE WITH YOU by Mark and Nancy Wallace.
We are excited to share our children's favorite bedtime songs with you, arranged and sung by a very talented couple. This tape was made especially as a companion to *MODELS OF LOVE*, to help parents put their children to sleep in a conscious way. Side one includes original compositions (even one by us) to sing to your children as they drift to sleep. Side two contains exquisite harp music to ensure sweet heavenly sleep.

Cassette with lyrics included $9.95

WINGS TO MY HEART by Rosey Lovejoy.
This is a lively and touching recording for children of all ages. We listen to this tape over and over.

Cassette with lyrics included $9.95

I CLAIM A MIRACLE also by Rosey.
This recording is filled with joy and heart. We and our children love to sing these songs.

Cassette with lyrics included $9.95

And finally, three delightful instrumental tapes by Steven Bergman:

SLUMBERLAND
Beautiful, soothing quiet-time music for children and adults.
SWEET BABY DREAMS
A very special tape! Orchestrated lullabye music incorporating the nurturing sound of a pregnant mother's heartbeat.
LULLABIES FROM AROUND THE WORLD
Lovely orchestral interpretations of the world's lullabies.

Each cassette, $9.95

Ordering information:

- Order any 4 items—get any 5th item free
- Shipping: $1.00 first item; $0.50 each additional item
- California residents add 6.5% sales tax
- Send order to: RAMIRA PUBLISHING
  P.O.BOX 1707
  APTOS, CA 95001